The witness of the New Testam
darkness of the natural human n
Holy Spirit if ever we are to unc
very strong; yet in current theology and devotion it is often ignored.
So Paul Brown's careful combing through relevant passages is as
timely as it is important, and I heartily recommend it.

J.I. Packer,
Regent College, Vancouver

I heartily commend this book to you for two reasons. One reason is
that the author highlights a major New Testament emphasis for us.
The emphasis is that an understanding of biblical truth is given by the
Holy Spirit; His work is to reveal and teach. Sadly, it is an emphasis
which has been neglected in recent decades. Secondly, the author
exegetes the relevant New Testament texts. And he does it in a way
that allows the New Testament to speak clearly to us. In understanding
and interpreting the Bible, in depending more on the Holy Spirit and
experiencing the power of the Bible in your life, this book can help
you. Buy a copy then read it slowly and prayerfully.

D Eryl Davies
Principal,
Evangelical Theological College of Wales

Paul Brown has done the Christian world good service in restating a
truth often dismissed or ignored in hermeneutical discussions, namely,
the crucial importance of the Spirit's work in interpreting the text of
Holy Scripture. In a day when the scholarly world is insisting that a
great gulf separates the original writers of the biblical text from the
modern readers, this little piece of work is a timely reminder that the
same Holy Spirit who enabled people to compose the God-breathed
Scriptures, is given to Christian readers today to help them understand the sacred text.

Philip H Eveson
Principal,
London Theological Seminary

Paul E. Brown is the minister of Dunstable Baptist Church in Bedfordshire, England. He has written *Churches in Trouble?* and is a sub-editor of *Grace* magazine.

The Holy Spirit

The Spirit's Interpreting role in relation
to biblical hermeneutics

Paul E. Brown

Mentor

© Paul Brown

ISBN 1857 92 654 4

Published in 2002 by
Christian Focus Publications,
Geanies House, Fearn, Ross-shire,
IV20 1TW, Great Britain

www.christianfocus.com

Cover design by Alister MacInnes

Printed and bound by
JW Arrowsmith, Bristol

Contents

Abbreviations

AB	Anchor Bible
AV	Authorized Version
BAGD	Bauer, Arndt, Gingrich, Danker; A Greek-English Lexicon of the New Testament
BNTC	Black's New Testament Commentaries
CGTC	Cambridge Greek Testament Commentary
CTS	Calvin Translation Society
EC	Epworth Commentaries
ICC	International Critical Commentary
LBC	Layman's Bible Commentaries
LXX	Septuagint
MNTC	Moffat New Testament Commentary
NAC	New American Commentary
NASB	New American Standard Bible
NCB	New Century Bible
NCBC	New Century Bible Commentary
NEB	New English Bible
NIBC	New International Biblical Commentary
NICNT	New International Commentary on the New Testament
NIGTC	New International Greek Text Commentary
NKJV	New King James Version
NLCNT	New London Commentary on the New Testament
NIV	New International Version
NTC	New Testament Commentary
NTCS	IVP New Testament Commentary Series
PE	Pastoral Epistles
REB	Revised English Bible
RSV	Revised Standard Version
RV	Revised Version
TDNT	Theological Dictionary of the New Testament; Kittel & Friedrich
TEV	Today's English Version
TNTC	Tyndale New Testament Commentaries
TPINTC	Trinity Press International New Testament Commentaries
WBC	Word Biblical Commentary
WC	Westminster Commentaries
WEC	Wycliffe Exegetical Commentary

PREFACE

This book began life as a study presented to the University of Glamorgan and carried out through the Evangelical Theological College of Wales. I am very grateful for the help received from Dr Eryl Davies of the Evangelical Theological College of Wales, Alan Hill of the University of Glamorgan and Professor Paul Helm of King's College, London; also Dr Tom Holland and John Kendall of the Evangelical Theological College of Wales. Particular thanks also to Richard and Jean Rowland who did the original word-processing for me, and who put up with endless revisions and attempts to get all the references correct. Thanks are also due to Bethel Evangelical Church, Hanley, and Dunstable Baptist Church, who gave me time, and the opportunity to go away to study. I am also grateful to Malcolm Maclean and the editorial team at Christian Focus for their work in restyling my manuscript for publication. My wife, Mary, has been a constant support and encouragement. I personally found it immensely rewarding studying all the references to the Holy Spirit in the New Testament and evaluating them with reference to my theme. I believe also that this enlarged my understanding of biblical interpretation and, in some measure, revitalised my ministry.

INTRODUCTION

This book considers what the New Testament says about the anointing of the Holy Spirit and his role as teacher and revealer.[1] It examines references which speak of his ministry in teaching and illumination, in relation to current issues in biblical hermeneutics. There has been a great deal of interest in the person and work of the Holy Spirit at a popular level as a result of the charismatic and house-church movements both within and outside the Christian denominations. However, this interest has not yet been matched by any significant increase in scholarly books dealing directly with the doctrine of the Holy Spirit,[2] although there has been some considerable research in certain related areas, notably that of prophecy.[3]

It is rather surprising that no detailed study has been done in recent years on what can be called the teaching ministry of the Holy Spirit.[4] While it would be wrong to consider the references to the Holy Spirit in the New Testament as sparse, they are not great in number[5] when compared, for example, with Christological references. Some of the most important references to the Holy Spirit, however, are concerned directly with the teaching ministry. It is a frequent emphasis in the New Testament writings, expressed in various ways, that understanding God and spiritual truth is not something which people are naturally capable of; rather it is only possible through the Spirit.[6]

The relationship between the Spirit and the Word is frequently considered in a general way, especially in less recent books on the Spirit.[7] The two themes which are usually explored are (1) the testimony of the Spirit to the Word, a theme which rose to prominence at the time of the Reformation, notably in the writings of Calvin,[8] but has suffered a considerable eclipse since then;[9] (2) the balancing of the Word and the Spirit in preaching and the life of the churches.[10] There does not seem to have been any major effort to extend the teaching and revealing ministry of the Holy Spirit into the realm of interpreting and understanding the Bible, apart from the work of the Puritan theologian John Owen.[11] Karl Barth might be regarded as an exception to this.[12] His emphasis upon the sovereignty of the Word of God confronting the reader in the text of Scripture is a crucial concept,[13] but his concern is not to work out the relationship of the Spirit's work to hermeneutics in detail.[14]

Hermeneutics itself, however, is an area which has seen considerable study recently.[15] Once biblical hermeneutics was no longer restricted to enunciating principles of interpretation,[16] but began to embrace the whole idea of the communication of understanding,[17] the way was opened up for a variety of hermeneutical approaches to the Bible.[18] Hermeneutics has now come to dominate theology so much that theologies are often the outworking of particular hermeneutical perspectives.[19] Moreover the linking of hermeneutics with praxis in liberation theologies has given an urgency and dynamic to what at one time seemed a static discipline.[20]

However, the word 'hermeneutics' has by now acquired somewhat elastic properties, and tends to be over-used. Two comments are relevant here. Firstly, if the practical question is asked, 'What is doing hermeneutics'?, the answer is not immediately apparent. Hermeneutics is generally thought of as an academic discipline which is taught and researched. But is that what biblical hermeneutics is about? At a more practical level in the life of the churches, hermeneutics is thought of as part of the preparatory work done by their pastors and teachers. More logically, though, 'doing hermeneutics' ought to be the art and act of interpreting and communicating the Bible to others.[21]

Secondly, looking at 'hermeneutics' in a broad way means it is not possible simply to stop with 'understanding' in the purely intellectual sense; a biblical text has not really been grasped until there has been appropriation and response.[22] As soon as concerns like these become included in the general meaning of hermeneutics it becomes apparent that we are entering an area that the New Testament certainly includes under the ministry of the Holy Spirit. In the New Testament the church, through its apostles and preachers, evangelizes and teaches by the Holy Spirit. Just as Christ received the anointing of the Spirit for his ministry, so the church has also received the Spirit to enable it to function as a living, dynamic body.[23] No-one has made this point more urgently or cogently than Dr J.I. Packer. He writes:

> Evangelical theology affirms a correlation between the rational process whereby principles, having been established from Biblical particulars, are applied to cases and persons, and the teaching ministry of the Holy Spirit, who enables our sin-darkened minds to draw and accept these correct conclusions as from God. Because correct application is a strictly rational process, most evangelical text-books on interpreting Scripture say little or nothing about the Holy Spirit, Scripture's ultimate author, as the great hermeneut who by leading and enlightening us in the work of exegesis, synthesis and application, actually interprets the Word in our minds and to our hearts.[24]

Biblical hermeneutics needs to be considered within the framework of the doctrine of the Holy Spirit. Just as Christian ethics has the Holy Spirit as its motivation and dynamic so also does biblical hermeneutics. There is room for considerable discussion about ethical questions, and indeed for disagreement, but ultimately the Christian's life, both as an individual and within the corporate life of the church, is a life under the impulse and leading of the Spirit.[25] So also, if biblical hermeneutics is going to be oriented within the life of the church and its proper dimensions retained, it needs to be correlated with the teaching ministry of the Holy Spirit.

Admittedly, many books and articles on hermeneutics refer to the Holy Spirit's work, but often this is only done briefly and superficially and no attempt at integration is made. Anthony Thiselton in *The Two Horizons* is concerned to show that considerations about the work of the Spirit do not bypass serious hermeneutical thought nor provide 'some esoteric gnostic route to knowledge'. This concern on the part of Thiselton gives his discussion a somewhat negative cast. However, he also hints at ways in which some hermeneutical conclusions harmonize well with an emphasis on the Holy Spirit,[26] and it is to such points of harmonization that this study looks.

There are two further preliminary matters to address. The first is to set out my reasons for approaching the exegetical task in the way that I have. My decision to work with the final form of the text is not simply a reflection of a commitment to a conservative evangelical view of Scripture, but also a practical necessity in attempting to survey data from the whole New Testament. It has, moreover, been argued recently that 'this is the form of the text most suitable for theological use'.[27] Therefore I have not involved myself in questions of source or redaction criticism, nor, apart from a brief discussion below, in questions of authorship. In this I have followed the example of H. B. Swete:

> In pursuing this aim I have not thought it necessary to spend many words upon the questions of literary and historical criticism which are raised by every book in the New Testament. The testimony which the writers bear to the belief or the experience of their age is but seldom, and in a relatively low degree, affected by questions of this kind...and whatever views may be held as to the historical character of certain books, the New Testament as a whole speaks with a voice too clear and full to be overpowered by the din of our critical controversies. In the following pages I ask the reader to listen to that voice, as it tells him what the presence and working of the Spirit of Christ meant to the first generation of believers.[28]

I assume that Swete is right in what he says in his last two sentences.

Several comments need to be made regarding the Pauline literature.

It is beyond the scope of this study to discuss questions of authorship. The main candidates for doubt over Pauline authorship are Ephesians, Colossians, 2 Thessalonians and the Pastoral Epistles. Recently there has emerged a greater recognition of the possibility that the Pastorals may, after all, be from the hand of Paul,[29] though doubts continue to be expressed about the authorship of Ephesians.[30] In arguing for Pauline authorship some point to the possible involvement of a secretary, which would account for variation of style and language.[31] On the other hand those who argue for a Deutero-Paulinist (or Deutero-Paulinists) contend that he came from the Pauline circle and his concern was to commend Paul's theology to a new generation and use it to confront heresy and establish sound doctrine.[32] In any case as all the letters claim to be from Paul the burden of proof is on those who deny this. Moreover, this claim is decisive for letters written under the inspiration of the Spirit.

Another problem concerns the fairly large number of references where it is uncertain whether the translation should be Spirit or spirit. There is considerable disagreement in the commentaries on this matter and individual cases will need to be considered as they arise. However, in many places, the very uncertainty indicates that perhaps the exact translation, or deciding definitely between one or the other, is not so important. One reason for this is that 'Spirit' is a dynamic concept and even if it refers to human disposition or quality very often this is the result of an activity of God, which in Paul's thought was effected by the Spirit. Sometimes the word leans more to the Spirit personally, at other times more to a gift or operation of the Spirit. In both cases, it is appropriate to use the capital 'S' especially as this indicates unambiguously the source or origin of the gift or disposition. This will become evident when considering the Pauline material.

This study does not look for evidence of any development of thought in the doctrine of the Spirit in Paul's letters. Its general assumption is that Paul had a highly developed understanding of the Holy Spirit's role in Christian conversion and the Christian life; for him the Christian life is divinely initiated, sustained and developed and this is by the Holy Spirit. This is seen particularly clearly in some letters but forms the sub-stratum in which all references to the Spirit are to be understood. The frequency with which he speaks of the Spirit in the various letters depends on the circumstances and subjects of the letters.

Secondly, it is also necessary to focus this work and my focus is that there is a clear strand of thought running through the New Testament that an understanding of Christian truth does not come simply through the use of human reason, but rather is given by the Holy Spirit. An important part of the Holy Spirit's work according to the New Testament is to reveal and teach. It is this strand which is now to be followed and examined by a general survey of material from the whole of the New Testament. In the course of doing this, it is hoped to show that a broad spectrum of commentators have understood the texts in the way they are understood here. I have tried to consult classic commentaries as well as the most recent. I have tended to concentrate on commentaries rather than journal articles and research papers as the amount of literature is enormous and the major commentaries critically utilise the latter. To some extent the weight of evidence is cumulative. Certain texts are more crucial than others and will be given careful evaluation.

My view of biblical hermeneutics has been enlarged and modified in the course of this study. Anthony Thiselton says, 'In a co-operative shared work, the Spirit, the text, and the reader engage in a *transforming* process which enlarges horizons and creates *new horizons*.'[33] I assume a hermeneutical model in which each of these three components, God (I prefer to say 'God' rather than 'Spirit' here, to retain the thought of the word of God), the text and the reader are given due weight and brought together in the process of hermeneutics.

CHAPTER ONE

THE SYNOPTIC GOSPELS

This study of the New Testament evidence of the work of the Holy Spirit in teaching, revealing and anointing begins with a consideration of the Synoptic Gospels, but as the beginning and ending of Luke's Gospel contain material which is peculiar to Luke this is considered along with Acts. This approach would be unsatisfactory if particular attention needed to be given to the specific contribution of each Gospel writer, but in a general survey of the New Testament it seems the best way to proceed. I will be following the general framework of Matthew's Gospel as the largest number of references pertinent to this study have been identified in Matthew (excluding the peculiarly Lucan material in the opening and closing of that Gospel). Nearly all the references are paralleled in either Mark or Luke, though only a few in both. The earlier Matthean material (following Matthew's structure) tends to be paralleled in Luke and the later Matthean material in Mark.[1]

Taking Matthew as the main basis for study the material presented can be classified in three ways:

First, general considerations which relate to the theme, indicating the need for special understanding if Christian truth[2] is to be grasped.

Second, references which speak of revelation and understanding being given by God inwardly within the mind and heart of the subject.

Third, direct references to the Holy Spirit.

It is to these matters we now turn.

The need for special understanding to grasp Christian truths
There are some general considerations which relate to this theme, indicating the need for special understanding if Christian truth is to be grasped.

The general state of need

Matthew 4:16 (REB³)

The people that lived in darkness have seen a great light; light has dawned on those who lived in death's dark shadow.

When Matthew applies these words of Isaiah 9:1–2 to the ministry of Jesus begun in Galilee he clearly sees the condition of darkness described by Isaiah as appropriate to the people of that region. Jesus is the great light who by his character, deeds and teaching will illuminate them. The background in Isaiah 8 is one in which the message and instruction, presumably of Isaiah, though it could be interpreted more widely of the message of God, have been sealed up and people turn to the spirits of the dead for some word of hope. However, 'everywhere is distress and darkness inescapable' (Is. 8:22, REB). The darkness, then, is one which includes ignorance of God's word, and the light one which involves revelation and illumination.

The state of the heart
Secondly, note should be taken of Jesus' teaching which implies that people may be inwardly evil and therefore unable to think aright or understand as they should. The first example is in Matthew 6:22–23 (Luke 11:34–36) where Jesus speaks of the eye either being good (ἁπλοῦς – clear, sound, healthy, BAGD)[4] or bad (πονηρὸς). The suggestion is that light and understanding depend on the state of the heart – for 'in all this the eye is an analogue for the heart (see v. 21)'.[5]

Another example occurs in Matthew 12:33–36 (see also Luke 6:43–45 and Matthew 7:16–20). Here the thought primarily concerns the origin of the words people utter: 'it is from the fullness of the heart that the mouth speaks' (v. 34, REB). An evil heart will lead to evil words. The picture is very similar in both instances, though in one case it is light which should shine in, and in the other it is words that go out expressing what is within. If the heart is evil, a person is in darkness, and words will betray that condition.

Lack of insight in the Jewish leaders

There is also the description given in the Gospels of the lack of understanding shown by the Jewish priests and teachers of the law, men whom one would anticipate would have considerable insight into the Old Testament, commensurate with the amount of study devoted to it. In fact, however, one of the focal points of the clashes between Jesus and the Jewish teachers was over the understanding of Old Testament scripture. Matthew early on shows the extraordinary attitude of the chief priests and scribes when he describes them telling Herod where the messiah was to be born, and yet apparently not taking the slightest interest in the possibility that this momentous event had taken place (2:3–6).

Of greater significance are the two occasions when Jesus chides the Pharisees for failing to understand the words of Hosea 6:6, 'I desire mercy, not sacrifice' (Matt. 9:13; 12:7). His words, 'Go and learn what this text means' and 'If you had known what this text means' (REB) are a strong indictment of the spiritual insensitivity of his opponents. They knew the existence of the text itself, but its meaning and application to life in the present were completely missed.

In Matthew 21:15–16 Jesus rebuts the indignation of the chief priests and scribes aroused by children crying out in the temple, 'Hosanna to the Son of David', by quoting Psalm 8:2, 'Have you never read the text, "You have made children and babes at the breast sound your praise aloud."' Another example comes in Matthew 22:29 (Mark 12:24) where Jesus says, 'How far you are from the truth! You know neither the scriptures nor the power of God', and follows with '... have you never read what God himself said to you ...' (v. 31; Mark 12:26; Luke 20:37 – 'even [και].Moses showed in the burning bush passage ...' [NKJV]).[6]

Spiritual blindness

Closely related to this lack of insight into and understanding of the Scripture, is the spiritual blindness Jesus discerned in the Pharisees and scribes which is expressed particularly vividly in his words recorded in Matthew 23. Five times Jesus calls them 'blind', making it clear that they are spiritually incapable of getting their priorities right and of recognizing the difference between details and the weightier matters of the law. For Jesus, it appears, understanding the law of God is more than just a matter of intellectual ability and close study. Those who were foremost among his contemporaries in both of these were castigated by him because they were morally and spiritually blind and lacked any proper understanding of the truth. Here were living examples, as Jesus saw it, of those whose hearts were bad.

God's chosen have knowledge and insight
The converse of this is seen in the words of Jesus in the eschatological discourse of Matthew 24. In verse 24 (Mark 13:22) Jesus is recorded as saying, 'For false messiahs and false prophets will arise, and they will perform great signs and wonders, so as to lead astray, if possible, even the elect.' The clear implication of the words is that for all the subtlety and deception of the false messiahs and prophets the elect cannot be led astray (εἰ δυνατόν 'if it were possible'). While the scholars and leaders, for all their knowledge, remain in the dark, God's chosen, even when surrounded by the most convincing of impostors, cannot be led astray. They have a knowledge and insight which enables them to see through and resist the most persuasive of errors.

Inward revelation and understanding given by God
The second strand of evidence consists of those verses which speak of revelation and understanding being given by God. Some of the most important passages in the Synoptic Gospels on this subject belong under this heading. Five references and their parallels will be examined.

Matthew 5:8

Blessed are the pure in heart, for they will see God.

There is a link here with those passages, reviewed above, which speak about a good heart (or eye). If the ultimate object of religious and spiritual truth is a knowledge of God – the beatific vision, seeing God[7] – then Jesus here teaches that the inner quality of the heart is essential; only the pure in heart can see God. True knowledge of God depends upon the moral and spiritual condition of the heart. Neither the scriptures themselves, nor even the words of Jesus, can give such an understanding by themselves.

Matthew 11:25–27 (Luke 10:21–22):

At that time Jesus said, 'I praise you, Father, Lord of heaven and earth, because you have hidden these things from the wise and learned, and revealed them to little children. Yes, Father, for this was your good pleasure. All things have been committed to me by my Father. No-one knows the Son except the Father, and no-one knows the Father except the Son and those to whom the Son chooses to reveal him.'[8]

The Lucan introduction to these words contains a significant reference to the Holy Spirit, 'At that moment Jesus exulted in the Holy Spirit...' (REB). This indication of the role of the Spirit in this exalted prayer of Jesus demonstrates that the Spirit is the active, inward-working power of God, whose presence and working is not always explicitly stated, but can be assumed as he acts as agent of Father or Son.[9]

Matthew 11:25 encapsulates the point made earlier that the wise and learned do not, by the mere fact that they are so, understand spiritual truth. However, there are two more comments to be made. Firstly, Geldenhuys is justified in saying, 'The contrast posited by the Saviour is not that between "educated" and "uneducated" but between those who imagine themselves to be wise and sensible and want to test the Gospel truths by their own intellects and to pronounce judgement according to their self-formed ideas and those who live under the profound impression that by their own insight and their own reasonings they are utterly powerless to understand the truths of God and to accept them.'[10]

In addition, Jesus makes it clear that God has hidden (ἔκρυψας)[11] these things from the one group and revealed (ἀπεκάλυψας – paronomasia for emphasis and effect) them to the other; this was the Father's choice (REB – εὐδοκία; more literally 'thus it was pleasing before you' where ἔμπροσθέν σου gives an added reverential note in addressing God, BAGD]). This same emphasis is seen in verse 27: 'those to whom the Son chooses to reveal him.'

Verse 27 emphasizes that all things have been given to Jesus as the Son and no-one knows the Father except those to whom (ᾧ ἄν) the Son chooses to reveal him. Suzanne de Dietrich comments, 'Reflect a moment on this word "know". In the Bible it never means merely intellectual knowledge, but rather a living relationship which engages the whole person.'[12] While this is, in general, true, the words 'to reveal him', suggest understanding and insight more than relationship. Moreover Luke writes 'no-one knows who the Son is (τίς ἐστιν ὁ υἱός) ... or who the Father is (τίς ἐστιν ὁ πατὴρ)', which seems to place the emphasis on the intrinsic nature of the Father and the Son, and on the distinctiveness of each. Luke also uses γινώσκει while Matthew has ἐπιγινώσκει, but it is doubtful whether any difference of meaning should be discerned as ἐπιγινώσκειν is frequently used without any emphasis on the preposition.[13]

The characteristic words of Calvin appear justified in summarizing this passage and its relevance to this study, 'Therefore his meaning is that none can reach faith by his own intelligence but only by the secret illumination of the Spirit.' 'It all comes back to this: It is the Father's gift that the Son is known, for by His Spirit He opens the eyes of our minds and we perceive the glory of Christ which otherwise would be hidden from us. But the Father, who dwells in light inaccessible and is Himself incomprehensible, is revealed to us by the Son, His lively image, and in vain do we seek him elsewhere.'[14]

Matthew 13:10–17 (Mark 4:10–12; Luke 8:9–10)

The disciples came to him and asked, 'Why do you speak to the people in parables?' He replied, 'The knowledge of the secrets of the kingdom of heaven has been given to you, but not to them. Whoever has will be given more, and he will have an abundance. Whoever does not have, even what he has will be taken from him. This is why I speak to them in parables: "Though seeing, they do not see: though hearing, they do not hear or understand." In them is fulfilled the prophecy of Isaiah: "You will be ever hearing but never understanding; you will be ever seeing but never perceiving. For this people's heart has become calloused; they hardly hear with their ears, and they have closed their eyes. Otherwise they might see with their eyes, hear with their ears, understand with their hearts and turn, and I would heal them." But blessed are your eyes because they see, and your ears because they hear. For I tell you the truth, many prophets and righteous men longed to see what you see but did not see it, and to hear what you hear but did not hear it.'

This is Jesus' explanation for his use of parables. Matthew's account is by far the fullest; Luke's is the briefest.

All three accounts agree, with very similar wording, that to know the secrets (μυστήρια)[15] of the kingdom of heaven has been given to the disciples. Matthew adds the negative, 'but to those (i.e. the people in general to whom he spoke the parables) it has not been given'. Alexander gets to the heart of what Jesus says when he comments, 'The difference between these classes was not one of personal intrinsic merit, but of divine favour. To you it has been given, the perfect passive form, implying an authoritative predetermination, being common to all three accounts ... given, not conceded as a right, but granted as a favour.'[16]

Verse 12 in Matthew's account (Mark 4:24–25; Luke 8:18) indicates a principle behind Jesus' adoption of the parabolic method at this time. The majority of the people had already heard Jesus speak. Those who had listened and begun to respond would receive more through his parables; but those who had never really listened would find the parables interesting but would completely miss their significance. This also arises, in part at least, from the nature of parables. 'Parables both reveal and conceal truth; they reveal it to the genuine seeker who will take the trouble to dig beneath the surface and discover the meaning, but they conceal it from him who is content simply to listen to the story.'[17]

This point is underlined by the quotation from Isaiah. As a result of the condition of mind and heart, however much the people listen, they will never understand. Their mind is dulled and they have stopped their ears and shut their eyes. So Calvin says, 'The Gospel is not the cause of blindness properly speaking or in itself or in its nature, but only in the event. It is like the dim-sighted going into the sunshine. It only makes their eyes weaker still. Yet the fault lies, not in the sun, but in their eyes.'[18]

The words in verse 11, 'To you it has been given ... to those it has not been given' imply that the disciples themselves would have been dull and unreceptive apart from the ability to know granted to them, 'natural insight is not enough; spiritual enlightenment is given'.[19] This passage is emphatic in its teaching that spiritual understanding, the ability to know the secrets of the kingdom of heaven, is a gift from God.

In verses 16–17 Jesus pronounces a blessing (μακάριοι) on the disciples because they do see and hear. This is to be linked with verse 11: 'To you it has been granted to know the secrets of the kingdom of heaven.' W. C. Allen comments on the emphatic position of ὑμῶν δὲ at the beginning of the sentence, 'The ὑμῶν is emphatic, and contains a direct contrast to those referred to in αὐτοῖς, vv. 10–13, ἐκεῖνοι, v. 11, and in vv. 13–15.'[20] Interestingly Luke does not have this saying at this point but in 10:23–24, immediately after the previous passage considered.[21] In that context it suggests that the Son is choosing to reveal to them the things which they see and hear. Both contexts suggest that the disciples are not simply blest because they are seeing things that had not happened previously – many other Jews saw most of them too – but they are blest because insight into the spiritual realities of the kingdom is being granted to them but not to others.

Matthew 16:13–23 (Mark 8:27–33; Luke 9:22–27)

When Jesus came to the region of Caesarea Philippi, he asked his disciples, 'Who do people say the Son of Man is?' They replied, 'Some say John the Baptist; others say Elijah; and still others, Jeremiah or one of the prophets.' 'But what about you?' he asked. 'Who do you say I am?' Simon Peter answered, 'You are the Christ, the Son of the living God.' Jesus replied, 'Blessed are you, Simon, son of Jonah, for this was not revealed to you by man, but by my Father in heaven. And I tell you that you are Peter, and on this rock I will build my church, and the gates of Hades will not overcome it. I will give you the keys of the kingdom of heaven; whatever you bind on earth will be bound in heaven, and whatever you loose on earth will be loosed in heaven.' Then he warned his disciples not to tell anyone that he was the Christ. From that time on Jesus began to explain to his disciples that he must go to Jerusalem and suffer many things at the hands of the elders, chief priests and teachers of the law, and that he must be killed and on the third day be raised to life. Peter took him aside and began to rebuke him. 'Never, Lord!' he said, 'This shall never happen to you!' Jesus turned and said to Peter, 'Get behind me, Satan! You are a stumbling-block to me; you do not have in mind the things of God, but the things of men.'

The important verses for this study are 17 and 23. Initially it can be noted that there is no parallel to verse 17 in either Mark or Luke; nor is there any parallel to verse 23 in Luke. Probably the main reason for this difference lies in the different purposes of the gospel writers. Luke, in particular, appears to be leading up to the climax of the transfiguration (Luke 9:28–36) and his focus is on Jesus himself. Matthew is clearly much more concerned to show Peter's role and to make it evident that his confession of Jesus' messiahship and Sonhood was not the result of human deduction or intuition, but of revelation from the Father, in this exemplifying the words of Jesus already recorded in 11:25–26. Several points can be noted:

Firstly, the fact that Peter has come to understand who Jesus is by revelation is emphasized in the words that Jesus speaks to him. First of all Jesus says, 'Blessed are you' (REB: 'you are favoured indeed'). Jesus is not congratulating Peter on the perspicacity of his spiritual insight; rather, Peter has been graciously favoured by the Father. Secondly, the words, 'my Father who is in heaven' contrast markedly with 'flesh and blood'; this is revelation from above, from a different realm altogether. This is further accentuated by the word 'my'. Peter has confessed Jesus as the 'Son of the living God'; it is that living God, 'my Father', who has revealed this truth to Peter. The negative is also important here. 'Flesh and blood', that is, human nature – human understanding, human resources, human learning – 'has not disclosed this to you'. The emphasis here is not on the heart being evil or the mind prejudiced, as in previous passages; human nature itself is inadequate for grasping such truth. As Calvin says, 'From this we infer that human minds lack the ability to perceive the mysteries of heavenly wisdom hidden in Christ; more, all human senses fail in this respect until God opens our eyes to see his glory in Christ.'[22] Linking this verse with 1 Corinthians 12:3, 'No-one can say "Jesus is Lord" except by the Holy Spirit', Suzanne de Dietrich comments: 'The entire Apostolic Church recognized that the divinity of Jesus Christ is a mystery of faith, inaccessible to human wisdom alone, which is otherwise called, according to a classic Hebrew expression, "flesh and blood" – the natural man.'[23]

It is very likely that this is to be seen against the theological background of the fallenness of human nature, but it is simply human nature as it is now that is in focus here. This is not a Pharisee or Sadducee, it is one of the earliest and most eager of Jesus' disciples, yet even he cannot grasp the truth of who Jesus is by unaided human powers.[24] He is granted revelation by the Father.

The sequel in verse 23 is extraordinary. Here is a reversal of verse 17; Peter thinks as a man thinks when he rebukes Jesus for his words about his death. Ridderbos says, 'Remarkably, however, Jesus' explanation in both cases refers to the very same things: in verse 17 He contrasts what is revealed by man with what is revealed by the Father: in verse 23 He contrasts minding the things of God with minding the things of man.'[25] Here is an underlining of the fact that when men think, using natural human powers, they get things wrong. The things of God require revelation and illumination if human beings are going to think them.[26]

Matthew 17:5 (Mark 9:7; Luke 9:35)

This is my Son, whom I love; with him I am well-pleased. Listen to him.

'The added words *listen to him* are probably to be seen as an echo of Deuteronomy 18:15, 18 where the same demand is made in reference to the promised prophet like Moses. In this context there is perhaps an implied rebuke of Peter's failure to grasp Jesus' teaching about the Messiah's role (16:21–23).'[27] The account of the transfiguration, coming immediately after the account of Peter's confession at Caesarea Philippi, and the prominence given to Peter in both passages, lends weight to France's contention that there is an implied rebuke here. But the connection between the two passages is much more than this. To begin with, the heavenly voice confirms the confession that Peter has made. Moreover the inference is that it was only after Peter's confession that it was appropriate for Jesus to reveal his glory as the divine Son. Nowhere does Jesus command or demand recognition of his Sonship by revealing his supernatural glory. It is after the inward revelation to Peter and his confession before the disciples that there comes the brief external revelation of glory, and the voice confirming Peter's confession and in this way accepting it.

The words from heaven also highlight the incongruity of Peter's reaction in 16:22. If Peter has confessed Jesus as Messiah and Son of God, to rebuke him (ἐπιτιμᾶν), dissenting strongly from his words (Ἵλεώς σοι – '[God] be merciful to you, Lord', that is, 'may God spare you this'), is highly incongruous and a contradiction of what his own confession implies. If Jesus is the divine Son, the object of the Father's love and approval, listening to him is the only response. To think the things of God means listening to the Son.

Being held responsible for lack of understanding
At this point an objection to what has been educed so far may be considered. This arises from those passages in which people are held responsible for not understanding the things which were said to them. The importance of preaching and teaching is emphasized in the Synoptic Gospels, especially the preaching and teaching ministry of Jesus (e.g. Matt. 3:1ff; 4:17, 23; 5–7; Mark 1:14, 21, 38, 39; Luke 23:47) and people were expected to listen and respond to what they heard: 'If you have ears, then hear' (Matt. 11:15). It is

striking that in Matthew 11, immediately before Jesus' words about hiding these things from the wise and learned and revealing them to little children, we find his denunciation of impenitent towns where his miracles had been performed. His words, 'If the miracles performed in you had taken place in Tyre and Sidon, they would have repented long ago in sackcloth and ashes' are sharply to the point here, for it cannot be supposed that Jesus is suggesting that Tyre and Sidon or Sodom would have been recipients of revelation from the Father. One of the clearest places where this is expressed is at the conclusion of the sermon on the mount in the parable of Jesus about the two houses (Matt. 7:24-27). Here the person who hears Jesus' words and does them is likened to a wise man and the person who hears but does not act is likened to a foolish man. This suggests that the problem with the people that Jesus confronted was not one of understanding, but of obedience. Three responses can be made to this.

Firstly, some would doubtless argue that this is another strand of thought that emerges from the Synoptics (and, indeed, the rest of the New Testament), and therefore that a choice has to be made between these two divergent emphases.

However, another way of looking at this would be to say that the understanding spoken of in the passages reviewed is not simply mental apprehension but includes receptivity and response. The mind receives the teaching and understands the sense of the words but there is no inclination to receive it as true or welcome it and obey it because the heart (i.e. the whole inner being) is predisposed by sin. Some of the passages suggest this, though others appear to go beyond it.

Thirdly, it can also be said that this is part of the wider difficulty of understanding the place of human responsibility within the activity of the grace of God. Many writers call in the concept of paradox at this point.[28]

References to the Holy Spirit

The references to the Holy Spirit in the Synoptic Gospels are not many[29] (12 in Matthew; 6 in Mark; 15 in Luke of which 7 occur in the first two chapters) but, as James Dunn has shown,[30] the significance of the Spirit for understanding the ministry of Jesus is of crucial importance. These references can be divided into four general groups: those which belong to the birth narratives; those which cluster around the baptism of John and the commencement of Jesus' ministry; those which relate to Jesus' ministry of casting out demons; and finally those which relate to the Old Testament, prophecy and speaking on special occasions. For this study it will sometimes be necessary to take a cluster of references together. There is little evidence directly linking the work of the Holy Spirit with the giving of understanding, but there are hints pointing in that direction.

Jesus' baptism and early ministry
The early references in Matthew to the conception of Jesus by the Holy Spirit have no relevance to this study, but those which relate to the beginning of his ministry are very important in understanding that ministry. The crucial event which heralded the beginning of his ministry was his baptism by John. On this occasion he publicly identified himself with sinful people by submitting to a baptism for the forgiveness of sins, and the Holy Spirit came upon him in the form of a dove (Matt. 3:16; Mark 1:10; Luke 3:22). Thus it can be said that Jesus was baptized with water and the Holy Spirit. The Spirit then led him into a desert region where he was tempted by the devil (Matt. 4:1–11; Mark 1:12–13; Luke 4:1–13). Victorious over the tempter, Jesus now began his ministry. Luke's account is particularly significant: 'Then Jesus returned in the power of the Spirit to Galilee ...' (Luke 4:14). Luke goes on to record Jesus' visit to the synagogue in Nazareth where Jesus read from Isaiah 61:1: 'The Spirit of the Lord is on me, because he has anointed me to preach good news to the poor. He has sent me to proclaim freedom for the prisoners and recovery of sight for the blind, to release the oppressed, to proclaim the year of the Lord's favour' (Luke 4:18–19 NIV).

There can be no doubt that all the synoptics present the baptism as the time when Jesus was anointed and equipped with the Holy Spirit for his ministry. His ministry was a ministry in the power of the Spirit (Luke 4:1).[31] James Dunn writes: 'His consciousness of a spiritual power so real, so effective, so new, so final, was the well-spring of both his proclamation of the presentness of the future kingdom and his authority in deed and word.... His awareness of being uniquely possessed and used by divine Spirit was the mainspring of his mission and the key to its effectiveness.'[32]

This ministry in the Spirit was understood by Jesus and the gospel writers in terms taken especially from the book of Isaiah 61:1–2, (as already noted) and 42:1–4 (Matt. 12:18–21). There does not appear to be any explicit allusion to Isaiah 11:1–15 in the gospels, but it is frequently assumed that this passage too, lay in the background of the thought of the writers when they considered the relationship of the Spirit to Jesus.[33] It is difficult to think that this passage would not be in the mind of Jesus also as he considered his messianic calling and equipping by the Spirit.

These references in Isaiah show the breadth of influence which the Spirit was understood to have had upon Jesus. His character and attitudes, as well as his ministry, were formed under the influence of the Spirit on him. For the purposes of this study it can be noted that Isaiah 11 speaks of the Spirit in terms of wisdom, knowledge and understanding. There is no difficulty in accepting that the Gospel writers would have considered that Jesus' insight and knowledge of the Old Testament, of the will of his Father, and the wisdom shown in his dealings with people, was the result of the Spirit upon and within him. It is possible to see hints of this in his very use of Isaiah 61:1–4; in Luke 10:21 (insight into the will of his Father); and in Matthew 12:17–21 (dealing with people); as also possibly Matthew 10:20, 'the Spirit of *your* Father', was, first of all, the Spirit of *his* Father; cf. also Luke 21:15 where Jesus says, 'I will give you words and wisdom...', yet elsewhere it is the Spirit who does so.

One reference in the narratives connected with Jesus' baptism and the beginning of his ministry remains to be considered. This records the words of John the Baptist, 'He shall baptize you with the Holy Spirit and fire' (Matt. 3:11; Mark 1:8; Luke 3:16). There are a number of difficulties connected with this verse, in particular the meaning of 'and fire' at the end of the verse.[34] A number of recent writers suggest that there is an allusion here to Isaiah 4:4

which speaks of washing and purging 'by the spirit of judgement and by the spirit of burning'.[35] Mark does not include the words 'and fire' and it is also significant that when baptism with the Spirit is alluded to in the rest of the New Testament fire is not mentioned. This suggests that concentration should be on the phrase 'with the Holy Spirit'. Denney goes so far as to say, 'The work of Christ was summed up in the words; "he shall baptize with the Holy Spirit."'[36] The significance of John's words seems to be this: the Holy Spirit, which Jesus had received with all the richness of influence already mentioned, would be poured out in rich effusion upon those who believed in him. And this is the Spirit of Isaiah 11, the Spirit who brings wisdom and understanding, counsel and knowledge. Because the Spirit had come upon Jesus he was able to baptize others with the Spirit: 'On Jesus, the Spirit came in fullness and came to remain for ever. For this reason, it was possible for Jesus to fulfil the mission of which John spoke.'[37] The term 'baptism' indicates that this is an initiatory experience of the Spirit, as well as emphasizing the comprehensiveness of being 'immersed' in the Spirit. The term 'receive' the Spirit, which is used of the same experience, emphasizes that the Spirit takes up residence in the Christian. His very presence has implications for understanding and knowledge and also for many other areas of life.

Jesus' exorcisms by the Spirit
A second group brings together the three references to the Holy Spirit in Matthew 12:28, 31–32 (12:28 being paralleled, with a notable difference by Luke 11:20; 12:31 by Mark 3:29; 12:32 by Luke 12:10). The occasion for these words of Jesus was the Pharisees' explanation for his casting out of demons: 'It is only by Beelzebub prince of devils that this man drives the devils out' (Matt. 12:24; REB). These verses are not directly relevant to this study but they do provide indirect strengthening of what has been seen in the references at the time of Jesus' baptism.

Jesus' exorcisms by the Spirit of God (Luke 11:20, 'finger of God', possibly an allusion to Exodus 8:19, and certainly an indication of the power of God in action) were the sign that the kingdom had come with power. James Dunn expresses the point like this, 'So far as Jesus was concerned, the exercise of this power was evidence that the longed-for kingdom of God had already come upon his hearers.' 'The eschatological kingdom was present for Jesus only because the eschatological Spirit was present in and through him.'[38] The exorcisms demonstrated that the Spirit had come in all his fullness so that all the messianic expectations concerning the Spirit and the kingdom were being fulfilled.

The two verses referring to the blasphemy against the Spirit underline this conclusion. While superficially these verses appear to introduce a contrast between Jesus and the Spirit – one in which the Spirit appears to have a greater dignity than Jesus – in fact they show a very close relationship between Jesus and the Spirit. James Denney explains: 'The Holy Spirit is not here (Mark 3:20–35) set in any contrast with Jesus, as though to blaspheme Jesus were a venial fault, but to blaspheme the Spirit an unpardonable one: on the contrary, the Holy Spirit is blasphemed when malignant hearts harden themselves to say of Jesus, "He has an unclean spirit."'[39]

The moral power of the Spirit is especially conspicuous in Jesus' exorcisms, and they serve to highlight the fact that the ministry of Jesus is a ministry in the power of the Spirit. It is the same Spirit which Jesus imparts to his followers.

Other references to the Holy Spirit
There are also several isolated verses speaking of the Holy Spirit which need to be commented on.

Matthew 10:20 (Luke 12:12; Mark 13:11):

For it will not be you speaking, but the Spirit of your Father speaking through you.

This is the promise of Jesus that when his disciples are brought before the authorities 'the words you need will be given you' by 'the Spirit of your Father'. Three points may be noticed. Firstly as M. B. B. Turner notes, 'This promise (Matt. 10:19–20, par.) assumes the disciples will already have the Spirit promised by Joel (it is only the words of defence that are given "in that hour"; not the gift of the Spirit itself.)'[40] Secondly, the Spirit is here described, uniquely in the New Testament, as 'the Spirit of your Father'. This suggests at least that disciples are brought into a relationship with God in which it is only to be expected that they will partake of the Spirit. As the voice of the Father attested the sonship of Jesus when the Spirit came upon him at his baptism, so for disciples also possession of the Spirit and sonship belong together. Thirdly, the Spirit here is clearly the Spirit of wisdom (cf. Luke 21:14–15) who gives 'the gift of a message fitting the circumstances'.[41] While these circumstances are particular, and this promise carefully limited in scope (the promise is not of understanding or insight, but simply of appropriate words) it is nevertheless the Spirit who gives them because it is part of the role of the Spirit to act in this way.

Luke 11:13 (Matt. 7:11):

If you then, though you are evil, know how to give good gifts to your children, how much more will your Father in heaven give the Holy Spirit to those who ask him!

At this point it is necessary to look at Luke's account because where Matthew records Jesus' promise, 'how much more will your heavenly Father give good things' Luke has 'how much more will your heavenly Father give the Holy Spirit to those who ask him!' (REB). The Holy Spirit is here 'the all-inclusive gift'.[42] As human fathers give good things to their children, so all the spiritual good things given by the heavenly Father are summed up in the Holy Spirit.

Matthew 22:43 (Mark 12:36):

He said to them, 'How is it then that David, speaking by the Spirit, calls him "Lord"?'

Here Jesus refers to David speaking in Psalm 110 'by the Spirit' (Mark has 'Holy Spirit'). Jesus is looking upon David as a prophet and expressing what for the Jews was the most characteristic way of understanding the Spirit.[43] It is enough for our purpose at this point to note that in the New Testament the Spirit who is given to disciples is one and the same with the Spirit of prophecy.

Matthew 28:19:

'Therefore go and make disciples of all nations, baptising them in the name of the Father and of the Son and of the Holy Spirit.

The Trinitarian formula for the baptism of disciples indicates the continuing importance of the Holy Spirit down to 'the end of time' (REB). As Father, Son and Holy Spirit were each specifically active in the baptism of Jesus, so disciples are baptized into a relationship with each one, not least the Holy Spirit who was received by Jesus in his fullness and is bestowed by him on them.

Summary

A number of passages indicate that the spiritual darkness which characterized the times of Jesus' life and ministry was the result of evil in the people's hearts leading to spiritual blindness. This was exhibited particularly by the Jewish religious leaders. On the other hand, the pure in heart see God and the elect cannot be led astray.

Other passages show that revelation and understanding are given by God. Truths hidden from the wise are revealed to babes by the Father; and it is the Son who reveals the Father. While the minds of many are dulled, disciples have the mysteries of the kingdom given to them. In particular it is the Father who reveals to Peter that Jesus is the messiah, the Son of the living God. However, when Peter thinks like a man he is seriously wrong.

This is to be seen against the background of the moral responsibility of people to listen and obey the words of Jesus. Spiritual blindness is the result of sin for which people are responsible.

The Synoptic Gospels do not speak directly of a work of the

Spirit in giving understanding or revealing when speaking of disciples. They do, however, speak of the Spirit coming upon Jesus to equip him for every aspect of his ministry and the Spirit is understood in terms drawn from the Old Testament which includes the Spirit, not only as the Spirit of prophecy, but also as the Spirit of wisdom, understanding, counsel and knowledge. Jesus, having been anointed with the Spirit, baptises with the Spirit, so that the same Spirit fills disciples too, equipping them for their lives and ministry.[44]

CHAPTER TWO

LUKE and ACTS

In his writings Luke lays particular emphasis on the work of the Holy Spirit. The first two chapters of his Gospel contain at least seven references to the Spirit.[1] There are nine references in the rest of the Gospel and their number and distribution are convincingly explained by Fitzmyer: 'What seems, then, to be important for Luke is that various stages of his narrative be initiated under the influence of the Spirit.'[2] In the Acts of the Apostles the Spirit appears fifty-seven times,[3] more than twice as many as in any other book of the New Testament, and a quarter of the total for the whole New Testament.

Luke

The birth and infancy narratives
Some of the references to the Holy Spirit in these narratives are directly concerned with the birth of Jesus. Comment will be made on five relevant passages.

Luke 1:15–17

For he will be great in the sight of the Lord. He is never to take wine or other fermented drink, and he will be filled with the Holy Spirit even from birth. Many of the people of Israel will he bring back to the Lord their God. And he will go on before the Lord, in the spirit and power of Elijah, to turn the hearts of the fathers to their children and the disobedient to the wisdom of the righteous – to make ready a people prepared for the Lord.

This passage speaks of John the Baptist being filled with the Holy Spirit from his mother's womb and as a result fulfilling a prophetic ministry, bringing back many from Israel to the Lord their God. A major theme in these narratives is 'prophetic inspiration heralding the arrival of the new era',[4] and the prominent emphasis in Luke is on the Holy Spirit as the Spirit of prophecy.

Luke 1:41–44

When Elizabeth heard Mary's greeting, the baby leaped in her womb, and Elizabeth was filled with the Holy Spirit. In a loud voice she exclaimed: 'Blessed are you among women, and blessed is the child you will bear! But why am I so favoured, that the mother of my Lord should come to me? As soon as the sound of your greeting reached my ears, the baby in my womb leaped for joy.'

Here there is a second example of a person who is filled with the Spirit, though this time it appears to be a temporary experience.[5] 'Because she [Elisabeth] is filled with the Spirit, her words will express the divine perspective and insight. What she says results from an inspired interpretation of the movement of the unborn child (as v. 44 makes explicit).'[6] Presumably it was the Holy Spirit who enabled her to realize that Mary was 'the mother of my Lord'.

Luke 1:67–79

His father Zechariah was filled with the Holy Spirit and prophesied: 'Praise be to the Lord, the God of Israel, because he has come and has redeemed his people. He has raised up a horn of salvation for us in the house of his servant David (as he said through his holy prophets of long ago), salvation from our enemies and from the hand of all who hate us – to show mercy to our fathers and to remember his holy covenant, the oath he swore to our father Abraham: to rescue us from the hand of our enemies, and to enable us to serve him without fear in holiness and righteousness before him all our days. And you, my child, will be called a prophet of the Most High: for you will go on before the Lord to prepare the way for him, to give his people the knowledge of salvation through the forgiveness of their sins, because of the tender mercy of our God, by which the rising sun will come to us from heaven to shine on those living in darkness and in the shadow of death, to guide our feet into the path of peace.'

In the third reference to being filled with the Spirit, Zechariah prophesies, uttering what Marshall calls 'a psalm of praise giving a divinely inspired commentary on the significance of the events which have begun to take place'.[7] As has been frequently noted this is full of 'OT ideas and phraseology'.[8] What is important here is the way the Spirit gives Zechariah a particular insight into the promises of the Old Testament. He is not simply speaking as a prophet, or a psalmist, but as an inspired interpreter of the Old Testament scripture, seeing it in the light of the new age that is dawning with the birth of John and the Most High who is, in some way, yet to come.

Luke 2:25–35

Now there was a man in Jerusalem called Simeon, who was righteous and devout. He was waiting for the consolation of Israel and the Holy Spirit was upon him. It had been revealed to him by the Holy Spirit that he would not die before he had seen the Lord's Christ. Moved by the Spirit, he went into the temple courts. When the parents brought in the child Jesus to do for him what the custom of the Law required, Simeon took him in his arms and praised God, saying, 'Sovereign Lord, as you have promised, you now dismiss your servant in peace. For my eyes have seen your salvation, which you have prepared in the sight of all people, a light for revelation to the Gentiles and for glory to your people Israel.' The child's father and mother marvelled at what was said about him. Then Simeon blessed them and said to Mary, his mother: 'This child is destined to cause the falling and rising of many in Israel, and to be a sign that will be spoken against, so that the thoughts of many hearts will be revealed. And a sword will pierce your own soul too.'

This passage speaks of the Holy Spirit coming upon Simeon resulting in the revelation that he will not die until he has seen the messiah. He is guided to the temple when Jesus is there (v. 27); he breaks out into a short psalm of praise (vv. 28–32); and he prophesies concerning the future of the infant messiah (vv. 34–35). Involved in these activities is spiritual knowledge concerning the significance of the occasion and the identity of the child: 'Simeon has now seen

God's promised salvation in that his eyes, opened by the Spirit of God (Schurmann, 125) have been enabled to recognise in this child the promised messiah (cf. v. 26).'[9]

Luke 2:40–52

And the child grew and became strong; he was filled with wisdom, and the grace of God was upon him. Every year his parents went to Jerusalem for the Feast of the Passover. When he was twelve years old, they went up to the Feast, according to the custom. After the Feast was over, while his parents were returning home, the boy Jesus stayed behind in Jerusalem, but they were unaware of it. Thinking he was in their company, they travelled on for a day. Then they began looking for him among their relatives and friends. When they did not find him, they went back to Jerusalem to look for him. After three days they found him in the temple courts, sitting among the teachers, listening to them and asking them questions. Everyone who heard him was amazed at his understanding and his answers. When his parents saw him, they were astonished. His mother said to him, 'Son, why have you treated us like this? Your father and I have been anxiously searching for you.' 'Why were you searching for me?' he asked. 'Didn't you know I had to be in my Father's house?' But they did not understand what he was saying to them. Then he went down to Nazareth with them and was obedient to them. But his mother treasured all these things in her heart. And Jesus grew in wisdom and stature, and in favour with God and men.

This appears to be an unlikely passage to occur in a discussion of the teaching ministry of the Holy Spirit, but two quotations deserve consideration. Firstly, while commenting on this passage, Fitzmyer says, 'pressing beyond Bultmann's singling out of the wisdom of Jesus, some commentators have tried to find further significance in the mention of Jesus' comprehension (2:47) and wisdom (2:52) in this scene. These are supposed to be reflections of divine Wisdom revealing itself, as it is described in Sirach 24:1-12 ... But in Sirach Wisdom is depicted as a woman.... Moreover, Wisdom is identified in Sirach with the Torah. It is farfetched to extend these to the person of the adolescent Jesus.'[10] There is little difficulty in agreeing with

Fitzmyer here, but a similar point has also been made recently by Turner: 'The outcome of Jesus' conception by the Spirit is portrayed in Luke 2:41–52, which is understood against the background of messianic hopes for a ruler endowed with wisdom (Is. 11:2–4; Pss. Sol. 17:37; 1 Enoch 49:2–3; etc.) and God's grace (cf. 2:40). Already Jesus shows a wisdom that startles the leaders of Israel ...'[11] There is much more ground in Luke itself for expressing the point in this way. The passage stresses the growing wisdom of Jesus (v. 52; and especially v. 40: πληρούμενον σοφίᾳ) and illustrates it by the incident in the temple. It does not seem farfetched to see this as 'the outcome of Jesus' conception by the Spirit'.

The resurrection narratives

Luke 24:25–27

He said to them, 'How foolish you are, and how slow of heart to believe all that the prophets have spoken! Did not the Christ have to suffer these things and then enter his glory?' And beginning with Moses and all the Prophets, he explained to them what was said in all the Scriptures concerning himself.

These verses recount how the risen Jesus taught the two disciples on the road to Emmaus about the messiah from the Old Testament. In common with the other disciples they had not understood that the messiah was to rise from the dead. So Jesus rebukes them for their dullness of mind and for their slowness to believe all that the prophets had said. This is Jesus teaching in person, but the verses highlight the need even for disciples to be given special instruction about and insight into the Old Testament scriptures.

Luke 24:31–32, 45:

Then their eyes were opened and they recognised him, and he disappeared from their sight. They asked each other, 'Were not our hearts burning within us while he talked with us on the road and opened the Scriptures to us?'... Then he opened their minds so they could understand the Scriptures.

These verses further on in the same account are noteworthy for the repetition of the word διανοίγεῖν – to open. In verse 31 it is the eyes of the disciples which are opened to recognize Jesus; previously they had not realized who he was (v. 16). In verse 32 they speak of how their hearts burned within them as he opened the scriptures to them. Further, to anticipate, verse 45 speaks of Jesus opening the minds of his disciples to understand the scriptures. In the last two cases it is Jesus that does the opening, and in none is there any mention of the Holy Spirit. However, the references underline the need of Jesus' disciples for divine illumination, whether it is to recognize him or to understand the scripture.

Luke 24:44–49

He said to them, 'This is what I told you while I was still with you: Everything must be fulfilled that is written about me in the Law of Moses, the Prophets and the Psalms.' Then he opened their minds so they could understand the Scriptures. He told them, 'This is what is written: The Christ will suffer and rise from the dead on the third day, and repentance and forgiveness of sins will be preached in his name to all nations, beginning at Jerusalem. You are witnesses of these things. I am going to send you what my Father has promised; but stay in the city until you have been clothed with power from on high.'

Three comments will be made about these verses.

First is the significant way in which understanding the scripture is related to the disciples' task of proclaiming repentance and the forgiveness of sins in the name of the messiah. As Fitzmyer says, '[The OT scriptures] become the basis for the testimony that the disciples are to bear and the preaching that they are to carry out in his name. Eye-witnesses have to become testifiers and indeed "ministers of the word" (1:2).'[12] Minds opened to understand the scriptures are a prerequisite for those who will fulfil the dominical injunction to proclaim the gospel to all nations.

Second, reference also needs to be made to the comment of Godet on this passage and particularly verse 45:

Jesus closes these explanations by an act of power for which they were meant to prepare. He opens the inner sense of His apostles, so that the Scriptures shall henceforth cease to be to them a sealed book. This act is certainly the same as that described by John in the words (20:22): '*And He breathed on them, saying, Receive ye the Holy Ghost.*' The only difference is, that John names the efficient cause, Luke the effect produced. The miracle is the same as that which Jesus shall one day work upon Israel collectively, *when the veil shall be taken away.*[13]

Plummer appears to agree with linking this passage with John 20:22, while Arndt is very doubtful.[14] There seems to be nothing to justify the dogmatic 'This act is certainly the same', and although the suggestion is interesting, it remains nothing more than a suggestion.

Third, we note Fitzmyer's comment on the position of δύναμιν at the end of verse 49:

The word δύναμις comes emphatically at the end of the verse and it rings a bell for the careful reader of the Lucan Gospel. For it was 'with the power of the Spirit' that Jesus himself withdrew to Galilee after his encounter with the devil (4:14). Moreover, it was with 'the power of the Lord' (Kyriou = Yahweh, 5:17) that he healed people. And the power that 'went forth from him' (6:19) is precisely the 'power' with which his disciples are now to be invested (see Acts 2:32–33). Though it is not yet made clear what 'my Father has promised' (24:49) is, that will be clarified in Acts 1:4b, 5b; 2:2–4, 32–33.[15]

This is a further reminder that it is the same Spirit who filled Jesus who is the promised gift of the Father, and it prepares the way for the Spirit's role and activity in Acts.

Acts

As already noted there are some 57 references to the Holy Spirit in Acts and concentration will be on some of these. Acts being primarily narrative, and the recorded sermons being mainly addressed to those who had not yet believed in Jesus, there is not the same direct teaching to be found as in the Gospels, nor is it so easy to draw deductions.

General comments on the Holy Spirit

First of all, it is surprising in view of the word 'power' in Luke 24:49 and Acts 1:8 that the Holy Spirit is so little connected with miraculous acts and healings. There are only three references of which this is possibly true (10:38, 13:9–11 and 4:31), and of these, the most definite (10:38) is speaking of Jesus' ministry. There are also three references in which the Holy Spirit is the inspirer of the Old Testament scriptures (1:16, 4:25, and 28:25). There are a significant number of references in which people speak out under the influence of the Spirit, often having been filled by the Spirit for this purpose (1:2; 2:4, 18; 4:8, 31; 6:10; 21:11 and possibly 7:51 if Stephen's words are to be referred to as the Spirit speaking through the prophets). There are also a number of references in which the Holy Spirit guides, speaks or warns, sometimes through prophets (8:29, 39; 10:19; 11:12; 13:2, 4; 15:28; 16:6, 7; 20:22, 23; 21:4, 11). Some of these have some significance for the present thesis.

The largest number of references refer to those who are baptized by, filled by, or who receive the Spirit. Omitting references to people described as full of the Spirit, which appears to refer to character, and what appear to be temporary fillings for a particular purpose, we still have 1:5, 8; 2:4, 17–18, 38; 8:16, 17, 18, 19, 20; 9:17; 10:44, 45, 47; 11:15, 16; 15:8; 19:2, 6. James Denney says, 'And more important than any single observation is the fact that in Acts, as elsewhere in the NT, the reception of the Spirit is the whole of Christianity. "They received the Holy Spirit even as we did" (10:47; 11:15; 15:8ff.). All that makes a man a Christian is in this ... In receiving the Spirit a person receives all that the Spirit is, and the Spirit begins to act within and through that person.'[16] So if the Spirit is the Spirit of wisdom and understanding then these qualities will belong to all Christians.

Acts 1:2

Until the day he was taken up to heaven, after giving instructions through the Holy Spirit to the apostles he had chosen.

This verse speaks of Jesus giving instructions to the apostles 'through the Holy Spirit'.[17] This seems to suggest that the period of instruction by Jesus was now drawing to an end and the era of the Spirit's teaching was dawning. The transition is marked by the risen Jesus giving his final orders (ἐντειλάμενος) through the Spirit.[18] It is also possible to see, with Calvin, that the witness of the apostles would be with the authority of God from the Spirit.[19]

Acts 1:8

But you will receive power when the Holy Spirit comes on you; and you will be my witnesses in Jerusalem, and in all Judea and Samaria, and to the ends of the earth.

Two comments will be made on this verse. Firstly, in the words of Williams, 'This commission obviously had a special reference to the apostles, who would uniquely authenticate the gospel data ...'[20] Secondly, however, this is a repetition of Jesus' words in Luke 24:49, a promise which was fulfilled on the day of Pentecost which inaugurated the era of the Spirit and formed the disciples of Jesus into one body,[21] the community of the Holy Spirit (1 Cor. 12:13).[22]

Acts 2

The second comment on 1:8 has already anticipated the significance of the outpouring of the Spirit at Pentecost recorded in this chapter. The main point to be stressed here concerns the preaching of Peter. What is especially significant about it is its use of the Old Testament; it is largely structured around the exposition and application of Joel 2:28–32 and Psalm 16:8–11. There are two aspects noted here. First of all it is possible to see Peter's sermon as an example of Christian prophecy, a fulfilment *par excellence* of the Joel prophecy.[23] But, secondly, of greater interest for our study, is the evidence it gives of Peter's insight into Old Testament scripture. It is true, of course, that the pattern for Christological interpretation of the Old Testament had been given by Jesus himself, but it is certainly reasonable to see Peter's understanding of the Old Testament as a function of the Holy Spirit's illuminating work.[24]

A note can be added on verse 38 where Peter promises that all who repent and are baptized will not only have their sins forgiven but will also receive the gift of the Holy Spirit. This emphasises the fact that every believer receives the full benefit of the promise of the Father; those coming after Pentecost enter into the fullness of the blessing of the Spirit which it brought.

Acts 4:8–12, 25, 26, 31

Then Peter, filled with the Holy Spirit, said to them: 'Rulers and elders of the people! If we are being called to account today for an act of kindness shown to a cripple and are asked how he was healed, then know this, you and all the people of Israel: It is by the name of Jesus Christ of Nazareth, whom you crucified but whom God raised from the dead, that this man stands before you healed. He is "the stone you builders rejected, which has become the capstone". Salvation is found in no-one else, for there is no other name under heaven given to men by which we must be saved.... You spoke by the Holy Spirit through the mouth of your servant, our father David: "Why do the nations rage and the peoples plot in vain? The kings of the earth take their stand and the rulers gather together against the Lord and against his Anointed One".... After they prayed, the place where they were meeting was shaken. And they were all filled with the Holy Spirit and spoke the word of God boldly.'

These references illustrate what has already been seen, that the Spirit is the inspirer of scripture, the giver of the response when Jesus' disciples are brought before the authorities (Luke 12:11, 12; 21:14, 15), and the One who enables God's word to be spoken with boldness. As in Acts 2 we also see here a particular use of Old Testament Scripture.

First of all Peter, filled with the Holy Spirit, makes an apposite application of Psalm 118:22 to Jesus and his rejection by the Jewish leaders. It is not just insight into the meaning of the text which is seen here, but its appropriateness to the situation. Peter's grasp of this, as well as his boldness in expressing it, is most suitably to be attributed to his being filled with the Spirit.

The same appropriateness of application is seen in the prayer of the church in verses 24–26. In Psalm 2:2 there is the link word 'anointed', 'Christ', but the continuation of the prayer in verses 27–28 shows how the church realized that the opening words of the Psalm expressed precisely the situation revealed by the rejection and crucifixion of Jesus, a situation which was still continuing.

However we are precisely to regard 'they raised their voice with one accord to God', it seems clear that all who gathered together joined in the prayer. It is not directly stated that the Spirit gave them a collective insight into the meaning and suitability of Psalm 2, but they were all filled with the Spirit (v. 31) and there is at least a suggestion that this is what happened.

Acts 5:32

We are witnesses of these things, and so is the Holy Spirit, whom God has given to those who obey him.

This verse contains a unique description of the Spirit as a witness, along with the apostles, of the resurrection, exaltation and saviour-hood of Jesus. Williams says that the Spirit's witness can be understood in two ways; first his very coming at Pentecost was evidence of these things (cf. 2:33), but he also bore witness with the apostles 'with the further thought that the Spirit brings this witness home to the people's hearts, convincing them that the apostolic testimony is true'.[25]

Acts 6:3, 10

'Brothers, choose seven men from among you who are known to be full of the Spirit and wisdom. We will turn this responsibility over to them' ... 'but they could not stand up against his wisdom or the Spirit by whom he spoke.'

In these two references wisdom and the Spirit are joined together. In the case of verse 3 perhaps practical wisdom is intended,[26] but in verse 10 we have a fulfilment of Jesus' words in Luke 21:14–15,

'So resolve not to prepare your defence beforehand, because I myself will give you such words and wisdom as no opponent can resist or refute' (REB). While 'wisdom' and 'Spirit' could be thought of as co-ordinate, several writers suggest rather that wisdom is 'a particular manifestation of the Spirit's work'.[27] Hull comments, 'It is, however, at Acts 6:10 ... that Luke actually joined the words "wisdom" and "Spirit" ... It was not knowledge in general but theological insight in particular that Luke had in mind when describing Stephen's powers of debate ... this insight is a gift of the Spirit.'[28]

Acts 7:55–56

But Stephen, full of the Holy Spirit, looked up to heaven and saw the glory of God, and Jesus standing at the right hand of God. "Look," he said, 'I see heaven open and the Son of Man standing at the right hand of God.'

In these verses Stephen's vision of the glory of God and Jesus standing at God's right hand is linked to his being filled with the Holy Spirit.

The use of the phrase ὑπάρχων δὲ πλήρης πνεύματος ἁγίου indicates that this was a continuing condition of being filled with the Spirit, and not an infilling on that occasion.[29] Perhaps the implication is that this vision was the culmination of a life filled with the Spirit.

Williams seeks to draw out the implication in this way, 'It was to the Spirit, therefore, that he owed his theological insights ... and now by the same Spirit – for this is the implication of the passage before us – those insights took a definite shape in his mind's eye.'[30]

Williams also links this with the vision of the Son of Man in Daniel 7:13ff. This must be a possibility as this is the only place outside the Gospels and apart from the words of Jesus himself where Jesus is called the Son of Man. If so, even at his death, Stephen, filled with the Spirit, sees the exalted Jesus in terms drawn from the Old Testament. Bearing in mind the sovereignty, glory and eternal kingdom of the Son of Man as described in the Daniel prophecy it was most fitting for Stephen to see Jesus at this time in this way.[31]

Acts 8:35:

Then Philip began with that very passage of Scripture and told him the good news about Jesus.

In this verse Philip, in response to the question of the Ethiopian eunuch, began to tell him about Jesus from Isaiah 53. Bearing in mind the role of the Spirit in verses 29 and 39 it seems reasonable to consider Philip as under the constant impulse of the Spirit. Swete's comments therefore appear justifiable: 'In Philip's interview with the Eunuch we observe the same skill in interpreting the OT which marked the Apostles after the coming of the Spirit ... It may be that the Christian interpretation of this prophecy was already familiar to Philip, for our Lord had applied this passage to Himself; but it is not quoted elsewhere in the Acts, and the meaning of Isaiah 53 may have been suggested by the same Spirit that had bidden Philip to join the eunuch.'[32]

Acts 9:3 (22:6; 26:13); 26:18:

As he neared Damascus on his journey, suddenly a light from heaven flashed round him ... 'to open their eyes and turn them from darkness to light, and from the power of Satan to God, so that they may receive forgiveness of sins and a place among those who are sanctified by faith in me.'

These verses are linked together here because the bright light seen by Saul on the road to Damascus in some ways can be considered symbolic of the spiritual experience that he had, and of the ministry of conversion to which he was called.

The great light, in which Saul saw the risen Christ (Gal. 1:16; 1 Cor. 9:1; 15:8), clearly speaks of revelation from God.[33] Some writers suggest that the words of 26:18 'to open their eyes and to turn them from darkness to light' reflect on Paul's own experience.[34] Opening eyes and turning from darkness to light are activities which are not normally attributed to people, but rather belong to God. So Calvin says, '... for we know that the eyes of the mind are enlightened only by the Holy Spirit.... But it is a common thing for God to transfer to his ministers the honour due to Himself alone, not in order to take anything away from Himself, but to commend the efficacy of His Spirit, which He puts forth in them. For He does not send them to work so that they may be dead instruments, or as if they were play-actors, but so that He may work powerfully with their assistance.'[35]

Acts 15:28

It seemed good to the Holy Spirit and to us not to burden you with anything beyond the following requirements.

The Council of Jerusalem, as it is usually described, had an exceptionally difficult task before it. On the one hand it wanted to assert the full acceptance of the Gentiles into the church (v. 19), on the other it did not want to offend the susceptibilities of Jews who might be turned from the gospel (v. 21). In the letter which was written to the congregations in Antioch, Syria and Cilicia, the apostles and elders say, 'It seemed good to the Holy Spirit and to us ...' In the debate, doubtless also in the selection and use of Amos 9:11–12 (vv. 16–18), and in the decision and the letter itself the guidance of the Spirit is recognised. The understanding needed to reach a satisfactory conclusion is acknowledged to be the work of the Holy Spirit.

Acts 16:14

One of those listening was a woman named Lydia, a dealer in purple cloth from the city of Thyatira, who was a worshipper of God. The Lord opened her heart to respond to Paul's message..

Rackham[36] links the opening[37] of Lydia's heart here with Luke 24:45 and Jesus opening the minds of his disciples to understand the scripture. Although she was evidently a religious woman, hearing the gospel preached by Paul was not enough; she needed her heart to be opened. There is no mention of the Spirit here but it would not be untrue to the ethos of Acts to suggest that Luke would have understood the Spirit to be the agent used by the Lord in this act (cf. 1:2).

Acts 17:11

Now the Bereans were of more noble character than the Thessalonians, for they received the message with great eagerness and examined the Scriptures every day to see if what Paul said was true.

Over against the example of Lydia is that of the Bereans. They are commended for their diligent study of the scriptures as they tried to establish the truthfulness of what Paul was teaching. However, if Lydia needed her heart to be opened to receive what Paul said, it would seem to be perverse to understand this verse as suggesting that diligent study alone could result in determining the truth. In the context of Acts Calvin's comment seems justifiable, 'If anyone objects that this kind of examination will be ambiguous, since Scripture is so often obscure, and twisted to yield different meanings, I say that we must at the same time bring in the judgement of the Spirit, who is not called the Spirit of discernment without good reason.'[38]

Summary
In Luke the birth and infancy narratives provide some indications of the Holy Spirit giving knowledge. Elisabeth recognizes Mary as the mother of 'my Lord'; Zechariah has an insight into Old Testament scriptures; Simeon knows that the babe is the messiah. There may be a connection between Jesus' conception by the Spirit and his growth in wisdom. The resurrection narrative stresses the need for minds to be opened to understand the scriptures; this will be necessary for the future witness of the disciples. This is particularly significant in view of what we find in Acts.

In Acts the role of the Spirit in giving understanding of the Scriptures is a prominent feature. It can be seen in Peter's sermon in chapter 2, and in his words before the Sanhedrin in chapter 4. It is also seen in the case of Stephen, and probably Philip; and in the conclusions of the council of Jerusalem. 6:3 and 10 both bring the Spirit and wisdom together.

Hull's conclusion on the role of the Spirit in giving understanding of Scripture is justified: 'But it would be a mistake to limit the role of the Spirit, where the understanding of the Scriptures is concerned, merely to that of Christ's "remembrancer". If the Fourth Gospel claimed that the Spirit would call to mind all that Christ had said (14:21), it also claimed that the Spirit would guide into all the truth (16:13). And in Acts we see this second promise being fulfilled as the Spirit leads the Church into all the truth, of which understanding of Scripture formed a vital part.'[39]

Chapter 3

JOHN'S GOSPEL

The Johannine literature[1] is of considerable importance for the consideration of the subject of this book. In the conclusion of his recent study of the Holy Spirit in the Johannine Tradition, Gary M. Burge summarises thus: 'The Spirit would primarily recall the words of Jesus and thus sustain his case before the world. But in addition the Spirit would lead the community into the depths of these truths, inspiring reflection and development.'[2] Particularly in this latter activity we see the relevance of the Spirit's work for hermeneutics. The fourth Gospel gives particular emphasis both to the Holy Spirit and to truth. In the Paraclete sayings these themes coalesce and the Holy Spirit is described by Jesus as the Spirit of truth. The material bearing on our subject in this Gospel is considerable and the discussion therefore will need to be succinct. This material will be considered thematically.

1. Light and darkness

The light/darkness motif is the first to be introduced in John's Gospel. It is applied in several rather different ways and the longest passage is where it is exemplified in the healing of the man born blind in chapter 9.

1:4-13: Initially the light is here identified with the life that was in the Word (v.4), but in verses 8 and 9 the light is contrasted with John the Baptist and is presented as coming into the world. In verses 10ff. the light is referred to as 'him', and in verse 14 the light is also clearly the Word. This identification of Word and light is very suggestive and also links with the description of Jesus as the truth (14:6).

Over against the light is the darkness.[3] It appears that it is mankind that is in the darkness and thus needs the light (vv.4, 5). The reception

51

given to him who is the light in verses 10 and 11 suggests that the balance of probability is that verse 5 should be translated 'the darkness has not grasped – or apprehended – it.'[4] Even when the light came into the world personally the darkness did not recognize or accept him. Those in the darkness who did so, were those born of God (v.13).

The implications of this are that human beings are in the dark and they need enlightening. This enlightening comes from the Word, but even then it is not accepted except where a person is born of God. Human resources (v.13a) are totally inadequate.[5] This is underscored by Jesus' words to Nicodemus in 3:3: 'unless a person has been born again, he cannot see the kingdom of God.'

3:19-21

This is the verdict: Light has come into the world, but men loved darkness instead of light because their deeds were evil. Everyone who does evil hates the light, and will not come into the light for fear that his deeds will be exposed. But whoever lives by the truth comes into the light, so that it may be seen plainly that what he has done has been done through God.

In this passage the light stands more for what illuminates and exposes. Coming to the light thus involves having one's deeds brought out into the open for scrutiny. The thought seems to imply that coming to Christ or God means coming into a circle of light. Those whose deeds are evil therefore hate and avoid the light, preferring the concealment of the darkness. There are those, however, who do – or perhaps 'live out'[6] – the truth; these come to the light, but when they do so it is seen clearly that their deeds have been done 'in God'. In this passage there is an identification of darkness with evil, and of right living with living the truth; those in the dark prefer it that way because they hate the light, while the deeds of those who come to the light are done because of the action of God in them.[7]

Chapter 9: There can be little doubt that John records the miracle of restoring the sight of the man born blind not just as a sign of Jesus being the Christ (v.22) and the Son of Man (v.35), but also because it exemplifies the way Christ acts as the light.[8] This becomes clear in verses 39–41:

> Jesus said, 'For judgment I have come into this world, so that the blind will see and those who see will become blind.' Some Pharisees who were with him heard him say this and asked, 'What? Are we blind too?' Jesus said, 'If you were blind, you would not be guilty of sin; but now that you claim you can see, your guilt remains.'

These verses vary the motif to that of sight/blindness. The man born blind – a salient point, typifying the existing condition of people when Jesus came – had his sight restored by the power of Christ, who is the light. Now he can see, and the spiritual significance of this is evidenced in verses 30–33, and finally in verse 38. On the other hand, the Pharisees, relying on their own insight, are blind, and their blindness is culpable because they claim to see.[9]

12:35-41

Then Jesus told them, 'You are going to have the light just a little while longer. Walk while you have the light, before darkness overtakes you. The man who walks in the dark does not know where he is going. Put your trust in the light while you have it, so that you may become sons of light.' When he had finished speaking, Jesus left and hid himself from them.

Even after Jesus had done all these miraculous signs in their presence, they still would not believe in him. This was to fulfill the word of Isaiah the prophet: 'Lord, who has believed our message and to whom has the arm of the Lord been revealed?' For this reason they could not believe, because, as Isaiah says elsewhere: 'He has blinded their eyes and deadened their hearts, so they can neither see with their eyes, nor understand with their hearts, nor turn – and I would heal them.' Isaiah said this because he saw Jesus' glory and spoke about him.

There are references to Jesus as light in 8:12 and 12:46, but of more significance is this section which contains references both to light and to blindness. In verses 39 and 40 John uses Isaiah 6:10 to explain the unbelief of Jesus' contemporaries, a verse which we have already seen used by Jesus in the Synoptics (Matt. 13:14,15; Mark 4:12; Luke 8:10), and also by Paul as recorded by Luke in Acts 28:26 and 27. This further reference underlines the importance of this Old Testament text amongst the early Christians for understanding the lack of belief shown by so many Jews towards Jesus. It also strongly supports the Synoptic record that Jesus himself first used the text in this way.

What is to be noted about John's use of the Isaiah text is the way he says, 'They *were not able* to believe.' This is probably to be understood in the way that the concept of hardening is in Paul, that is, as judicial, depending on previous unbelief and rejection. Carson speaks here of a 'realized eschatology of condemnation'.[10] Coming as it does in the context of an appeal by Jesus, 'While you have the light, believe in the light' (v.36), it indicates that light rejected leads to blindness.[11]

2. The action of God in salvation through Jesus
This can first be considered against the background of a general rejection of Jesus and his claims. The fact of such a rejection is set out early in the Gospel, in 1:11: 'He came to his own, and his own people would not accept him' (REB). Similarly in 6:36 Jesus says, 'But you, as I said, have seen and yet you do not believe.' In 8:55 Jesus says to the Jews concerning God, 'You do not know him.'[12] This last reference is significant for the fact that it indicates that lack of knowledge of God is the reason for rejecting Jesus as messiah.

In other references various reasons are given for rejecting Christ (3:19-21; 8:15; 12:42,43). In 5:38–44 these are shown to be particularly deep-seated; the Jews do not have God's word abiding in them; they search the Scriptures but do not see Jesus in them as messiah;[13] they are not willing to come to him; they do not have the love of God in them.[14] It is significant that they need understanding of the Scriptures; the understanding which comes when God's word dwells within a person.[15]

Some references indicate that it is impossible for people to believe in Jesus without the action of God; this is explicitly expressed in 6:44 and 10:26, and is a clear inference in 8:34.[16]

The character of the world, that is the world made up of sinful humanity, means that it rejects Jesus. Some references indicate that the world hates Jesus (7:7; 15:18; 17:14); 8:23 and 24 indicate that there is a complete disparity between Christ and the world; he is from above while those who belong to the world are from beneath. Other references show that the world does not know who Jesus is (1:10; 17:25); 14:17 is similar but refers to the Holy Spirit.

Against this background, salvation, described in various ways, is shown to be *entirely an act of God*. It is a new birth (1:13; 3:3, 5–8). This carries the implication of a new life with a new understanding and perceptions. Salvation also involves being drawn by God to Jesus Christ, 6:44–46, 65.[17] Included in this is the idea of being taught by God: 'It is written in the prophets, "And they shall all be taught by God."[18] Therefore everyone who has heard and learned from the Father comes to me.'

In chapter 17 those who believe in Jesus are those who have been given to him by the Father (vv.2, 6, 9, 12, 24).[19] In verse 6 Jesus says, 'I have manifested your name to those whom you have given me.' This links with the assertion of verse 3: 'This is eternal life, that they may know you, the only true God, and Jesus Christ.' Verse 8 also speaks of Jesus giving them 'the words which you have given me'. Being given to Jesus he reveals God's character and words to the disciples.

Other references indicating the action of God are 3:27; 6:37 and 15:16. Two others can be commented on. 8:47 says, 'He who is of God hears God's words; therefore you do not hear, because you are not of God;' while 10:27 says, 'My sheep hear my voice...'[20] The result of belonging to God or Jesus is hearing words or a voice.

The Spirit is only mentioned infrequently in these verses[21] but there is a clear indication of a need for a work of God if people are going to come to Jesus and receive his salvation; that this does happen is expressed in a number of ways. Implicit in this is the granting of knowledge and understanding which is an essential part of salvation.

3. Knowledge and Truth

These are key concepts in John's Gospel. This section discusses a number of verses which imply that knowledge of the truth is not something which people can attain by themselves, rather it is received from God through Jesus Christ.[22] Prefaced as it is by the phrase 'No-one has seen God at any time', 1:18 shows that a true knowledge of God is only possible through Jesus Christ. The clause 'who is in the bosom of the Father' (NKJV), paralleling 13:23 and suggesting the most intimate communion with the Father, indicates that the making known, or 'narrating'[23], of the Father is not just by teaching, but by deeds and the very character of Jesus.[24] The rest of the Gospel implies that this knowledge is only revealed to faith. Unbelievers do not see the Father in Jesus.

In 3:9–13 Jesus expresses his surprise at the ignorance of Nicodemus, a teacher of particular eminence in Israel.[25] In verse 12 there is a difficult comparison between 'earthly things' and 'heavenly things'. 'Earthly things' appears to refer to basic truths such as being born again by the Holy Spirit, which had been foreshadowed in the Old Testament (eg. Ezek.36:25–27). 'Heavenly things' would then refer to truths not yet revealed.[26] In verse 13 Jesus refers to himself as the one who has come down from heaven, which implies that he is the one who is able to teach such things. Nicodemus, and in this he is a typical example of the Jews,[27] is unable to receive such knowledge.

In 7:16–18 Jesus affirms that his teaching derives from the one who sent him. The person who will know that this is so, is the person who desires (θέλῃ) to do God's will.[28] This is an important principle. Such knowledge is not merely theoretical, which a person can accept or reject as he pleases. It is only the person who desires practically to do God's will who will know 'concerning the teaching' (περὶ τῆς διδαχῆς). True knowledge is not speculative, and the person who simply wants to know will find he cannot reach the truth; only with the disposition to obey does true knowledge come.

Jesus implies in 7:28 and 29 that the reason the people of Jerusalem did not really know him – as distinct from knowing some things about him – was because they did not know God. There is a paradox here. Those who know God will know who Jesus is; those who know Jesus will know God, for Jesus knows God. As in the previous passage it is the disposition which is all important. It is not just a matter of having Scripture; a disposition of faith and obedience is necessary for true knowledge.

In 8:31 and 32 Jesus is speaking about those who have believed in him, though the clear implication is that this believing may be only superficial. Hence Jesus says, 'If you continue[29] in my word, you are truly my disciples and you will know the truth and the truth will set you free.' Here knowing the truth is linked with a faith that continues to hold on (cf. NIV) to Jesus' teaching. It is such a faith which enables disciples to understand the teaching and know the truth which liberates.[30]

8:43 and 47 contain a very sharp assertion by Jesus that the spiritual condition of the Jews prevents them from receiving his word and knowing the truth. God is not their Father (v.42), rather they are of their father the devil (v.44). Consequently they are not able really to hear Jesus' word. His words are the truth (v.46), and they are God's words (v.47); but as his opponents are not of God they cannot hear them.

The opposite of this is asserted by Jesus in 10:4, 14, 26, 27 where he pictures himself as the good shepherd. Those who are his sheep recognize his voice; they hear his voice and follow him. Those who do not believe show that they are not his sheep, because these things are not true of them.

17:3 and 8 indicate that eternal life is knowing God and Jesus Christ. This knowledge comes through receiving Jesus' words;[31] words given him by the Father. Receiving these words has brought certainty that Jesus came from the Father, being sent by him.

4. The Holy Spirit
This section looks at the general teaching of John's Gospel regarding the Holy Spirit.

In 1:32–34 John the Baptist sees the Spirit descend upon Jesus. It is not mentioned that this took place at Jesus' baptism. The first two references have the definite article before the word πνεῦμα:

Then John gave this testimony: 'I saw the Spirit come down from heaven as a dove and remain on him. I would not have known him, except that the one who sent me to baptize with water told me, "The man on whom you see the Spirit come down and remain is he who will baptize with the Holy Spirit." I have seen and I testify that this is the Son of God.'

This by itself would not indicate that John thinks of the Spirit in personal terms, but it does anticipate the definite and much more personal description of the Spirit as the παράκλητος in chapters 14–16. There is no article before the last reference in verse 33 but it does not seem that too much should be made of this as the article is commonly omitted in prepositional phrases. There is an emphasis upon the fact that the Spirit remains on Jesus, and this seems related to the fact that Jesus baptizes in the Holy Spirit. The Spirit came upon him, remains with him, and he then baptizes others in, or with, the Spirit.[32] The main emphasis of the passage appears to be this; Jesus is the one who baptizes with the Holy Spirit. Coming in this way at the very beginning of the Gospel, John's teaching about the Spirit needs to be considered in relation to this description of Jesus.

This raises the question of what precise connotation is to be given to the word 'baptize' in connection with the Spirit. This is scarcely ever considered, perhaps because there is no obvious answer.[33] The usage is metaphorical and stands in contrast to, or at least is compared with, John's baptism in water. Possibly the word 'baptize' here is an inclusive word for giving the Spirit, with all that is involved in that.[34]

In 3:3–8 the Spirit is described as the author of a second birth, or a birth from above. Verses 6 and 8 both clarify the concept, verse 6 emphasizing that this is not something which belongs to flesh, that is human nature in this context, while verse 8 stresses the power, invisibility and will of the Spirit in this birth. This spiritual birth makes the person who experiences it a spiritual person (v.6). This passage does not speak of any activity of Jesus in relation to the Spirit, but it is interesting to try and relate this to the previous passage.[35] It is tempting to see a correlation in this way; the person baptized in the

Spirit[36] becomes a spiritual person. But it may be that verse 8 rules this out.[37]

Of particular importance is the fact that one of the effects of birth by the Spirit is the ability to 'see'[38] the kingdom of God (3:3). This clearly links in with the themes of light, blindness and sight, and understanding. The term 'kingdom of God' is a broad one and, used as it is with a man of training and knowledge of the Old Testament, it indicates that a real understanding of truths about God and the spiritual realm are only possible when a person has had an experience of the Spirit[39] of such depth and far-reaching consequence that it can only be described as another birth.

In 3:34 (For the one whom God has sent speaks the words of God, for God gives the Spirit without limit), πνεῦμα again has the definite article. The main questions to be settled are, who gives, and who receives, the Spirit? It is very widely agreed, and the context appears to support this, that it is God who gives the Spirit without measure to Jesus, described in verse 28 as the Christ and in verse 35 as the Son.[40] There is a clear connection between the words 'he whom God sent utters the words of God', and the receiving of the Spirit without measure. The Spirit causes Jesus to speak the words of God. It is not difficult to link this ministry of the Spirit with the later description of the Spirit as the Spirit of truth. The emphasis of this verse (taken in conjunction with verse 35) is that the complete equipping of Jesus for his ministry is by the Spirit. As Jesus is also the baptizer in the Spirit this has implications for the lives and ministries of those thus baptized.

4:10 and 14 make no explicit mention of the Spirit, yet in this Gospel it seems difficult to suppress the implication that the 'living water' is ultimately a reference to the Spirit.[41] This is made explicit in 7:37. Even without referring to the last reference, if it is right to emphasize that Jesus is the baptizer with the Spirit, then the inference seems a strong one that giving living water is another way of referring to baptizing with the Spirit. It may be possible to see a contrast here with water baptism. In verses 1 and 2, both John and Jesus' disciples are baptizing in water, but Jesus does not do this. This is immediately followed by an event in which Jesus promises to give living water which will spring up within a person. This strengthens the argument for an allusion to the Spirit. Moreover it appears that just as Nicodemus, a Jew, needed a new birth by the Spirit, so also the Samaritan woman equally needed what can also be described as a life-changing experience; the two experiences appear to be the same thing described in different terms.

If then it is appropriate to consider what Jesus was offering in terms of the Spirit these features ought to be noticed. This 'water' is given by Jesus; it remains within the heart of the person who receives it (just as the Spirit remains on Jesus, 1:32, 33); and it brings eternal life, another comprehensive term referring to a life of spiritual and eternal dimensions.

On the surface it does not seem as if there is any explicit reference to the Holy Spirit in the term 'in spirit and truth' (4:23, 24). In each verse both nouns are governed by the one preposition, which seems to rule out such an understanding. However verse 24 begins, 'God is spirit...', and this is the reason why worship must be in spirit and truth; it is to be in accordance with the reality that God is spirit.[42] This raises the question of how Jesus, and John, envisaged it would be possible to worship 'in spirit and truth'. In 3:6 Jesus says, 'What is born of the Spirit is spirit.' The Nicodemus interview, and perhaps Jesus' words about 'living water', suggest that such worship would be the outcome of birth by the Spirit,[43] or of the gift of the water of the Spirit.[44]

It may also be that 'in truth' is not to be taken as 'sincerely', but rather as 'in accordance with the truth'. Perhaps Jesus is saying that two factors govern worship: it must be in spirit because God is spirit, and it must be governed by the truth about God. So there is a close link between 'spirit' and 'truth'. Both are effects of the Spirit; and in worship the Spirit enables the worshipper to worship according to the truth about God.[45]

The first thing to be determined in 6:63 ('The Spirit gives life; the flesh counts for nothing. The words I have spoken to you are spirit and they are life') is whether there is any reference or allusion to the Holy Spirit. Translations vary. REB and RSV have 'spirit' with a small 's' in both occurrences, while versions like the AV, NKJV and NIV have the first occurrence with a capital, 'Spirit'. This is a matter of judgment but there are certain pointers which suggest that 'Spirit' is appropriate and might also be better for both occurrences. The phrase 'the Spirit is the lifegiver' seems more dynamic and more likely than 'the spirit', and might also have the suggestion of personality about it.

The importance of this verse is the way in which it links Jesus' words with the Spirit and with life.[46] In the context what Jesus seems to be saying is that the flesh, that is Jesus' literal flesh and blood, cannot impart life, it is his words which actually do that. His words explain the significance of his self-giving in death, and the Spirit makes his words life-giving. It is in this way that he is the living bread, and in this way that he satisfies thirst (linking with 4:10–14 and 7:37–39).[47]

7:37–39 take up the familiar themes of 'thirst', 'water', 'Spirit', and 'life'.[48] What is significant here is that John adds the comment that the fulfilment of these words awaited the glorification of Jesus, that is by his death and resurrection. This is a Johannine reference to the Pentecost event. This introduces a tension into this Gospel, one that will become apparent also in 14:17. On the one hand Jesus gives the living water of the Spirit, on the other this awaits a future event. John's words are striking, 'For the Spirit was not yet...' Taken with the Paraclete passages this indicates that, at the least, the fullness of the Spirit awaited the glorification of Jesus.[49]

Burge says of 20:22: 'Few passages in John present the interpreter with so many problems and options as are inherent in 20:22.'[50] Consequently it is difficult to assess the significance of these verses for the present study. If, to quote Burge again, 'one emphasis is certain: the Fourth Evangelist considered John 20:22 to be the fulfillment of his expectation so carefully developed in the Farewell Discourses',[51] then this verse is important because this giving of the Holy Spirit involves all that the Gospel has indicated the Holy Spirit will do. Even if this event is viewed as a symbolic act anticipating an endowment of the Spirit yet to come,[52] the same importance belongs to the words, 'Receive the Holy Spirit.' However, here the gift of the Spirit is only linked with the ministry of forgiveness, and although this is probably to be understood as proclamatory,[53] any other reference to the teaching work of the Spirit only arises because this is the culmination of other passages in John, notably the Paraclete passages.

Summary

Before turning to the Paraclete passages it may be valuable to summarize what has been seen in John so far.

1. The earliest Johannine motif is that of light and darkness. While Jesus is the light, the world is in darkness and rejects the light unless there has first been a birth from God. Those in the dark do not come to the light; only those whose works are done 'in God' come. While Jesus gives light, those who rely on their own understanding become blind, and indeed, are blinded so that they do not see or understand.

2. Another theme is that salvation is the action of God. This is seen against a background of the rejection of Jesus. This rejection arises from the character of the world; it is in fact impossible for people to believe in Jesus apart from the action of God. Salvation is entirely of God; it is a new birth; it is being drawn to God and being taught by him. Implicit in salvation is the giving of knowledge and understanding. The Spirit is the agent in the new birth.

3. Knowledge and truth are key concepts in John. Knowledge of God is only through Jesus. Even eminent teachers do not understand apart from new birth. Knowledge is given to those who desire to do God's will. Knowing the truth comes from a faith that continues in Christ's word. Only those who have God as their Father are able to hear Christ's word, while all those who are his sheep recognize his voice.

4. John lays emphasis on Jesus as the baptizer in the Spirit. He received the Spirit without measure and speaks the words of God; he imparts the same Spirit. New birth by the Spirit enables a person to understand the kingdom; the same experience of the Spirit's transforming power is described in other terms; this is the event which constitutes a person a Christian. The Spirit enables worship

in accordance with truth; is the dynamic force in Jesus' words; but was only given in his fullness after the glorification of Jesus. Implicit in this teaching about the Spirit is that the Spirit is God's agent in salvation bringing light, knowledge and truth to those in the dark.

5. The Paraclete passages

14:15–17

If you love me, you will obey what I command. And I will ask the Father, and he will give you another Counselor to be with you forever – the Spirit of truth. The world cannot accept him, because it neither sees him nor knows him. But you know him, for he lives with you and will be in you.

There are a number of points in the first passage which must be discussed. First, the precise meaning of the word παράκλητος is hotly debated, and there seems to be little certainty about it.[54] On the whole the context seems to favour Barrett's proposal that the Holy Spirit is the one who brings the exhortation, or encouragement, of the gospel.[55] This fits in with the title 'Spirit of truth', and also his teaching ministry to the disciples and his witnessing ministry to the world. Moreover in this respect the Spirit would take the place of Jesus himself, who had been the teacher and guide of the disciples.[56]

Secondly, the last sentence raises the question of the relationship of the Paraclete to Jesus himself. There is a strong implication that the Paraclete takes the place of Jesus; Jesus is returning to the Father, but the Paraclete will be given to the disciples and will remain with them for ever. The Spirit fulfils some of the functions at present fulfilled by Jesus. There is a further implication that the Spirit is personal.[57]

Thirdly, the Paraclete is given the descriptive title 'the Spirit of truth'. Being deprived of the teaching ministry of Jesus who is the truth and spoke the truth (1:14; 14:6; 3:33,34; 6:63; 18:37,38), the disciples are given the Spirit of truth. How the Spirit makes known the truth is not specified in this passage, but clearly fulfilling this function is implied in Jesus' words.[58]

Fourthly, the relationship of the Paraclete to the world and to the disciples is set out. With regard to the world, the world is not able to receive him, because it neither sees nor knows him. The world cannot receive the Spirit of truth, and therefore the ministry of the Spirit is primarily one towards the disciples; though later it is indicated that the Spirit has a ministry to the world through them. The world may feel the impact of the Spirit, but it cannot receive him while remaining the world.

The last sentence of verse 17 is extremely difficult to understand. Perhaps in this context, the meaning is that the disciples know the Spirit because he is in Jesus, and hence with them (παρ' ὑμῖν).[59] This seems possible as μένει is contrasted with ἔσται, and therefore only refers to the present (hence the translation 'dwells', 'lives'). This is not to say that the disciples have not already experienced the transforming power of the Spirit (as in 3:3–8; 4:10–14), only that the Spirit who has been given without measure to Jesus and by whom he utters the words of God (3:34) will be given them so that they might know and speak the truth of God.

Fifthly, one further question arises out of the relationship between verse 17 and verse 18. At first sight it seems surprising that Jesus should say that God would give the disciples another παράκλητος and then follow that by saying, 'I will not leave you as orphans, I will come to you.' The implication, and rationale, of what seem to be almost contradictory sentences, is that Jesus would come to his disciples in some way by the Spirit.[60] So Jesus is also able to add: 'In a little while the world will see me no longer, but you will see me; because I live, you too will live. When that day comes you will know that I am in my Father, and you in me and I in you' (vv.19, 20 REB). The Spirit, then, is, in a clearly identified way, the Spirit of Jesus, and his coming mediates the presence of Jesus, so that disciples see him, live by him and are one with him. This is further borne out by Jesus' answer to Judas' question (14:22–24).

14:25, 26

All this I have spoken while still with you. But the Counselor, the Holy Spirit, whom the Father will send in my name, will teach you all things and will remind you of everything I have said to you.

The introductory words in verse 25 suggest that Jesus is indicating that it is only after the Holy Spirit has been sent that the disciples will really understand the meaning of what he is saying. The Spirit will both bring back Jesus' words and also teach the disciples all they need to know about them.[61] The παράκλητος is here identified with the Holy Spirit, indicating that 'Spirit of truth' in verse 17 is not to be in any way distinguished from the Spirit already spoken of in John. The Spirit being sent by the Father is another way of expressing the fact that he is given (v.16), but there is a new element when Jesus adds 'in my name'. 'In my name' does not appear to mean 'on my authority', as this is inappropriate; it might mean something like 'in answer to my request' (cf. v.16). The phrase seems to tie the Spirit very closely to Jesus, emphasizing this feature in these passages.

The Spirit will fulfil a twofold function. Firstly, 'he will teach you all things.' Two questions immediately arise: in what way does he teach? and, what does 'all things' comprise? It may be that the second activity of the Spirit, 'remind you of all that I told you', is at least a partial answer to these two questions.[62] However the contrast between ταῦτα (v.25) and πάντα (first occurrence in verse 26) suggests that the Holy Spirit will do more than simply remind of words spoken by Jesus. Moreover the words 'will teach you all things' seem redundant if they are to be wholly understood in terms of what follows. The last two Paraclete passages will clarify this matter further, but this is a distinct promise of a wider teaching role for the Spirit with regard to the disciples.[63]

The second function also raises two questions: how will this take place? and, what purpose does the reminding serve? The first question can only be answered by assuming that Jesus is indicating that the Spirit will work in the disciples' memory, prompting them and enabling them to remember accurately and comprehensively.[64] This suggests that the teaching ministry of the Spirit is also to be of a similar inward nature; the inference is that it involves direct revelation.[65] As for the purpose, this will also become clearer in considering the next passages. However, as the words that Jesus spoke were words that covered a whole variety of subjects, spoken for a variety of purposes, and demanding a variety of responses, it is impossible to narrow down the purpose of the reminding too much. Jesus' words will be remembered so that they can continue to fulfil the purposes for which they were originally spoken.[66] This raises another question which has a considerable bearing on the subject of this book: is this promise simply for the eleven disciples in their character as apostles, or is it a promise for all disciples in all ages? As the promise of remembering is only actually applicable to those who heard Jesus, the former would seem to be the correct answer. The implication of this would then seem to be that this remembering was to enable the apostles to pass on their memories of Jesus' words to others (including by writing them down). This would suggest that being taught all things by the Spirit was particular revelation enabling them to teach the next generation of believers.[67] However, in the immediate context, and in the context of 14:15–17, there are a number of other consequences of the donation and coming of the Spirit which it seems difficult to restrict to the apostles. Perhaps the right way would be to consider that these passages indicate that the coming and ministry of the Spirit applies to all disciples, but has particular relevance and application to the apostles.

15:26, 27

When the Counselor comes, whom I will send to you from the Father, the Spirit of truth who goes out from the Father, he will testify about me. And you also must testify, for you have been with me from the beginning.

The context of this passage is different from that of the previous two passages, and is concerned with persecution. The disciples live in a world which hates them (v.18), and as a result they are likely to face exclusion from the synagogue and even death itself (16:2). Against this background comes the third promise of the παράκλητος. In view of this it is difficult to suppress the thought that the παράκλητος will strengthen the disciples and enable them to remain faithful to Jesus (16:1). Perhaps the stress on the fact that the Spirit comes from the Father (παρὰ τοῦ πατρὸς, twice in two consecutive clauses) is intended in part to underline that they will receive divine help. However the main stress is on bearing witness, and once again the παράκλητος is described as the Spirit of truth. The witness is twofold. First the Spirit of truth bears witness concerning Jesus. The title links back with 14:26 and the thought of being reminded of all that Jesus spoke. This witness must be in the minds of the disciples. As the Spirit of truth the παράκλητος enables them to remember the words of Jesus and understand the truth about him. They then are also (καὶ) to bear witness;[68] knowing the truth about Jesus they can bear their testimony to him. They are able to do this because they have been with Jesus from the beginning of his ministry. This emphasizes the element of memory in the Spirit's work. The Spirit of truth works on what the disciples already know of Jesus by personal experience. Although it is not expressed in this way there seems to be a causal relationship between the witness of the Spirit and the witnessing of the disciples.[69] The emphasis again is on these disciples as the first witnesses who are especially enabled for this by the Spirit. The witness is to Jesus.

The thought of witnessing to Jesus in a hostile and unbelieving world seems to be carried on into chapter 16 and to verses 7–11.[70] In 14:17 the world does not receive the Spirit, nor sees or knows him, but here the world comes under his influence through the witness of the disciples. The work of the παράκλητος as the Spirit of truth is therefore both to and through the disciples.[71] These passages are also not simply independent descriptions of different aspects of the Spirit's ministry, they add to each other to build up a total picture of the Spirit's work as the παράκλητος.

16:7–11

But I tell you the truth: It is for your good that I am going away. Unless I go away, the Counselor will not come to you; but if I go, I will send him to you. When he comes, he will convict the world of guilt in regard to sin and righteousness and judgment: in regard to sin, because men do not believe in me; in regard to righteousness, because I am going to the Father, where you can see me no longer; and in regard to judgment, because the prince of this world now stands condemned.

Our main concern here is the convicting ministry of the παράκλητος. In this passage the REB translation of παράκλητος as 'advocate' is most justified, as the picture of a prosecuting counsel bringing a charge seems the most apt. The translation of ἐλέγξει is also a difficult point. Is it convict or convince? That is to say, is there a subjective element involved so that people in the world are actually convinced of sin, righteousness and judgment? The word itself can be used in either way and its usage in the rest of the New Testament is not decisive.[72] At first sight 'convict' seems the most likely.[73] However, against this is the fact that as the Spirit's work is within the disciples, we should also expect the same to be true of his work with regard to the world. It is difficult to think that this is just an objective laying of a charge through the disciples speaking, rather this convicting is more likely to be envisaged within the conscience of members of the world.[74] This however does not mean that they will all submit to such a conviction.[75] To that extent 'convict' seems better than 'convince'.[76]

A further question concerns the purpose of this convicting of the παράκλητος; what is the end in view? As this comes after Jesus has spoken of the disciples bearing witness (15:27), and seems to refer to the Spirit's assistance in their witness-bearing, and as this witness is to Jesus himself, it appears that the purpose is not simply conviction in itself, a mark of disapproval of the world's hostility and unbelief. Rather it is much more likely that the purpose is evangelistic, and the conviction is in order to lead to faith in Jesus.[77] This also strengthens the idea that conviction has a subjective element to it.

Conviction is of sin, righteousness or justice, and judgment. The reasons given for this conviction cannot be discussed in detail but the second and third ('because I go to the Father, and you see me no more' and 'because the ruler of this world is judged') refer to realities which are not open to observation and which can only operate as reasons if the world comes to know their reality. This seems to imply that the Holy Spirit impresses these things upon the minds, or perhaps consciences, of people of the world. In the yet-to-take-place glorification of Jesus by death, resurrection and return to his Father, the ruler of this world will be judged. That guarantees that those who belong to his rule will also be judged. There is an eschatological element here. The judgment of the last day is brought into the court of conscience by the Holy Spirit; and the purpose of this is to call to repentance and faith.[78] The instrument which the Spirit uses in this is the witness of the disciples to Jesus.

16:12–15

I have much more to say to you, more than you can now bear. But when he, the Spirit of truth, comes, he will guide you into all truth. He will not speak on his own; he will speak only what he hears, and he will tell you what is yet to come. He will bring glory to me by taking from what is mine and making it known to you. All that belongs to the Father is mine. That is why I said the Spirit will take from what is mine and make it known to you.

It is better to consider this passage separately from verses 7–11 because these verses deal once again with the work of the Spirit of truth with relation to disciples. Verse 12 indicates that there are still many things that Jesus is unable to speak to them,[79] but the Spirit will guide them into all the truth when he comes. As in 14:26 this must refer to direct revelation, supplementing,[80] and perhaps giving enlarged understanding of, what Jesus already said.

Once again the Spirit is described as the Spirit of truth, underlining his function to guide into truth. The word 'guide' is used in the Hermetic Literature of leading souls to knowledge[81]. ἐν is unexpected; if it is to be accepted as the best reading, then perhaps the suggestion of Carson is correct, '*in* all truth suggests an exploration of truth already principially disclosed.'[82] 'All truth' must be qualified by the context and the other Paraclete passages, here meaning 'all truth about Jesus which you need'. However this is to be interpreted in no narrow way, for all that the Father has also belongs to Jesus, and what belongs to Jesus the Spirit makes known to the disciples (vv.14, 15). What we have then is revelation about the Father as well as Jesus the Son.[83] In making known to the disciples the truth about the Son, based on what the disciples had already seen and heard of him, the Spirit also reveals to them truth about God. In verse 13 it is also said that the Spirit will make known 'things to come'. It is not clear precisely what this means.[84] It has already been suggested that in verses 8–11 the Spirit anticipates the judgment of the last day, bringing home the reality of this to the consciences of those from the world. Perhaps it is in that sort of way that this phrase is to be understood. Especially the future revelation of the glory of the Christ at the parousia, and the assurance of his final victory with his disciples over the world and the devil, would seem to be included.[85] So rather than revealing details about the future the Spirit gives assurance and hope while the disciples are suffering in the world.

It is also emphasized in this passage that the Spirit does not speak on his own authority or initiative. He only speaks what he hears[86] and what he makes known are the things of Christ. Perhaps this is to emphasize the complete congruity of the disciples' future knowledge with what Jesus has already taught them. There is not the slightest 'wedge' between the teaching of Jesus and the teaching of the Spirit; the truth is a seamless whole.

Because of the importance of these passages they will now be considered as a whole and various points examined:

1. As the Spirit of truth the παράκλητος does not simply reveal new truth to the disciples. He does do this; things the disciples were not able to bear at that time would be taught them later by the Spirit. But his teaching is closely tied both to what they have heard from Jesus and what they have seen, having been with him from the beginning. Even what is new is perhaps more an enlarged understanding of what they have heard than something entirely new. The teaching ministry of the Paraclete is a ministry which is based on, and gives insight into, truth about Jesus already known.

2. These passages are an integral part of a discourse in which Jesus is preparing his disciples for the new conditions which will

obtain when he has returned to the Father. Given that this is so, a great deal of what he says is applicable to all those who will live in the new era which will come about by his return to heaven and the giving of the Holy Spirit. It is also the case that some things are more directly and specifically applicable to those who live at the time of transition. Moreover these particular eleven disciples, who are going to be commissioned as apostles (20:21), are the link both between the life and ministry of Jesus and future disciples, and Jesus and the unbelieving world which needs to hear witness concerning Jesus. In both respects their ministry is of crucial importance. In these circumstances it seems right to consider both a special application of the Paraclete promises to the eleven and a general application to succeeding believers who are going to receive the Spirit, living in the era after his giving.[87]

3. Various aspects of the work of the Spirit outlined here can be set down: It is a ministry which makes known the truth, as the title given to the Spirit here makes explicit. It is a ministry which centres in the person of Jesus; he is at the centre of the truth made known; it is 'things concerning him' which are made known; his life and words are brought to mind; he is glorified in it all. It is a work within the memories and minds of the disciples. It does not bypass their own faculties, though the indication is that in their case the Spirit makes known to them insight and truth which they could not otherwise know. It appears that his work in the world is analogous, conviction being in the conscience.

In this work the Spirit is not to be considered as acting independently. He only speaks what he hears (as was true of the Son, 8:26). It is probably immaterial whether the hearing is to be thought of as from the Father or the Son; once the Son has returned to heaven they speak with one voice (cf. 14:20, 23, 24). Moreover in making known the things that belong to Jesus, the Spirit also makes known what belongs to the Father (16:14, 15). Further the Spirit is clearly the Spirit of Jesus, who brings the presence of Jesus to his disciples for their comfort and assurance. This ministry of the Spirit brings them into contact and fellowship with the Father and Son, and therefore must not be considered just in intellectual terms, for it involves a spiritual relationship with the exalted Jesus and with the Father through him. This ministry of the Spirit is of the very essence of the new relationship disciples have with Jesus after his return to the Father.

4. This ministry has various effects. It has effects for the disciples themselves first in terms of their own understanding, and the reassurance this would bring. It has effects for their witness to the world, and by implication, to the next generation of disciples. This ministry was not solely for the disciples' own personal benefit; it enabled them to function as effective witnesses for Jesus. It enabled them to remain faithful even in persecution; and more importantly to bring home to the world the condemned position in which it stood in the light of its own refusal to believe in Jesus, his exaltation and the condemnation of the ruler of the world.

5. This has considerable consequences for biblical hermeneutics. The church lives and studies the Bible in the age of the παράκλητος. Just as the Spirit of truth operated primarily with truth already known to the disciples, so the ministry of the Spirit is needed for real understanding of the truth that centres in Jesus. Even with the disciples their own faculties were involved. The work of the Spirit is an inward work which perhaps defies explanation, but there is no tension between the work of the Spirit and the full use of human faculties in seeking to understand the truth of God.

This understanding and guiding into truth were also inextricably bound up with a spiritual relationship and fellowship with Jesus as the exalted Son and the Father. Interpretation cannot be divorced from devotion and Christian experience. They take place together by the influence of the Spirit.

Understanding and knowledge of truth are not ends in themselves for the church. They come in the context of being strengthened and equipped for life in a hostile world, and to fulfil a commission to the next generation and particularly to the world. The Spirit's witness to Jesus is to enable the church to witness to the world. Understanding cannot stand by itself, only in relation to other realities and possibilities. Interpretation for its own sake is self-defeating; it is to enable the church to function in the world and towards the world.

CHAPTER 4

ROMANS

The material in Romans will be considered under five headings. With the exception of the references that explicitly speak of the Holy Spirit these will largely follow the order of the letter itself.

The effects of sin upon the mind

1:18–23

The wrath of God is being revealed from heaven against all the godlessness and wickedness of men who suppress the truth by their wickedness, since what may be known about God is plain to them, because God has made it plain to them. For since the creation of the world God's invisible qualities – his eternal power and divine nature – have been clearly seen, being understood from what has been made, so that men are without excuse. For although they knew God, they neither glorified him as God nor gave thanks to him, but their thinking became futile and their foolish hearts were darkened. Although they claimed to be wise, they became fools and exchanged the glory of the immortal God for images made to look like mortal man and birds and animals and reptiles.

The argument in this passage, which is widely[1] considered to be Paul's description of the condition of the Gentile world and God's condemnation of it, depends upon divine revelation. In verse 19 Paul emphasizes that 'what is known of God' (τò γνωστòν τοῦ θεοῦ)has been plainly shown to people.[2] The eternal power and Godhead, or deity, θειότης, of God are seen from the things that he has made. People have the truth. There are several points which are relevant for this study:

First, though they have the truth, they suppress it in

unrighteousness. It is difficult to be certain about the exact meaning of κατεχόντων. The word could be translated 'suppress', 'hold down', or 'restrain' (2 Thess. 2:6) or even 'possess'.[3] The last alternative would perhaps throw the emphasis more on 'in unrighteousness', but the final sense is not greatly altered. People have the truth, but they do not respond to it; in unrighteousness they do not allow it to have its effect upon their lives and behaviour.

Secondly, the consequence of this suppression is that they are 'without excuse'. It is not that people are constitutionally incapable of appreciating what can be known of God, nor that the evidence is uncertain or ambiguous, 'For all that can be known of God lies plain before their eyes'.[4] The problem is a moral and spiritual one, according to Paul.

Thirdly, as a result of suppressing the truth and not allowing it to produce the proper response of glorifying God and expressing thanks to him they became (aorist) futile in their thinking and their foolish – foolish because suppressing the truth about God must be so – hearts (probably almost synonymous with 'mind' here) were darkened. This suggests a condition where thinking has become vain, and in which the light of God is no longer able to shine into their minds. As Käsemann puts it, 'He (the person who disregards the truth) becomes incapable of discriminating perception, loses any grasp of reality, and falls victim of illusion.'[5]

Fourthly, the effect of this darkness and folly, Paul says, can be seen in the fact that they have exchanged the glory of the immortal God for images which they fabricate themselves. They think they are wise, but their actions show their folly.

Fifthly, as a result the next verses speak of God giving people up, in verse 24 to the 'desires of their hearts', in verse 26 to 'shameful passions', but in verse 28 to 'a debased mind',[6] ἀδόκιμον νοῦν; νοῦν here probably meaning *way of thinking* as the sum total of the whole mental and moral state of being'.[7] There is a play on words in this verse, perhaps to show the grim appropriateness of God's action, which might be expressed something like this, 'As they did not see fit to hold God in their knowledge, he gave them over to an unfit mind ...' though 'unfit' considerably weakens the sense of ἀδόκιμον. This passage, then, which begins by showing how people sinfully reject the truth about God made known to them, demonstrates how this leads to a deeper futility and darkness (v. 21), one which is deepened and accentuated by the righteous judgment of God who gives people over to 'their own depraved way of thinking'.[8]

The next two chapters show the same basic point expressed in different ways. In chapter two the focus of attention switches from the Gentile to the Jew, but here also the same spiritual blindness and inability to grasp the truth about God, as it should be grasped, is expressed. Romans 2:5 speaks about 'your hardness and impenitent heart', heart here probably being used in the broad sense to include the whole inner being and attitudes including those of the mind.[9] Romans 2:8 speaks of those who 'do not obey the truth, but obey unrighteousness'.[10] The contrasting of truth with unrighteousness is significant, and suggests that the moral bent of the inward being means that even when the truth (truth as in 1:18, i.e. the truth about God and what he requires) has been revealed, or is known, people prefer to obey unrighteousness.

2:17–24

Now you, if you call yourself a Jew; if you rely on the law and brag about your relationship to God; if you know his will and approve of what is superior because you are instructed by the law; if you are convinced that you are a guide for the blind, a light for those who are in the dark, an instructor of the foolish, a teacher of infants, because you have in the law the embodiment of knowledge and truth – you, then, who teach others, do you not teach yourself? You who preach against stealing, do you steal? You who say that people should not commit adultery, do you commit adultery? You who abhor idols, do you rob temples? You who brag about the law, do you dishonour God by breaking the law? As it is written: 'God's name is blasphemed among the Gentiles because of you.'

This section is important for the way in which it confronts Jewish pride in the knowledge of God and his ways and prepares the way for Paul's indictment of both Jew and Gentile in 3:9ff. The Jews appear to have a great advantage in terms of knowledge and understanding, but Paul will show that this is not really so. Three comments will be made on this section:

Firstly, there is a strong emphasis here on knowledge and the resulting ability to teach others, 'you know his will; ... you know what really matters; you are confident that you are a guide to the blind, a light to those in darkness, an instructor of the foolish, and a teacher of the immature ... you possess ... the embodiment of knowledge and truth.'[11] There is a heavy irony here as Paul is going to make clear. The Jews, or at least the Jewish teachers, were sure they knew, and as a result were confident they were neither blind, in darkness, foolish nor immature.

Secondly, the reason why the Jew was so confident that he knew was because he had the law, 'you ... rely on the law ... you know his will ... taught by the law you know what really matters ... you possess in the law the embodiment of knowledge and truth'.[12] This of course was true. The Jews did have the law, and they knew it and studied it. Yet Paul's series of rhetorical questions, 'You teach others, then; do you not teach yourself?' calls the reality of this knowledge into question and leads up to the denouement of verses 23–24, 'You who make your boast in the law, do you dishonour God through breaking the law? For, "The name of God is blasphemed among the Gentiles because of you," as it is written.'[13]

Thirdly, the only conclusion that can be drawn from this is that the sort of knowledge that the Jews had of the law was an inadequate knowledge, a surface knowledge which meant that they had neither grasped all that was involved in the law nor obeyed it as it was intended to be obeyed. In terms of verse 8 they did not obey the truth, which they had in the law; they obeyed unrighteousness. They did, of course, obey the law in an outward way, and that was one reason why they felt competent to teach others, but their moral and spiritual understanding was lacking.[14] As Paul goes on to show in the next verses they were circumcised externally, but their hearts were not circumcised; their inner being was affected by sin so that they neither understood the law aright, nor were their attitudes right;

they were proud and self-confident, commending each other, but not commended by God.

This leads on to chapter three and the last passage to be considered under this heading,

3:9–18

What shall we conclude then? Are we any better? Not at all! We have already made the charge that Jews and Gentiles alike are all under sin. As it is written: 'There is no-one righteous, not even one; there is no-one who understands, no-one who seeks God. All have turned away, they have together become worthless; there is no-one who does good, not even one. Their throats are open graves; their tongues practise deceit. The poison of vipers is on their lips. Their mouths are full of cursing and bitterness. Their feet are swift to shed blood; ruin and misery mark their ways, and the way of peace they do not know. There is no fear of God before their eyes.'

In verse 9 Paul summarizes the charge or indictment he has already brought in the first two chapters against both Jews and Greeks. Elsewhere Paul has used both the words Greek and Gentile (1:14, 16; 2:9, 10; 1:5, 13; 2:14, 24), but he probably uses the word Greek (NIV is inaccurate here) because he is thinking of people at their most religious (Jews), and at their most cultured and educated (Greeks).[15] These, he says, we have indicted as being 'under sin', that is, under the power or control of sin. It is this that accounts both for spiritual ignorance and blindness, and for moral delinquency.

Both of these are stressed in the catena of quotations from the Old Testament that Paul uses. In particular we notice verses 11–12a, 'There is no-one who understands; there is no-one who seeks God; all have turned aside' presumably from the way or from God himself.[16] This is the root of the trouble and the debased behaviour results from a condition in which God is neither known or revered: verse 18, 'There is no fear of God before their eyes.'[17]

We can now sum up this section. For Paul all men and women are 'under sin'.[18] This means that sin rules in their hearts, or inner being, and has effects in every part of their life, including their thinking and general behaviour. As a result of this people reject the truth which is made known to them in creation and their minds are closed to the truth of God. This inevitably leads to perverse behaviour.

God's hardening work in the impenitent

The concept of hardening occurs in chapters 9 and 11, but as already noted it is anticipated in the first chapter. In that chapter the emphasis is on God giving people up to their own sinful desires and passions, as if God removed restraints thus permitting them to go from bad to worse as their evil desires take them. In chapters 9 and 11, however, the emphasis is much more on obduracy of mind and attitude. 9:17 takes up the example of Pharaoh, referred to in the previous verse which is a quotation of Exodus 9:16, and generalizes from it, 'Therefore he is merciful to whom he wills, and hardens whom he wills.' Pharaoh's hardness of heart was seen in his refusal to let the Israelites depart from Egypt, which was ultimately a refusal to recognize Yahweh as the living God and submit to his will as mediated by Moses.

The contrast between the two components of the verse, and the context of election in which it occurs, suggests that 'hardens' is to be understood in a similar way to 'giving up' in chapter 1. However, there is this difference. Chapter 1 speaks only of general revelation through creation; in chapters 9 and 11 there is a rejection of more specific revelation from God, in the case of Pharaoh both of God's power and his word. In chapter 11 it is Israel itself, to which the oracles of God were committed (3:2), which is hardened. This means that hardening is more positive than merely 'giving up', but it is similarly judicial. So while God shows mercy in the sense of calling and revealing himself in salvation and grace to whom he wills, to others he does not do so but rather because of their rejection of his word gives them up to their own desires, confirming them in their hardness. Two further points need to be noted here. Firstly, the fact that God shows mercy indicates that people are here already contemplated as sinful before God. The situation is not a neutral one with God allotting some to this destiny and others to that, rather out of those already contemplated as sinful God shows mercy to some.[19]

Secondly, in the context there is a strong presumption that what Paul means is that God shows mercy to some, but hardens all the rest. The immediate focus on Pharaoh might suggest that God shows mercy to some, he hardens others and there is a great mass of others of whom neither is true. This leads us to the next reference.

In 11:7 Paul draws the conclusion suggested above, 'What Israel seeks, it has not obtained; but the elect have obtained and the rest were hardened.'[20] This is supported by what appears to be an interweaving of Deuteronomy 29:4 with Isaiah 29:10 and a citation of Psalm 69:22, 23. There are several points of interest here. Firstly, Deuteronomy 29:4 speaks of God not giving the Israelites eyes to see or ears to hear, indicating that without such a gift of God people do not in fact understand his word or ways. Secondly, the verses from Isaiah and Psalms are in the context of judgment which suggests that hardening is a judicial act. Thirdly, hardening here is interpreted primarily in terms of dulled senses, blind eyes and deaf ears,[21] eyes darkened and unseeing being repeated in the reference from Psalm 69.

There is a further reference to hardening in 11:25 which speaks of 'hardening in part' (πώρωσις ἀπὸ μέρους). This is not to be understood to mean partial hardening, in the sense that those who were hardened were only partially hardened. The immediate context suggests that 'in part' is to be understood in a temporal sense 'until the fullness of the Gentiles has come in', while the broader context would suggest that the hardening was always in part because there was always an elect remnant chosen by grace (vv. 5–7).[22]

Despite the complexities of this concept it seems clear that for Paul the explanation of the lack of response on the part of Israel to the Christian gospel lay in his understanding of hardening. Without exploring this any further it indicates, for the purposes of this study, that in Paul's mind it is not possible for people to understand God's word without his mercy. The alternatives are mercy or hardening, the latter mysteriously God's response to man's reluctance to listen or respond.

God's wisdom beyond human grasp

Chapter 11 comes to a remarkable climax with verses 33–36. Paul breaks out into an exclamation of awed wonder at the wisdom of God revealed in his plan for Jew and Gentile. Using Isaiah 40:13, Jeremiah 23:18 and Job 41:11 Paul describes the wisdom and knowledge of God as beyond the ability of the human intellect to discover; his judgments are inscrutable and his ways unsearchable. While this indicates the necessity for revelation, more is suggested, namely: that even when God's ways have been revealed they are still mysterious and defy full understanding; the human mind sees the tip of the iceberg but the depths are still hidden out of sight. Those who see something are left gasping with awe at the dim outlines of that which they cannot see. What we have here then is more than revealed fact, there is a sense of the greatness and grandeur of God's ways. There is a spiritual or pneumatic element[23] which is most convincingly explained as an elevation of mind brought about by the Holy Spirit.

Transformation by the renewing of the mind

The second verse of chapter 12 speaks of being transformed by the renewing of the mind so that the will of God can be found out in experience, δοκιμάζειν, and that it is good, acceptable and perfect.[24] It is Christians who are being spoken of here; those who have already believed the gospel and therefore who know the truth. However there is the danger that their outlook and attitudes will still be fashioned, συσχηματίζειν, according to the general outlook and values that belong to the unbelieving world and therefore a renewing of the mind is called for. Paul does not indicate here how this renewing of the mind comes about but it is not difficult to suggest that for him this would include two elements: firstly, God's revealed truths and values informing and moulding the mind, and secondly, God's Spirit[25] (see 8:5–8, a passage which will be considered under the next heading). Indeed it is the scope and fullness of Paul's teaching about the Spirit in this letter which make this almost certain.

The work of the Holy Spirit

There are probably some 29 references to the Holy Spirit in Romans, more even than in 1 Corinthians.[26] It is, perhaps, surprising to realize that Paul mentions the Spirit more in this letter than any other, the largest number of references (18) occurring in chapter 8. Not all the references are directly relevant to the present study.

1:4

and who through the Spirit of holiness was declared with power to be the Son of God, by his resurrection from the dead: Jesus Christ our Lord.

The only question which is relevant from this verse is whether ὁρισθέντος means 'to declare' or 'to appoint'. Modern versions of the Bible like the NIV and the REB favour the former, while Bromiley's summary of K. Schmidt's article in Kittel's *Theological Dictionary of the New Testament* maintains that it is not 'a matter of great urgency, since a divine declaration is also a divine appointment. In the light of Acts 10:42 and 17:31 what Christ is now declared or appointed to be is to be equated with what he already is from all eternity by divine appointment.'[27] However Acts 10:42 and 17:31 are not necessarily decisive for Paul's usage in Romans, and as this is the only place where Paul uses the verb, its precise meaning here can only be determined from the context. There are several imponderables which affect understanding at this point. For example, to link ἐν δυνάμει with ἐξ ἀναστάσεως (as REB does) tends to favour 'declare' (or 'proclaim', as REB), while to link ὁρισθέντος with ἐξ ἀναστάσεως throws an emphasis on υἱοῦ θεοῦ ἐν δυνάμει (Son of God with power) which might suggest a new status and would fit nicely with 'appoint'.

In addition the precise significance of 'according to the Spirit of holiness' (κατὰ πνεῦμα ἁγιωσύνης) is difficult to determine.[28] How far this phrase balances κατὰ σάρκα, and what this means for our understanding of it, and whether it is to be connected with τοῦ ὁρισθέντος or υἱοῦ θεοῦ or ἐν δυνάμει or ἐξ ἀναστάσεως are all significant but delicately poised questions. However, it is difficult to believe that some element of declaration, or at least *public* appointment,[29] is not intended by so decisive an event as the resurrection. Indeed an emphasis on 'the Son of God with power' might suggest that the resurrection was the public inauguration of a new phase in the life and ministry of Jesus (also Matt. 28:18). Whatever the precise connection of the Holy Spirit with the resurrection here it is certainly significant that in some way it is the Spirit who is involved in this act of God. If it is difficult to suppress the idea of proclamation, we also have to notice that it is particularly the Holy Spirit who is involved in this.[30]

2:29

No, a man is a Jew if he is one inwardly; and circumcision is circumcision of the heart, by the Spirit, not by the written code. Such a man's praise is not from men, but from God.

There is some doubt whether there is a reference in this verse to the Holy Spirit or not. REB, for example, translates, 'his circumcision is of the heart, spiritual, not literal.' On the other hand the parallel in 2 Corinthians 3:6 strongly suggests that the Holy Spirit is intended. The phrase οὐ γράμματος ἀλλὰ πνεύματος (2 Cor. 3:6) is so similar to ἐν πνεύματι οὐ γράμματι here that it suggests that Paul was accustomed to drawing such a contrast. As he clearly has the Holy Spirit in mind in 2 Corinthians 3 (v. 3, 'the Spirit of the living God', v. 6 'the Spirit gives life') it seems most natural to understand the same here. Even if it seems better in English to use 'spiritual' it would be preferable to capitalize as 'Spiritual' in order to indicate that the circumcision of the heart is a fruit of the work of the Spirit.[31]

Coming as it does at the end of chapter 2 this verse indicates that for Paul the real Jew is someone who has been circumcised inwardly, that is someone whose heart has been changed in such a way by the Spirit that he has a new disposition or attitude, one which is commended by God. Over against the blindness and misunderstanding of the law, which according to Paul characterizes the man who is named a Jew, Paul sets the real Jew (REB) whose difference springs from the work of the Spirit in his heart. Comment on 7:6 is appropriate at this point. Here too we have a contrast between the Spirit and the letter. As it stands this is as problematic as 2:29 but the considerations arising from 2 Corinthians apply here too, though perhaps 'newness of Spirit' in the context might tend to suggest the power of God's Spirit because of the connection with resurrection in verse 4. The emphasis here seems to be on the freshness and vigour of the new way which issues in fruit for God (v. 4). Any connection with understanding the law seems to be rather remote, and therefore this verse is not viewed as having any relevance to the present thesis.

5:5

And hope does not disappoint us, because God has poured out his love into our hearts by the Holy Spirit, whom he has given us.

This verse cannot be passed over because although its connection with our subject is only indirect there are two features that need comment. The first concerns the knowledge of God's love which is involved in the experience of the Holy Spirit described here. It is very widely agreed that the love of God here means God's love for us.[32] This sense and assurance of God's love is the basis for hope, so the meaning must be that the Holy Spirit who has been given brings with him an overflowing – outpoured – sense of God's love for us.[33]

The second comment relates to how far this awareness of God's love is to be understood in terms of the context, and particularly the development of Paul's thought in the verses that follow. There can be no doubt that for Paul the love of God has been given historical and concrete expression in the person and mission of Jesus Christ. The fact that Paul goes on to speak of the death of Christ and in verse 8 says, 'God demonstrates his own love towards us, in that while we were still sinners, Christ died for us'[34] shows that it is very unlikely that in verse 5 he is simply thinking of the Holy Spirit giving a sense that God loves us and no more. Rather the Holy Spirit illuminates and makes real and personal the love of God objectively made known in Jesus Christ, and especially in his death. If this is correct it is an interesting example of the Holy Spirit illuminating and applying objective truth subjectively in the hearts of those to whom he is given.[35]

8:5–6

Those who live according to the sinful nature have their minds set on what that nature desires; but those who live in accordance with the Spirit have their minds set on what the Spirit desires. The mind of sinful man is death, but the mind controlled by the Spirit is life and peace.

These verses occur in a chapter that has a considerable number of references to the Spirit. Because in some verses the word 'spirit' is unmistakably the Holy Spirit[36] the position adopted here is that it is the Holy Spirit who is referred to throughout the chapter. This is also supported by the contrast between flesh and Spirit (as also in Galatians 5:16–26), the fact that in verse 15 the Spirit is received, and the expression τὸ φρόνημα τοῦ πνεύματος in verse 27 where the Spirit is clearly meant.

The primary orientation of the passage in which these verses occur is ethical. Paul is concerned with the righteous requirement, τὸ δικαίωμα, of the law being fulfilled in the lives of those who walk, or live, according to the Spirit. In these verses he states that those who live according to the Spirit set their minds on the things of the Spirit, and this mind-set of the Spirit, or disposition arising from living according to the Spirit, is life and peace.

The primary meaning of the term 'the minding of the Spirit' refers to a disposition to live in a righteous way. Verse 7 indicates that it includes willing subjection to God and his law. At the same time it is possible to see an intellectual element in this phrase. This would include the idea of insight into the meaning of the law, and wisdom to apply the law to particular situations. The mind-set of the Spirit must include understanding.[37]

The mind-set of the Spirit is specifically 'life and peace'. 'Life' here contrasts with 'death' which is what the mind-set of the flesh leads to. However the addition of the word 'peace' is unexpected. It looks as if 'peace' contrasts with being at enmity with God in verse 7, the link being διότι in the beginning of the verse. The word 'peace' – and perhaps to some extent the word 'life' – indicates the breadth of the term, 'the minding of the Spirit'. To have a mind controlled by the Spirit not only leads to a life of righteousness, it means the person concerned has entered into a life in which there is no enmity with God, a life of peace; a life then in which God is known.

8:14–16

because those who are led by the Spirit of God are sons of God. For you did not receive a spirit that makes you a slave again to fear, but you received the Spirit of sonship. And by him we cry, 'Abba, Father.' The Spirit himself testifies with our spirit that we are God's children.

There are three comments I want to make on these verses.

The first is to note that this is a development of Paul's discussion from the beginning of the chapter. It could be argued that all the way through to verse 27 Paul is, in effect, working out what it means to live (περιπατοῦσιν) according to the Spirit (verse 4). This means that there is an underlying unity to all that he says about the Spirit here. To be indwelt by the Spirit (verse 9), is to be controlled by the Spirit (verse 4) and led by the Spirit (verse 14), and it is the one Spirit who sanctifies (verse 13), assures (verses 15, 16, 23), assists in prayer (verses 26, 27), and raises up the body to new life (verses 10, 11).

Second, as the Spirit of adoption, the Spirit enables God's children to recognize that God is their Father and to address him accordingly.[38] Fear and slavery have been removed and the implication seems to be that spontaneously, instinctively, the person who has received the Spirit cries out to God, 'Abba, Father.' The Spirit, therefore, when he comes, brings a consciousness of God as Father with him; not just a sense that it is right or fitting for God to be addressed in that way, but rather a warmth and intimacy that expresses a filial relationship whatever precise words may be used.

Third, it is not certain whether verse 16 is to be taken as a development of what has been said in verse 15, or as an explanatory expansion of it. On balance it seems better to understand it in the second way; we cry 'Abba, Father', because the Spirit bears witness with our spirits that we are the children of God; it is all part and parcel of the same experience. However, we must notice the clear 'bears witness with', or 'confirms to'.[39] Here is a work of the Spirit in which he speaks to the spirits of God's children assuring them of their new status. This is a very personal aspect of the teaching ministry of the Spirit.

8:26–27

In the same way, the Spirit helps us in our weakness. We do not know what we ought to pray for, but the Spirit himself intercedes for us with groans that words cannot express. And he who searches our hearts knows the mind of the Spirit, because the Spirit intercedes for the saints in accordance with God's will.

In some ways this verse speaks about a work of the Spirit which is the opposite of that expressed in verses 14–16. There it was the Spirit witnessing to the children of God concerning their adoption and hence enabling them to pray to God as Father. Here it is the Spirit pleading within the saints (ὑπερεντυγχάνει) and God, who searches hearts knowing what the Spirit says. There is also a link with verses 5–6 where the same phrase is used (τὸ φρόνημα τοῦ πνεύματος). However, it seems much more likely that this is a reference to the mind of the Spirit himself.[40] The mind of the Spirit thus means what the Spirit knows about the condition and needs of the person concerned, and his intercession on the basis of this. This tends to suggest that the phrase τὸ φρόνημα τοῦ πνεύματος has a strong sense of knowledge and understanding about it.

What is of interest is that the Spirit who teaches and witnesses to God's people, here also expresses the thoughts and yearnings which through weakness they are incapable of articulating in prayer to God. In this case God knows the mind of the Spirit, but it is his role in expressing thought, especially that which is almost beyond expression, which is important. The Spirit, then, is the Spirit of prophecy who speaks through the prophets God's words to men; he is the Spirit who gives understanding and insight into truth about God which otherwise remains unapprehended; he is the Spirit who assures of sonship; and he is the Spirit of prayer who intercedes for God's people according to God's will when they are scarcely able to pray for themselves.

9:1

I speak the truth in Christ – I am not lying, my conscience confirms it in the Holy Spirit.

This is the last reference to the Holy Spirit which will be commented on as the other references in the letter are not related to the theme. It is interesting to note the similarities between this verse and 8:16 centring on the use of the verb συμμαρτυρούσης. However, what is significant is the role Paul attributes to the Holy Spirit in enlightening – it seems justifiable for REB to use this word in translation – the conscience. Paul's point is simply this, that in speaking about his sorrow and grief for his own kinsmen, the Holy Spirit assures his conscience that he is speaking the truth. It is not just that he consults his conscience, for conscience can be faulty, but the Holy Spirit enables him to know the truth about himself,[41] so that he can speak with absolute sincerity and disingenuousness when he opens his heart to his readers.

Summary

The material in Romans was considered in five sections. The first concentrated upon the effects of sin upon the mind. 1:18–23; 2:17–24; 3:9–18 all show that sin rules in the hearts of people and this has effects for their thinking first, and then their behaviour. The next three sections show, first, that hardening is God's response to man's refusal to listen to God's word. It is only mercy that overcomes such human reluctance. Then in 11:33–36 Paul gives doxological expression to the fact that God's wisdom surpasses human understanding. Finally, 12:2 speaks of transformation by the renewing of the mind. All of these indicate the need for the work of the Spirit which is being considered.

Although there are more references to the Holy Spirit in Romans than in any other of Paul's letters, not many of them have a direct bearing on the teaching ministry of the Spirit. There may be a suggestion of declaration in 1:4. 2:29 suggests that the real Jew, circumcised in heart in the Spirit, has a different disposition than those who are blind to the truth. In 5:5 the Spirit gives a sense of God's love and this is related to the objective truth of Christ's death (v. 8). 8:5–6 speaks of the 'minding of the Spirit'. This has reference to disposition, but the primary orientation is ethical. In 8:14–16 the Spirit brings a consciousness of God as Father, while in 8:26–27 the Spirit helps in prayer. In 9:1 the Spirit enlightens the conscience. These indications of the Spirit's role in giving knowledge become stronger when considered against the background Paul has given of people 'under sin', and of the needs set out in the previous paragraph.

CHAPTER 5

THE FIRST LETTER TO THE CORINTHIANS

In looking at this letter I will comment on the various relevant passages as they occur and finish with a concluding observation on the subject of prophecy.

1:5–6

For in him you have been enriched in every way – in all your speaking and in all your knowledge – because our testimony about Christ was confirmed in you.

In these verses Paul is giving thanks because the Corinthians have been enriched in all (every sort of) utterance and all knowledge. It is probable that both words (λόγος and γνῶσις) were used frequently and in a particular way among the Corinthians.[1] Perhaps Paul is, in part at least, reminding them that these are gifts from God, riches that they have in Christ, and therefore nothing to be proud of or used in self-centred ways. In particular we note that knowledge is a gift. Probably God is to be understood as the one who enriches them in Christ.[2] Even granting a special nuance for the Corinthians, 'knowledge certainly refers to intellectual apprehension and application of Christian truth',[3] though the idea of insight should not be excluded either.[4] The emphasis, then, in this passage is that knowledge of the gospel and Christian truth is not something learned and grasped by natural ability but is a gift of God's grace in Christ.

This arises 'as the testimony of (about) Christ was confirmed in you'.[5] Writers on 1 Corinthians tend to start off disagreeing about the way in which the testimony of Christ was confirmed, but as they develop their understanding of it they begin to converge. Probably it is the spiritual gifts themselves which give the confirmation but Barrett seems justified in comparing with 2 Corinthians 1:21–22 and seeing the Holy Spirit as particularly the donor of all spiritual gifts (doubtless also with chapter 12 in mind).[6] It is particularly significant, because of the place the Corinthians gave to knowledge, to see how Paul emphasizes that it is a gift of God, one received in Christ, by the Holy Spirit.

1:18–31

For the message of the cross is foolishness to those who are perishing, but to us who are being saved it is the power of God. For it is written: "I will destroy the wisdom of the wise; the intelligence of the intelligent I will frustrate." Where is the wise man? Where is the scholar? Where is the philosopher of this age? Has not God made foolish the wisdom of the world? For since in the wisdom of God the world through its wisdom did not know him, God was pleased through the foolishness of what was preached to save those who believe. Jews demand miraculous signs and Greeks look for wisdom, but we preach Christ crucified: a stumbling-block to Jews and foolishness to Gentiles, but to those whom God has called, both Jews and Greeks, Christ the power of God and the wisdom of God. For the foolishness of God is wiser than man's wisdom, and the weakness of God is stronger than man's strength. Brothers, think of what you were when you were called. Not many of you were wise by human standards; not many were influential; not many were of noble birth. But God chose the foolish things of the world to shame the wise; God chose the weak things of the world to shame the strong. He chose the lowly things of this world and the despised things – and the things that are not – to nullify the things that are, so that no-one may boast before him. It is because of him that you are in Christ Jesus, who has become for us wisdom from God – that is, our righteousness, holiness and redemption. Therefore, as it is written: 'Let him who boasts boast in the Lord.'

These verses elaborate, among other things, the fact that true wisdom is a gift of God (v. 30). This develops what has been said about knowledge and shows that the sort of wisdom that the Christian gospel knows is not one which depends on human cleverness or learning (vv. 19–20), but is the wisdom of God which is found and made known in Christ (vv. 24–30).[7] There are three points which may be taken up in this passage.

Firstly, Paul uses Scripture, γέγραπται,[8] to show that God has brought the wisdom and cleverness of the wise to nothing. The way he has done this is by choosing to save people by the message of the cross. This overturns all the expectations of those who anticipate that it will be by human wisdom that salvation is effected and a knowledge of God achieved.

Paul then goes on to assert that the world has not in fact come to a knowledge of God by its wisdom (v. 21),[9] this negative conclusion demonstrating that if God is going to be known then this knowledge will have to come in a different way. In fact God in his wisdom ordained that the world should not reach him by its own wisdom, but chose rather by the foolishness of the gospel to save those who believe. The change of category from knowing God to being saved shows how in Paul's thought the whole question is not an intellectual one, but one which lies in what might be called the spiritual[10] realm. Those who emphasize human wisdom are thinking simply in terms of the use of the mind, whereas human fallenness demands that a person be saved in order to know God, and this is something that God himself must do.

This leads to the conclusion that there are two sorts of wisdom. There is human wisdom which has utterly failed, and which God has confounded (BAGD), but there is a wisdom from God which is found in Christ and his crucifixion (vv. 24–30).[11] This prepares the way for what Paul is going to say in chapter 2:6ff.

Chapter 2 is one of the most important passages in Paul for his understanding of the work of the Spirit in teaching and enlightening. Paul's first reference to the Spirit in this letter comes in this chapter and this is significant as the lengthy explanation of the effects of the Spirit's presence within Christians focuses on something quite other than what the Corinthians would have considered important.[12] In this chapter the contrast between the wisdom of this world (v. 6) and God's wisdom (v. 7) is developed further, and Paul stresses that God's wisdom is only made known by the Spirit.

2:4

　My message and my preaching were not with wise and persuasive
words, but with a demonstration of the Spirit's power.

The Spirit is first mentioned in this verse in which Paul reminds the
Corinthians of what had happened when he came and preached the
gospel to them.[13] In the preaching of the gospel the Spirit is the
agent of God in making the 'foolishness' of Christ crucified (1:18,
21, 22) the wisdom of God to those who hear – or at least to some
of those who hear. There is disagreement about what precisely the
'demonstration' (ἀποδέιξει) consisted of. Watson is possibly most
on target when he says, 'It is more likely that he [Paul] is thinking of
the internal testimony by which the Spirit had convinced his hearers
of the truth of his message, as well as its further work in liberating
and transforming their lives and endowing them with spiritual gifts.'[14]
　Paul is going to elaborate more clearly the role of the Spirit in
making known the gospel and its implications – the things which
God has prepared for those who love him (v. 9) – as the wisdom of
God.

2:6–16

We do, however, speak a message of wisdom among the mature, but
not the wisdom of this age or of the rulers of this age, who are coming
to nothing. No, we speak of God's secret wisdom, a wisdom that has
been hidden and that God destined for our glory before time began.
None of the rulers of this age understood it, for if they had, they
would not have crucified the Lord of glory. However, as it is written:
'No eye has seen, no ear has heard, no mind has conceived what God
has prepared for those who love him' but God has revealed it to us by
his Spirit. The Spirit searches all things, even the deep things of God.
For who among men knows the thoughts of a man except the man's
spirit within him? In the same way no-one knows the thoughts of God
except the Spirit of God. We have not received the spirit of the world
but the Spirit who is from God, that we may understand what God has
freely given us. This is what we speak, not in words taught us by

human wisdom but in words taught by the Spirit, expressing spiritual truths in spiritual words. The man without the Spirit does not accept the things that come from the Spirit of God, for they are foolishness to him, and he cannot understand them, because they are spiritually discerned. The spiritual man makes judgments about all things, but he himself is not subject to any man's judgment: 'For who has known the mind of the Lord that he may instruct him?' But we have the mind of Christ.

In reviewing verses 6–16 our main concern is to isolate the various aspects of the Spirit's work as expounded by Paul here.

Aspects of the Spirit's work
Firstly, Paul says that the things which God has prepared for those who love him, things which go beyond seeing, hearing or imagining,[15] God has revealed to us through the Spirit (vv. 9–10). These things form part of the content of the wisdom – God's wisdom hidden from those who rely only on human thought and understanding (vv. 6–7) – which Paul and his colleagues[16] do speak to the mature.[17] There is a question whether the 'us' in 'God revealed to us' (v. 10) refers to Paul and his fellow apostles and preachers or whether 'us' means 'us Christians'. If Fee is right in closely connecting 'us' with 'those who love him' in the previous verse (who are also the 'mature' of verse 6) then the latter is correct.[18] In this case the aorist ἀπεκάλυψεν must refer to the time of illumination when the gospel came with the 'demonstration of Spirit and power'.[19] When God calls (1:24), the Spirit reveals the truth, reality and implications of Christ and him crucified.

Secondly, in verses 10b, 11 Paul pursues an analogy in which he shows that just as only the spirit of a person knows what the person is really like, so only the Spirit of God knows what God is, and he knows even the deep things of God. In applying this Paul does not say that the Spirit reveals to us the deep things of God – we must look at what he does say in a moment – but the fact that he goes on to say that we have received the Spirit who is from God must indicate that the coming of the Spirit brings some knowledge of God with him. While Paul's stress may not be on this, the implication is unmistakable. This ties in with 1:21. The world by wisdom did not know God, but receiving the Spirit of God who knows the things of God (v. 11b – REB 'knows what God is'), we do know God. Thirdly, turning now to verse 12 with its emphasis on 'we' at the beginning there are four points which need to be commented on. The emphasis on 'we' appears to be an implied rebuke and a recall to the Corinthians: 'Now we have not received the spirit of the world...' If this is so it underlines the fact that the whole passage seems to stress that all Christians are given an understanding by the Spirit.

The same question can be asked of the aorist 'we have received' in this verse as of 'God has revealed' in verse 10. Because it is characteristic of Paul, and of the New Testament, to speak of the time of conversion as the time of receiving the Spirit,[20] this also links with 2:10, 2:4 and 1:24. What is particularly significant, especially in the context of this letter, is the purpose of receiving the Spirit as Paul expresses it here, 'that we may know the things freely given to us by God'.[21] Receiving the Spirit means knowing the things that God gives to us and has for us.

It is significant again that the verb 'have been freely given' (REB, 'has lavished') is χαρισθέντα. The Spirit gives knowledge of the good gifts of God. Later the activity of the Spirit as the distributor of spiritual gifts (12:11) will be explained, but here Paul emphasizes the Spirit as the one who enables God's people to know what God gives them in Christ. There may be some link between 'the things which have been freely given by God' in this verse, and 'the deep things of God' in verse 10. God's gifts spring from his purpose (cf. v. 7), and also from his nature. The things that he bestows are not totally unrelated to what he is, they spring from his love and grace. This is probably hinted at in χαρισθέντα, and is why Paul can say unexpectedly 'so that we might know the things freely given to us by God' rather than 'so that we might know the things of God'.

This prepares the way for verse 13 'which things we also speak'. Here Paul looks back to verse 6. 'These are the things we speak, and we speak them in words which the Spirit teaches' (looking back to vv. 1–4), 'interpreting spiritual truths to those who have the Spirit' (REB). This last phrase is a notorious crux of interpretation. Against the understanding represented by REB, Fee comes down on 'explaining the things of the Spirit by means of the words taught by the Spirit'.[22] The arguments are finely balanced and certainty seems unlikely. Perhaps the best thing is to agree with Watson when he says, 'Either way, the Spirit is the key to everything.'[23]

Fourthly, by contrast with the 'natural' or 'unspiritual' person the spiritual person receives and grasps the 'things of the Spirit' (v. 14),[24] but verse 15 goes further; he 'can judge the worth of everything' (REB). This seems to suggest that the person who is spiritual, having received the Spirit, has a basic standpoint and attitude from which he is able to assess everything. Perhaps in the context this means that he not only understands the things of the Spirit, but he is able also to see the wisdom of this world for what it is. Included in this would be the fact that he is able to judge and see through those who cling on to the wisdom of the world. By contrast he cannot be judged by anyone without the Spirit, because such a person lacks the insight necessary for this. Paul here is doubtless responding to, or perhaps anticipating, criticism of himself on the part of those Corinthians who emphasized wisdom as they understood it.

Fifthly, Paul backs up what he has said by a quotation from Isaiah 40:13. The point of the quotation appears to be that only someone who has the mind of the Lord is able to judge and understand the people who belong to him, and who have received his Spirit. This leads Paul to a last astonishing statement, 'but we have the mind of Christ'. As for him Jesus is Lord,[25] he speaks of Christ rather than God but this in no way lessens the force of what he is saying. It is a most striking climax to the chapter.

One of the reasons why Paul brings out these five different facets of the wisdom which is made known through the Spirit is because he wants the Corinthians to realize what is true of them, and to stir their minds to recall how they first received the gospel of Christ crucified. Paul is undertaking a very delicate task here. In 3:1 he is going to acknowledge that he is not able to speak to them as spiritual people, but it is clear that that is what they really are. He therefore appears to be trying to awaken them out of the folly of turning to human wisdom, and to do so he stresses the riches of the wisdom and knowledge which the Spirit makes known in Christ – even giving them the mind of Christ. So these two points emerge; all Christians have received the Spirit and insight into the wisdom of Christ, even if some turn aside to the wisdom of the world; and the knowledge and wisdom brought by the Spirit are far-reaching indeed.

3:18-20

Do not deceive yourselves. If any one of you thinks he is wise by the standards of this age, he should become a 'fool' so that he may become wise. For the wisdom of this world is foolishness in God's sight. As it is written, 'He catches the wise in their craftiness'; and again, 'The Lord knows that the thoughts of the wise are futile.'

In this short section Paul returns to the theme of wisdom and sets out 'Even more starkly than in the opening chapter ... the alternatives: either the wisdom of the world or the wisdom which counts in the sight of God.'[26] Though what Paul has already said has excluded the possibility, this clarifies even more the point that spiritual wisdom cannot be added on to, or grow out of, the 'wisdom of the world.'[27] The antithesis is complete. A person has to give up human wisdom and count it as folly in order to become 'truly wise' (REB). The negative side of what Paul has been arguing is seen here at its starkest. Its implications for biblical hermeneutics are considerable. Human wisdom simply cannot lead to a right understanding of spiritual truth; it has to be renounced as folly if there is to be understanding. The starting point for hermeneutics, therefore, must be the work of the Spirit, and dependence upon the Spirit must characterise all hermeneutical endeavours.

8:1-3

Now about food sacrificed to idols: We know that we all possess knowledge. Knowledge puffs up, but love builds up. The man who thinks he knows something does not yet know as he ought to know. But the man who loves God is known by God.

This passage recalls Paul's words in 2:9 and anticipates his far longer exposition of love in chapter 13. Here we can see very clearly how 'knowledge' can be totally inadequate and can lead to a distortion in Christian behaviour.[28] If verse 4 expresses the content of this knowledge then it was not incorrect, yet it was completely inadequate and the logic of simply acting in accordance with that knowledge led to further division in the church and to real spiritual harm to Christian brothers. Fee suggests the Corinthian attitude was like this: 'In their minds being spiritual meant to have received *gnosis*, meaning probably that the Spirit had endowed them with special knowledge which *all* believers should have, and which should serve as the basis of Christian behaviour.'[29] According to Paul a true knowledge, which must be a true knowledge of God, involves love. Knowledge without love cannot be true Christian knowledge, the knowledge of a person who is spiritual.

This is taken up again[30] in chapter 13 where in the opening verses Paul shows that understanding all knowledge and all mysteries is nothing without love. Here this knowledge appears to come via prophecy, but the point is still the same. The person who actually has insight into knowledge and 'hidden truth' (REB) is nothing without love. The Gospels provide many examples of those who had considerable knowledge of the Old Testament and, as they thought, the nature and ways of God, yet who proved by their resistance to Christ that they had no love and were in fact quite wrong – else they would not have crucified the Lord of glory (2:8). Similarly 1 Corinthians shows people who gloried in the gifts of the Spirit yet were without love and whose supposed knowledge by-passed Christ crucified and therefore demonstrated their real spiritual emptiness – 'I am nothing'.

Spiritual gifts

Chapters 12–14 cover the subject of spiritual gifts. Because many of the details of interpretation are disputed and their continuing direct relevance for the churches is perhaps problematic it is difficult to assess the teaching here without being drawn aside into discussions which are not relevant to the subject under consideration. However, it is necessary to examine the implications of this passage. The general approach adopted here to the gifts listed in chapter 12 is the one proposed by Gordon Fee, 'Indeed, the list of nine items in vv. 8–10 is neither carefully worked out nor exhaustive; it is merely *representative* of the diversity of the Spirit's manifestations. Paul's concern here is to offer a *considerable* list so that they will stop being singular in their own emphasis. All of this suggests not only that we do not have here a systematic discussion of "spiritual gifts", but also that there is some doubt as to whether the apostle himself had precise and identifiably different "gifts" in mind when he wrote these words.'[31]

12:3

Therefore I tell you that no-one who is speaking by the Spirit of God says, 'Jesus be cursed,' and no-one can say, 'Jesus is Lord,' except by the Holy Spirit.'

In this verse Paul is concerned to provide the evidence which will authenticate someone who professes to speak under the influence of the Spirit. Paul shows that it is the content,[32] not the manner of speaking, that provides this evidence, and that turns on what is said about Jesus. Negatively, no-one can say that Jesus is accursed under the influence of the Spirit;[33] positively no-one can confess that Jesus is Lord except by the Spirit.[34] The Christological nature of the test is marked and reminiscent of what Paul has said in chapters 1 and 2. The Spirit leads to a practical knowledge of Christ, one which manifests itself in actual commitment to his lordship.

12:8

To one there is given through the Spirit the message of wisdom, to another the message of knowledge by means of the same Spirit ...

In this verse Paul speaks of 'the word of wisdom' and 'the word of knowledge'. It is almost impossible to be sure of the exact nature of these gifts[35] but Fee is probably right both in emphasizing that it is the word, the 'utterance', which is the gift, and in linking wisdom with the gospel as in 2:4.[36] What is important is that both the utterance of wisdom, and the utterance of knowledge are gifts of the *Spirit*.

12:10

to another miraculous powers, to another prophecy, to another distinguishing between spirits, to another speaking in different kinds of tongues, and to still another the interpretation of tongues.

This verse speaks of four gifts which are relevant to the study; prophecy, discerning of spirits, kinds of tongues and the interpretation of tongues. Because of the importance of prophecy this needs a note to itself. Of the other three perhaps the first thing to stress again is that they too are gifts of the Spirit. Whatever is precisely intended by 'discerning' and 'interpretation' in the context they are both given by the Spirit, and are wholly congruous with what we have seen of the Spirit's work elsewhere, even if their meaning here is to be understood as a specialized one. Clearly tongues were highly valued at Corinth, over-valued in fact, but what their exact nature was is not clear. They appear to consist primarily of prayer (14:2, 16, 17; this apparently including sung praise as well), though this does not sit easily with 'he speaks mysteries' in 14:2 which suggests a form of prophecy (cf. Ephesians 3:3–5). Within the church tongues and interpretation needed to go together so that everyone could understand, profit from what was said, and add 'Amen' (14:2, 7, 5, 16). This at least gives a precise meaning to 'interpretation of tongues'.

Discerning of spirits is presumably the ability to distinguish between evil spirits and the Holy Spirit, or perhaps more specifically between words spoken under the influence of evil spirits and those spoken under the influence of the Holy Spirit (cf. 1 John 4:1–3). This would link 12:10 with 12:3 and one interpretation of 14:29.[37] This also makes 'discerning' of spirits a very specialized gift, but together with the interpretation of tongues it is possible to set these specialized gifts against the background of the general work of the

Spirit who gives discernment and understanding. These gifts of the Spirit are gifts of the *Spirit*, because it is the Spirit who is the Spirit of wisdom and understanding, and it is his ministry towards the people of God to give wisdom and understanding.

Prophecy

There is considerable difference of opinion over what is meant by prophecy in these chapters. The options range from preaching, inspired preaching, prophetic messages which nevertheless can be checked (14:29), to Spirit-directed speaking for God in the full Old Testament sense.[38] For the purposes of this study it is not necessary to come down on any one of these as the correct understanding. Rather these are the points which are important.

This is a gift of the Spirit. Even if prophecy means preaching, this passage indicates that some (prophets) are given the ability to articulate and communicate to people things that edify, stimulate and encourage (14:3; REB for last two). This might appear a very 'ordinary' gift, but it would underline the importance of the Spirit's help even in ordinary matters.

In prophecy, however understood, a message is presented,[39] ultimately believed to be from God. This means that it is the Holy Spirit who guides the mind to the message, who enables the one who will speak it to understand it, as well as granting guidance in the actual speaking. These activities of the Spirit within the mind are analogous to the ministry of the Spirit which he exercises in teaching and illuminating. It would be possible here also to see them as specialised applications of the general teaching ministry of the Spirit.

The relationship of New Testament prophecy to the Old Testament needs to be raised also. The book of Acts gives clear indication that the Holy Spirit gave understanding of Old Testament texts,[40] and Peter's preaching on the day of Pentecost, in particular, was structured around two such texts. As the Old Testament functioned as the 'Bible' of the early churches it is extremely likely that prophecy would involve Spirit-given insight into and exposition of the Old Testament.[41] It is true that the one book of prophecy in the New Testament (Revelation) does not do this in a formal way, but it is also true that Revelation is full of allusions to the Old Testament and Old Testament imagery, and brings together many Old Testament themes into their final form.[42]

14:24–25 indicates that prophecy acted with a convincing power upon the person who heard it. These verses suggest that the Spirit gave the prophet insight into the deepest needs and concerns of the human heart, which then resonated within the heart of the unbelieving visitor present in the congregation. It would be possible to deduce that there was a convincing or applicatory work of the Spirit in him, but this is not said,[43] nor is it strictly necessary to consider this within the context of this chapter, important though it is in itself.

In 14:36–38 Paul asserts that anyone who is a prophet or a spiritual person (πνευματικός) ought to recognize that what he writes is a commandment of the Lord. If a person who claims to be spiritual or a prophet does not in fact so recognize Paul's letter, he himself cannot be acknowledged to be what he claims to be (so REB). This agrees with what Paul has said earlier (v. 29) about the prophets judging what one of their numbers says, though it is widened by the inclusion of the term 'spiritual'. The point is that true prophets and spiritual people are able to discern when another prophet is speaking 'with the Lord's authority' (REB). So a person gifted by the Spirit, and particularly one gifted as a prophet, has also a discernment and ability to recognize the words of the Lord by the Spirit. All these points, in various ways, fit in to the overall pattern of the Spirit giving understanding and illumination to God's people.

Summary

The First Letter to the Corinthians contains a number of references which indicate that knowledge and wisdom are gifts of God. These are contrasted with human wisdom which has failed in its attempt to know God, and knowledge without love which simply leads to pride. In 2:4 'persuasive words of human wisdom' are contrasted with the 'demonstration of the Spirit and power'.

Chapter 2 is particularly important and five aspects of the Spirit's revealing ministry can be noted. Firstly, God has revealed to

Christians by the Spirit things that go beyond seeing, hearing or imagining. Secondly, Christians have received the Spirit of God who knows the things of God and searches the deep things of God. Thirdly, Christians have received the Spirit from God in order to know the things freely given them by God. Fourthly, in contrast to the 'natural man' Christians, being spiritual, can 'judge all things'. Fifthly, they now have the mind of Christ.

In chapters 12 to 14 the main subject is spiritual gifts, though 12:3 states that no-one can acknowledge the lordship of Jesus except by the Spirit. It is not possible to be certain about the exact nature of all the gifts enumerated, but several of them are closely connected to wisdom, knowledge and discernment. Though these gifts may be specialized it is significant that they are gifts of the Spirit. Prophecy seems to include insight both into Old Testament scripture and into present needs. Moreover prophets and spiritual people will recognize that Paul writes the commandments of God.

CHAPTER 6

THE SECOND LETTER
TO THE CORINTHIANS

In considering 2 Corinthians comment is made on the relevant passages as they occur, particular attention being given to Chapter 3 and the opening verses of Chapter 4.

1:21–22

Now it is God who makes both us and you stand firm in Christ. He anointed us, set his seal of ownership on us, and put his Spirit in our hearts as a deposit, guaranteeing what is to come.

It is possible that there is a threefold reference to the Spirit in these verses even though the Spirit is only explicitly mentioned once. Firstly, there may be an allusion to the Spirit in the word 'anointed'. This is the only occasion when Paul uses the verb χρίειν[1] but in view of its use in Luke 4:18 (this dominical use of Isaiah 61:1–2 doubtless remaining influential in the early church) and John's use of the noun χρῖσμα in 1 John 2:20, 27,[2] together with the reference to the Spirit in the next verse, it seems reasonable to see the anointing as being by or with the Spirit. In addition, in Ephesians 1:13 it is with the Holy Spirit that believers are sealed. So perhaps it is the Spirit who is the anointing, the seal and the deposit, or guarantee.[3] There are two points which are of interest to us in these verses.

The first depends on how far any of these terms reflect on the consciousness of those who receive the Spirit. The whole emphasis in these verses is on Christians being established, 'guaranteed as his', as REB translates. Quite clearly Paul is not reflecting simply on the objective fact; rather the presence of the Spirit in our hearts as a deposit, or first instalment, guaranteeing the final enjoyment of the consummation of all things, gives a subjective assurance of what is objectively true.[4]

103

This is strengthened by the link with the promises of God and the fact that God's word is not 'Yes' and 'No', but 'yes' in Christ Jesus. In Christ Jesus all the promises of God are 'yes' and 'Amen' and Christians are established into (εἰς) Christ,[5] thus entering into the certainty of the promises. The Holy Spirit in the heart, then, brings assurance, a sense of certainty. This is not precisely the same as his teaching ministry but it indicates the way in which he gives a type of knowledge, bringing home the reality of an objective relationship brought about by God. The link with the promises and so with the Old Testament scripture is also significant.[6]

2 Corinthians 3.

Three preliminary points may be made in coming to 2 Corinthians 3.

First, there are a number of references to 'spirit' in it, but, as in other parts of Paul's writings, there is no agreement that all of them should be understood of the Holy Spirit. The position taken here is that it is most likely that all the references are directly to the Holy Spirit, but the conclusions drawn do not depend on this being so.[7]

Second, there is considerable difficulty and uncertainty in understanding some parts of this chapter.[8] Part of this difficulty relates to understanding how Paul uses 'the Spirit', especially in verses 17–18. These uncertainties do not affect the general points to be considered in relation to the thesis.

Third, this chapter is not directly relevant to the thesis but it is significant for its contribution in understanding Paul's attitude to the new covenant and to his own ministry. There are some indirect points of contact which cohere with what has been seen elsewhere in Paul.

In verses 1–2, Paul, in speaking of letters of commendation, describes the Corinthians as a letter 'known and read by all men'. In the next verse he says that this letter has been written 'with the Spirit of the living God'. The implication, then, is that what the Spirit has written can be seen and understood by people looking on from outside. The Spirit's writing actually refers to what the Spirit does in the heart ('the tablet of fleshy hearts'), but the effects are manifest so that the Corinthians can be compared to an open letter.

In verse 6 Paul draws a contrast between the letter and the Spirit, a contrast which has since become proverbial. What Paul means by this needs clarifying as it has been understood in several ways.

It was on the basis of this verse that the teaching arose 'that the law may be understood in two senses: a literal and inferior sense and a spiritual and superior sense'.[9] From this arose the emphasis on allegorizing characteristic of a great deal of Old Testament interpretation prior to the Reformation.[10] An inference from this teaching would be that it is particularly the Spirit who enables an interpreter to discern the spiritual meaning of the text.

More commonly it is suggested that Paul is here making a contrast between what is actually written and the spirit of the law.[11] This is how the contrast has come to be understood and used in general speech. The inference from this would be that the Spirit enables Christians to keep the law in a spiritual as opposed to a merely outward and formal way.

However, neither of these views takes the context into sufficient account. In the context it is the law which was written on tablets of stone (verses 2, 7) and which, in itself, is an external code which can only kill, but cannot give life. On the other hand, the Spirit is identified with the new covenant of which Paul has been made a minister, and the new covenant is declared in the gospel of which Christ is the centre.[12] So this phrase does not indicate that the Spirit gives a special, esoteric insight into Old Testament scripture, nor even enables the law to be kept spiritually (however true that may be in itself), rather it is indicating that the new covenant ministry is pre-eminently a ministry of the Spirit who gives life.

The previous point leads to the positive assertion by Paul of the new covenant ministry as a ministry of the Spirit (v. 6). As such it is a life-giving ministry (v. 6), a glorious ministry (v. 8), a ministry which brings liberty (v. 17). In general terms this links in with his words in 1 Corinthians 2:1–5 and emphasizes the nature of the Christian gospel as dependent on the Spirit at every point. The content of the gospel is Christ, but the dynamic is the Spirit. In this respect the new covenant is superior to the old. In general this means that the gospel is life-changing by the Spirit, but specifically Paul will show that it also has implications for understanding.

Just as the Israelites of Moses' day had their minds hardened (literally, ἐπωρώθη; perhaps 'dulled' or 'closed' as REB), and this necessitated Moses putting a veil over his face, so that the people could not see the glory that shone there,[13] so Paul sees the same veil as still over the hearts of the Jews when the old covenant is read in the synagogue (vv. 13–15). The only antidote to this is the Spirit – when a person turns to the Lord who is the Spirit[14] the veil is taken away. In other words it is the Spirit who enables a person to understand the law and see its glory, and to see its fulfilment and completion in Christ (v. 14b).

In the concluding verse of the chapter Paul, contrasting Moses who alone saw the glory of God, says that all Christians see[15] the glory of the Lord and are consequently being transformed into his image, 'from glory to glory' and this by the Spirit.[16] Two points are important here. Firstly, this is a continuing work of the Spirit in Christians. Secondly, before transformation takes place, there has to be a 'beholding' of the glory of the Lord. It is not stated that this takes place in reading the scripture, but verses 13–16 strongly suggest that this is at least included. The phrase 'just as by the Spirit of the Lord' refers back to 'are being transformed' rather than 'seeing as in a mirror', but in view of the context it seems legitimate to see the whole process as taking place by the Spirit.[17]

2 Corinthians 4:2–6

Rather we have renounced secret and shameful ways; we do not use deception, nor do we distort the word of God. On the contrary, by setting forth the truth plainly, we commend ourselves to every man's conscience in the sight of God. And even if our gospel is veiled, it is veiled to those who are perishing. The god of this age has blinded the minds of unbelievers, so that they cannot see the light of the gospel of the glory of Christ, who is the image of God. For we do not preach ourselves, but Jesus Christ as Lord, and ourselves as your servants for Jesus sake. For God, who said, 'Let light shine out of darkness', made his light shine in our hearts to give us the light of the knowledge of the glory of God in the face of Christ.

These verses are an extension of Paul's discussion in the previous chapter and take up again the metaphor of veiling. At this point Paul is concerned to explain why the gospel message, which he has described as being of such surpassing glory (3:9, 11), is in fact often not received. He is probably here answering an implied criticism that his ministry was not all that successful.

Paul's answer to his critics is worth commenting on. The opening of verse 3 appears to be concessive.[18] In 3:15 the veil lay over the heart of the readers of the old covenant, while now Paul speaks of the gospel itself being veiled. However, it is probable that this is simply a variant way of considering the situation. A veil lies between the truth and the heart; from one viewpoint it lies over the heart, from the other it lies over the gospel. Paul's explanation of this is that the god of this age has blinded the minds of those who do not believe. There is the possibility, which arises particularly from the position of εἰς, that Paul is thinking of this in a judicial sense, at least to some extent. Because the basic attitude of the heart is one of unbelief this enables the god of this age to shut out of the mind the light of the gospel of the glory of Christ.[19]

The answer both to the blinding of the god of this age and the unbelief of the heart is put in personal terms by Paul in verse 6. While 'our hearts' may include the thought that what God has done for him, he does for all believers, it seems impossible to suppress Paul's personal experience on the road to Damascus when 'a light shone around him from heaven'.[20]

The direct divine action in shining into the heart is intensified by the comparison with the divine fiat at creation, 'Out of darkness light shall shine';[21] moreover it is God himself who has made his light shine. The only answer to the unbelief and blindness of people is the action of God.[22]

It is probably significant that the shining is 'in our hearts'.[23] The problem is deeper than a merely intellectual one.

The result of God's shining is a 'knowledge of the glory of God in the face of Jesus Christ'. There is probably the thought that this is true γνῶσις in contradistinction to the γνῶσις sought by some of the Corinthians. The terms used here suggest that for Christians γνῶσις is more than just an intellectual apprehension of truths, it also includes the illuminating and transforming power of knowing God in Christ.

In these verses there is no mention of the Holy Spirit. However in view of 3:17–18 it would be impossible to exclude from Paul's thought a role for the Spirit in the shining of God in the heart.

5:16

Therefore, from now on, we regard no one according to the flesh. Even though we have known Christ according to the flesh, yet now we know Him thus no longer (NKJV).

This is a very significant verse because it describes the new attitude which the Christian[24] has towards other people, and towards Christ himself. At the heart of the phrase 'according to the flesh' lies the thought of self-centred judging[25] and living – so, verse 15 'should live no longer for themselves'. In the second half of the verse Paul is most probably reflecting on the fact that in his pre-conversion days his attitude towards Christ was very much 'according to the flesh'; an attitude which led him to persecute Christ's followers bitterly (Acts 9:1; cf. 26:9–11). The next verse also seems to continue the thought because for someone in Christ old things have passed away and all things have become new; judging and living 'according to the flesh' has been replaced by a new attitude and a new way of thinking.

Paul does not spell out what the new way of knowing is. Other references (e.g. Rom. 8:4, 5, 12, 13) suggest that for Paul this would be 'according to the Spirit' (κατὰ πνεῦμα).[26] It is then suggested by some that Paul did not mention this because the Corinthians would have misunderstood this term.[27] However, following Martyn,[28] several writers suggest that in this context the contrast with κατὰ σάρκα would not be κατὰ πνεῦμα but κατὰ σταυρὸν.[29] This might be so; but there is no conflict between κατὰ πνεῦμα and κατὰ σταυρὸν as 1 Corinthians 2:1–5 makes clear; in fact knowing would be κατὰ πνεῦμα because it is κατὰ σταὐρον, for there is no understanding of the cross except by the Spirit (1 Cor. 1:18, 23; 2:10–14).

10:3–6

For though we live in the world, we do not wage war as the world does. The weapons we fight with are not the weapons of the world. On the contrary, they have divine power to demolish strongholds. We demolish arguments and every pretension that sets itself up against the knowledge of God, and we take captive every thought to make it obedient to Christ. And we will be ready to punish every act of disobedience, once your obedience is complete.

In the last section of this letter Paul turns decisively on those who were his opponents in Corinth – 'some, who think of us as if we walked according to the flesh' (v. 2). In verse 3 he introduces the metaphor of warfare into his discussion, as Hughes puts it 'a warfare against evil and error and the powers of darkness, and therefore against those who seek, as his enemies at Corinth were doing, to overthrow the truth and to gainsay the gospel of Jesus Christ'.[30]

Once again the phrase κατὰ σάρκα occurs. Here Paul argues that though he lives in the flesh (i.e. in the body) yet his warfare is not according to the flesh. This is a similar point to 5:16. He has a new way of conducting controversy. His opponents may accuse him of being fleshly rather than spiritual, but in fact he does not wage the war of ideas and words as those who are dominated by the flesh do.

Positively Paul asserts that the weapons he uses are 'mighty in God'.[31] He does not specify what these weapons (ὅπλα) are. Probably we should look back to 6:6–7 for the sort of qualities he has in mind.[32] If so it is appropriate to notice that he includes the Holy Spirit in his list in verse 6.

In this warfare Paul pulls down (καθαίρειν; used twice here) strongholds which consist of 'reasonings' and 'every high thing which raises itself up against the knowledge of God'. Paul anticipates that there is a spiritual power in the way he conducts himself and the words and arguments he uses which, by God's help, will demolish all the 'reasonings' which operate against the knowledge of God.

Having done so his 'weapons' take every thought captive to

obey Christ. This is the positive aim, which is also the way of thinking that belongs to Christians; their thoughts are subordinated to Christ, and so their attitudes and methods of controversy are not fleshly but spiritual, as befits those whose minds are now aligned with the mind of Christ (cf. 1 Cor. 2:16).

Summary

The central importance of the Holy Spirit for Paul is seen in 2 Corinthians, as in Romans and 1 Corinthians. The ministry of the new covenant can be described as 'the ministry of the Spirit' (3:8).

In 1:20–22 the work of the Spirit includes giving assurance to believers that they are established in Christ; it may also include testifying to the certainty of the promises of God.

In chapter 3 it is part of the work of the Spirit to remove the veil so that the glory of God might be seen when the scriptures are read.[33] With this can be linked the shining in of the glory of God at the time of conversion (4:4–6). It is not said that this is the work of the Spirit but the close ties between chapter 3 and chapter 4 make a link with the Spirit's ministry almost inevitable.

2 Corinthians 3:18 indicates a continuing work of the Spirit in believers. While this is primarily in the ethical realm – transforming according to the image of the Lord – yet the process of looking with unveiled face upon the glory of the Lord is also involved and there is a strong implication that this takes place, in part at least, in the reading of scripture.

Both 5:16 and 10:4–6 indicate in different ways that Christians have a new way of thinking and of conducting the battle for ideas. In both places this is sharply differentiated from thinking 'according to the flesh' and the inference is, supported in the latter case, that this new thinking is 'according to the Spirit'.

CHAPTER 7

GALATIANS

In the letter to the Galatians there is scarcely any material relevant to our present subject. Not that there are no references to the Spirit, quite the reverse. Indeed David Lull in his book, *The Spirit in Galatia,* says, 'In his letter to the Galatians, Paul gives the term πνεῦμα a prominent position; one might say, the *most* prominent position. Each time Paul uses the term πνεῦμα (pneuma) it denotes an experienced reality among the Galatians, of which Paul not only approves, but also of which he reminds the Galatians with many complicated arguments.'[1]

This being so, a brief inquiry ought to be made into why there is nothing here which really furthers the investigation into the work of the Spirit in teaching and illumination. The answer is that, unlike the situation at Corinth, the problems that Paul was tackling did not bear on these aspects of the Spirit's work. The problems here are connected with the gospel, with faith, justification, circumcision and the law, and with Christian living. As a result Paul has very little that bears on the question of understanding and knowledge. The nearest that Lull gets to speaking about these themes is when he says that '[life in the Spirit] is a new "self-understanding", but only as an understanding of the real presence of *Another.* For Spirit-centred existence is an effective, habitual appropriation of the personal presence of God.'[2]

Galatians 1 emphasizes that Paul received his gospel by revelation. He is very insistent about this in verses 11–12: 'through a revelation of Jesus Christ', probably meaning 'about Jesus Christ'.[3] In verse 16 he speaks about God revealing 'his Son in me', which in spite of the 'in me' is almost certainly a reference to his experience on the Damascus road. Though Paul saw a vision outwardly, this also had an impact within him. Ridderbos explains the verse like this: 'Paul's knowledge of Christ as the Son of God rested on God's immediate intervention. The film was, so to speak, removed from his eyes. Then he understood that the Jesus whom he persecuted and whose name he had up to this point hated and despised, was the Son of God.'[4]

It would be possible to consider what role the Spirit might have played in the experience of Paul, but as Paul is stressing the uniqueness of his calling as an apostle this has little bearing on the general work of the Spirit in all believers. The most that could be stated is that Paul's experience of Christ being revealed in him could be considered as having a less specialized reflection in the experience of other believers (so, e.g. 3:1).

A brief overview of the extensive material on the Spirit in Galatians shows how much Paul understood the Christian life as a life lived in the Spirit.

- 3:2–5, 14 refer to receiving the Spirit.
- 4:6 speaks of the Spirit as the pledge of adoption.
- 4:29 speaks of the one who is born 'according to the Spirit.'
- 5:5 speaks of awaiting hope through the Spirit.
- 5:16–18, 25 are ethical in content. The Spirit leads into right living and therefore should be followed.
- 6:1 explains that those who live by the Spirit should restore a fallen brother.
- 6:8 shows that those who sow to the Spirit will reap everlasting life.

Three of these references are worth commenting on further.

3:2

I would like to learn just one thing from you: Did you receive the Spirit by observing the law, or by believing what you heard?

Paul challenges the Galatians to remember how they received the Spirit; was this as a result of keeping the law or by what he calls the 'hearing of faith'? He repeats his question in verse 5, though here he is concerned about the continuing 'supply' (ἐπιχορήγειν) of the Spirit, and verse 14 adds that the Spirit is received by faith. There is no indication here of a work of the Spirit prior to, or perhaps even co-terminous with, believing the message heard. However, it is probable that this is simply the way Paul expressed himself in trying to make the contrast between keeping the law and hearing the message of the gospel. The similar passages in 1 Corinthians 2:4–5; 1 Thessalonians 1:4–6 give clear evidence of the work of the Spirit at the time of conversion. What Paul is emphasizing here is the reality of the Galatians' experience of the Spirit as they heard the gospel.[5]

4:6

Because you are sons, God sent the Spirit of his Son into our hearts, the Spirit who calls out, 'Abba, Father.'

Paul speaks of God sending the Spirit of his Son into the hearts of believers.[6] This is very similar to what he says in Romans 8:15 but there are some differences. The most important of these for the present purpose is that Paul says nothing here about the Spirit witnessing to sonship (Rom. 8:16). Thus, in spite of the similarities, and the fact that Paul is certainly speaking of an experienced reality ('into our hearts'), the expression of this is described in the cry to God, 'Abba, Father', but not in any effect upon believers themselves.

5:5

But by faith we eagerly await through the Spirit the righteousness for which we hope.

Finally in 5:5 Paul says of Christians ('we' again; against a background of 'you' before and after) that they eagerly await the hope of righteousness by faith and through the Spirit. It is in this verse that Paul comes closest to speaking of the Spirit teaching or bearing witness to a truth. The thought seems to be that it is the Spirit who gives assurance and certainty to the hope of righteousness which Christians are looking forward to with anticipation.[7] There is then a hint here of what is much more clearly stated in other Pauline writings.

CHAPTER 8

EPHESIANS

The letter to the Ephesians has a number of passages which are particularly relevant to the theme of this book. John Owen, whose treatise argues a similar case, states that he would be willing to hang his whole case on Ephesians 1:17-19.

1:8–9

that he lavished on us with all wisdom and understanding. And he made known to us the mystery of his will according to his good pleasure, which he purposed in Christ.

There are several points which can be seen in these verses.

Firstly, in the long paragraph in which these two verses are found Paul is speaking of what is true of all Christians, this is clear from verse 3 on. Among the spiritual blessings (v. 3) which God has bestowed on them are the riches of his grace which abound to us (ἐπερίσσευσεν) in all wisdom and understanding (σοφίᾳ καὶ φρονήσει).[1] Wisdom and understanding have come to expression in a knowledge of the mystery of his will; a mystery[2] which is now open and clear to Christians and is expressed particularly in verse 10, though the whole passage speaks of what God has made known. Wisdom and understanding are thus part of what God in his grace has lavished on Christians; this includes knowing the truths of salvation and God's purpose and also seems to involve an appreciation of their reality.

1:13–14

And you also were included in Christ when you heard the word of truth, the gospel of your salvation. Having believed, you were marked in him with a seal, the promised Holy Spirit, who is a deposit guaranteeing our inheritance until the redemption of those who are God's possession – to the praise of his glory.

115

It is likely that in these verses the Spirit is himself both the seal and the guarantee. This is explicitly the case with ἀρραβὼν, which refers to a deposit or first instalment guaranteeing the full inheritance in due time.[3] It would be possible to understand Paul to be saying that because a Christian knows he has received the Spirit that in itself is a guarantee to him. But that presupposes that he has some consciousness of the Spirit's presence. Probably both in the case of the Spirit as seal, and as guarantee, the thought is that the Spirit actually seals to the believer that he belongs to God – that is, he testifies inwardly to that, and similarly he witnesses to the reality of the inheritance yet to come. One of the reasons why Paul expresses himself in this eulogy of praise and expects the Ephesians to join him in it, is because he and they are conscious of their position before God and this consciousness is the effect of the presence of the Spirit as seal and guarantee. There is no doubt that for Paul the Spirit was an *experienced* reality.[4]

1:17–18

I keep asking that the God of our Lord Jesus Christ, the glorious Father, may give you the Spirit of wisdom and revelation, so that you may know him better. I pray also that the eyes of your heart may be enlightened in order that you may know the hope to which he has called you, the riches of his glorious inheritance in the saints.

This is a particularly important passage for this study.

In this passage Paul prays for his readers. This is the first of several prayers in this letter, and in Philippians and Colossians, in which he prays particularly for knowledge, understanding and wisdom for his readers. It is particularly significant that this seems to be his priority when he prays for the churches. In this case he prays (1) that God will give them the spirit of wisdom and revelation; (2) 'in the knowledge of him';[5] this indicates that it was through the spirit of wisdom and revelation that they would know God; (3) the eyes of their heart (lit.) having been enlightened; this appears to refer to the enlightenment they received at conversion;[6] the thought appears to be that having been enlightened, the spirit of wisdom and revelation will enable them to see, or to see more clearly, what they are now able to see;[7] (4) that they might know what the hope to which they are called is etc.

In praying like this Paul's purpose is that they would realise truths about God, and especially the present position of Christ, which would banish from their hearts the fear which they still felt to some extent because in the past their lives had been dominated by bondage to the principalities and powers (v. 21; 6:12; Acts 19:12, 18, 19).[8]

It can be strongly argued that πνεῦμα refers to the Holy Spirit here.[9] Paul is praying for a gift from God, so the wisdom and revelation are not natural qualities or abilities; even *a* spirit of wisdom and revelation would be the effect of the working of *the* Spirit.[10]

The word 'revelation' (ἀποκάλυψις) is unexpected as it is used much more frequently of the revelation of the gospel to the apostles or prophets, as for example in 3:3, 5. However it was argued that in 1 Corinthians 2:10 Paul uses the verb when thinking of all Christians, and though that referred to the initial illumination at conversion, the use of the word for those who are already Christians is not out of place in the context of the Ephesians' experience and need.[11] Christians though they were, they needed the veil to be drawn back so that they might see clearly their security in Christ from the powers that appeared to threaten them.

The prayer, then, is asking for the help of the Spirit in enabling the Ephesians, as those already enlightened, to see clearly and to grasp by faith things which they already knew, but which they either did not feel the power and reality of, or whose implications for their lives had not fully dawned upon them.[12] This puts a particular emphasis on the central phrase in verse 18 – εἰς τὸ εἰδέναι ὑμᾶς – and especially the word 'know', 'that you might *know*'.

This lies at the heart of the illuminating ministry of the Spirit in believers.[13] Things which they already know intellectually, or which they can be instructed in, or which they can read from Old Testament or letter, become real and the personal spiritual relevance is brought home to mind and heart by the Spirit.

2:1–3

As for you, you were dead in your transgressions and sins, in which you used to live when you followed the ways of this world and of the ruler of the kingdom of the air, the spirit who is now at work in those who are disobedient. All of us also lived among them at one time, gratifying the cravings of our sinful nature and following its desires and thoughts. Like the rest, we were by nature objects of wrath.

In these verses Paul looks back to the past experience of the Ephesians. Verse 2 probably has their particular situation as unbelievers in mind and probably reflects on the fear which they still felt to some extent. In helping them overcome this Paul has not only spoken in chapter 1 of the exaltation of Christ over all principalities and powers but here he shows them that they themselves have been delivered by being raised up and seated together with Christ in the same heavenly realm where he is (v. 6 with 1:20). There is here a vivid description of the condition of those who were once pagans, with several implications for knowledge and understanding.

The Ephesians were once dead in transgressions and sins. The word 'dead' suggests that they were incapable of understanding truth about God, of turning to him, and of living in a way which would please him, or of doing anything about this situation.[14]

In addition they 'followed the ways of this present world order' (REB) a translation which tries to bring out the meaning of both αἰών and κόσμος (and also the sense of περιεπατήσατε). They also followed, or lived according to, the ruler of the power of the air, something which was not peculiar to them as he is the spirit who now works in all the disobedient. Not only did their sins make them dead to the spiritual realm and so to understanding the things of God, but the ruler of the power of the air was actually at work *in* them, which must also have implications for their thinking as well as every other area of life.

Among whom, says Paul, we all once lived in the lusts of the flesh, practising the desires of the flesh and of our minds. In its first occurrence flesh refers to the 'sinful nature' (NIV), but in its second to physical desire.[15] The sinful nature expressed itself in physical desire and in the mind as well.[16] This shows quite clearly the mind being controlled by the principle of evil, or sinful nature. Just as it is the Spirit who is needed for growth in holiness (e.g.. Gal. 5:22–25; 6:8), so the Spirit is needed also to clear the mind and give understanding. In both cases this is not just an initial experience but a continuing process.

2:18

For through him we both have access to the Father by one Spirit.

The emphasis here is upon the *one* Spirit. Paul is speaking about both Jew and Gentile having access to the Father through Christ, but he adds this note, ἐν ἑνὶ πνεύματι. Presumably the thought is that because they approach the Father in one Spirit, the two are made one. What Christ has done through his cross (vv. 15–16) the one Spirit implements as they actually draw near to God. What is true objectively through Christ becomes true existentially through the one Spirit in prayer. But it is not exactly clear why Paul needs to mention the Spirit here. Isn't *Christ* one, and isn't it through his reconciling work that they come to the Father anyway? It may be that Paul's thought is basically trinitarian and he preserves certain distinctions in the way the Persons of the Godhead act. This means he thinks of the Spirit particularly as the One who enables Christians actually to draw near to God (cf. Rom. 8:26–27; Eph. 6:18).[17] This would indicate that in personal relationships with God the Spirit plays the leading role; this is so in drawing near to God, but it is also so in God revealing himself to people and giving them an understanding of himself.

3:3–5

that is, the mystery made known to me by revelation, as I have already written briefly. In reading this, then, you will be able to understand my insight into the mystery of Christ, which was not made known to men in other generations as it has now been revealed by the Spirit to God's holy apostles and prophets.

In these verses Paul speaks of the mystery which has been revealed to him, and to the holy apostles and prophets. This is clearly a revelation which was given to him as a minister (v. 7), so that he should preach the unsearchable riches of Christ among the Gentiles (v. 8). There are two points which will be taken up briefly.

Firstly, though this is a specific revelation given to particular people so they could make known the mystery to others, we can see this as a pattern. In a different and lesser sense it is also true that all believers receive revelation at the time of their conversion.[18] In both cases the agent of revelation is the Spirit.[19] In the one case they receive new truths which in past generations had not been made known to people; in the other those same truths, as they are preached, are made clear to the mind and heart.

Secondly, there is a very close parallel to this section in Colossians 1:24–26, especially verse 26. Once again Paul refers to the mystery (though the content is different here) which had been hidden for ages but has now been manifested (ἐφανερώθη) to his saints.[20] The last word is striking because it recalls the 'holy apostles' (ἁγίοις in both cases). However the point here is that the mystery is revealed to God's people rather than to apostles and prophets. This supports the analogy which was referred to above, and also shows that it was through the preaching (Col. 1:25, 28) of Paul and his colleagues that this revealing took place. There is no mention of the Spirit; Paul is very sparing in his use of 'Spirit' in Colossians, probably because he wants to focus all attention on Christ himself.

3:15–19

from whom his whole family in heaven and on earth derives its name. I pray that out of his glorious riches he may strengthen you with power through his Spirit in your inner being, so that Christ may dwell in your hearts through faith. And I pray that you, being rooted and established in love, may have power, together with all the saints, to grasp how wide and long and high and deep is the love of Christ, and to know this love that surpasses knowledge – that you may be filled to the measure of all the fulness of God.

This brings us to a second prayer of Paul for the Ephesians.

The heart of the prayer is probably verse 19a: 'to know the love of Christ which surpasses knowledge'. The following clause seems to signify result, as REB, 'So may you be filled with the very fullness of God.' It is a prayer for knowledge, yet not just for intellectual knowledge; it is for a knowledge that surpasses knowledge. It desires that all the dimensions of Christ's love (v. 18) may be made known to the Ephesians.

In verse 18 Paul prays that his readers may be able to comprehend (καταλαβέσθαι – 'grasp'[21] may be the most vivid translation here) this love with all the saints.

The idea of 'grasping' or 'comprehending' clearly refers firstly to the mind and yet goes beyond the mind. How can a mind be capacious enough to grasp the breadth, length, height and depth of the love of Christ? It is not just intellectual; it is also experiential, because Paul clearly desires the Ephesians to have a sense of this love, to feel that Christ loves them and to know all that this love has done and what it means.

This grasping is 'with all saints'. That is, it is not merely an individualistic knowledge. It is in the fellowship of the saints that people attain, or begin to attain, to it, and perhaps we are to understand that only the joint understanding of the saints can approach to a grasping of it. The corporate dimension of understanding seems important here.[22]

The Spirit is referred to in this passage but this comes earlier than might be anticipated, and rather than asking for the Spirit to reveal the love of Christ, Paul's prayer is that the Spirit might strengthen his readers with power in their inner-being. This is an extremely interesting petition for it implies that it needs an inner strength to be able to grasp such an ungraspable reality as the love of Christ. Although separated by a verse it may be that the strengthening by the Spirit connects with the beginning of verse 18: 'that you may be strong enough to grasp ... ἵνα ἐξισχύσητε.' For example, Robinson says, 'In the original the expression is yet more forcible: "that ye may have the strength to comprehend". The clause depends on the participles "rooted and founded"; but it has a further reference to the words "to be strengthened with power by His Spirit in the inner man". [23] Even if it is very doubtful whether ἵνα εξισχύσητε can be connected grammatically with κραταιωθῆναι διὰ τοῦ πνεύματος αὐτοῦ εἰς τὸν ἔσω ἄνθρωπον it is quite certain from the flow of the passage that the Spirit plays a key role in the fulfilling of this prayer and in the saints coming to a comprehension of the surpassing love of Christ. [24]

4:17–24

So I tell you this, and insist on it in the Lord, that you must no longer live as the Gentiles do, in the futility of their thinking. They are darkened in their understanding and separated from the life of God because of the ignorance that is in them due to the hardening of their hearts. Having lost all sensitivity, they have given themselves over to sensuality so as to indulge in every kind of impurity, with a continual lust for more. You, however, did not come to know Christ that way. Surely you heard of him and were taught in him in accordance with the truth that is in Jesus. You were taught, with regard to your former way of life, to put off your old self, which is being corrupted by its deceitful desires; to be made new in the attitude of your minds; and to put on the new self, created to be like God in true righteousness and holiness.

There are three main points which can be considered in this paragraph.

First of all Paul, in describing the way the Gentiles live, uses a number of words that refer to the mind and thinking. He makes it quite clear that a great problem with these people is that they are unable to understand God and his ways and as a result they give themselves over [25] to a dissolute way of life. In verse 17 he refers to the 'futility of their minds', in verse 18 to their 'understanding being darkened' and later on in the verse to the 'ignorance that is in them, due to the hardness of their hearts'. In verse 19 they are described as 'having lost all sensitivity' (NIV: ἀπηλγηκότες, a hapax in the New Testament). [26] It seems as if Paul is multiplying words and phrases to emphasize the inner spiritual darkness of the minds of those who have not been illuminated by Christ.

In verses 20–21 Paul speaks of the difference that has happened to his readers and says, 'But you have not so learned Christ.' In the context, as verse 22 makes clear, Paul is saying that the ethical outcome of the Gentiles' way of thinking in lust and impurity, is not one which the Ephesians can in any way share. They have learned Christ which means putting off all the deceitful lusts that belonged to the old life. Paul does not explain what 'learning Christ' means, though he does go on to add, 'if you have heard him and were taught by him, as the truth is in Jesus'. Does this mean that the solution to the mental/spiritual darkness in the previous verses is simply a matter of teaching? Three reasons would suggest this is not so.

First, the very terms used in verses 17–19 seem to indicate that teaching alone will not get a response.

Second, the NIV translates 'were taught in him' (ἐν αὐτῷ). This seems to suggest that the translators understood Paul to be continuing his practice, seen especially in the opening of this letter, of looking upon believers as 'in Christ',[27] standing in a particular relation to him by faith. If this seems unlikely in the context of teaching, we ought to notice that he says the truth is 'in Jesus', and he also speaks of 'learning Christ', not learning *of him* (accusative not genitive). All this suggests a relationship to Christ out of which the Christian way of life springs.

The third reason is also the third point which needs to be considered from these verses. In verse 23 Paul says, 'and be renewed in the spirit of your mind'. Leaving aside, for the moment, the exact meaning of 'spirit', this indicates that teaching alone is not enough. In fact Paul is speaking here to Christians, to those who have already learned Christ; yet they still need to be renewed in mind (cf. Rom. 12:2). Is 'spirit' here a reference to the Holy Spirit or does it mean something like 'attitude' (NIV)? Commentators differ, but the genitive, 'of your mind' does seem difficult to understand if the reference is to 'the Spirit'.[28] However it is also in order to ask how Paul would understand this renewing to come about. Titus 3:5 speaks about the 'renewing of the Holy Spirit' so the Spirit's work may be in the background of Paul's thought at this point.[29]

4:30

And do not grieve the Holy Spirit of God, with whom you were sealed for the day of redemption.

This verse looks back to 1:13–14; by adding 'for the day of redemption' to 'sealed' it seems to link the eschatological sense of the guarantee to sealing by the Spirit. The word 'grieve' (λυπεῖτε) is unusual in reference to the Spirit and contrasts with the impersonal 'quench' of 1 Thessalonians 5:19.[30] It is a personal word and suggests a highly personal relationship with the Spirit, together with a sensitivity on the Spirit's part towards those he has sealed (cf. 2 Cor. 2:1–15; 7:8–11 for Paul's use of σφραγίζειν and its cognates). The implication of the words is that grieving the Holy Spirit will adversely affect the relationship between him and those he has sealed. This in turn speaks of a cognitive element in sealing. There is no reflection here on teaching or illumination as such, but the sentence presupposes a relationship which is known or felt and the communion this involves can be spoilt (there is no suggestion that a believer can be, as it were, 'unsealed' by the Spirit).

5:8–14

For you were once darkness, but now you are light in the Lord. Live as children of light (for the fruit of the light consists in all goodness, righteousness and truth) and find out what pleases the Lord. Have nothing to do with the fruitless deeds of darkness, but rather expose them. For it is shameful even to mention what the disobedient do in secret. But everything exposed by the light becomes visible, for it is light that makes everything visible. This is why it is said: 'Wake up, O sleeper, rise from the dead, and Christ will shine on you.'

In this passage Paul is urging the Ephesians to walk as children of light. Two aspects may be commented on.

Paul says of them, 'You were once darkness.' This is a very striking expression.[31] In the context it relates primarily to moral darkness, but it suggests an inner darkness which would include the understanding (cf. 4:18). The darkness of ignorance of God and what is holy leads to the unfruitful works of darkness (v. 11, which are often committed in the darkness, so that they can be hidden). But now, Paul says, 'you are light in the Lord'.[32] This may look back to 1:18, 'the eyes of your heart having been enlightened'. Some see verse 14 as a baptismal chant uttered at the time of emerging from the water in baptism.[33] There is a complete reversal: those who were 'darkness' are 'light' in the Lord; they have been enlightened inwardly and they are to express this in a consistent, progressive ('walk') life as 'children of light'. These verses, while primarily ethical in concern, indicate the radical change which takes place when people become Christians, and speak of the complete enlightenment which this involves and the way this is to be lived out continually. It is almost certain that verse 9a should read, 'the fruit of the light' but it is significant that the alternative reading 'the fruit of the Spirit' (presumably by scribal error from Galatians 5:22[34]) should come to a strong position in the Greek textual tradition. Elsewhere in Paul the contrast is between 'flesh' and 'Spirit' rather than 'darkness' and 'light' (e.g. Rom. 8:4–13; Gal. 5:16–25).

5:18–20

Do not get drunk on wine, which leads to debauchery. Instead, be filled with the Spirit. Speak to one another with psalms, hymns and spiritual songs. Sing and make music in your heart to the Lord.

There is wide agreement that here 'spirit'[35] is a reference to the Holy Spirit; apart from any other consideration the parallel with 'wine' suggests it. There is probably a link with verse 17 where Paul says, 'Do not be foolish, but understand what the will of the Lord is.' To get drunk leads to foolishness, but to understand the will of the Lord one needs to be filled with the Spirit. This is indicated by the parallelism of verses 17–18, but the phrase 'be filled with the Spirit' primarily looks forward, and the effects of being so filled are expressed in verses 19–21, and probably on through the succeeding verses. Being filled with the Spirit leads to singing praise to the Lord,[36] to thanksgiving and mutual submission. Included also is 'speaking to yourselves in psalms and hymns and spiritual songs'. In view of the close proximity of 'Spirit' in the previous verse, 'spiritual songs' would seem likely to be songs composed under the influence of the Spirit, perhaps spontaneously at the time of singing (cf. 1 Cor. 14:15). 'Speaking to yourselves', that is, 'to one another', suggests that these different types of songs are not only directed to God, but also have an edifying effect upon the congregation of God's people. In this connection the parallel passage in Colossians is significant, 'teaching and admonishing one another' (διδάσκοντες καὶ νουθετοῦντες, Col. 3:16).[37] The same combination occurs in Colossians 1:28 also (in reverse) and it perhaps seems rather strange that in singing there should be an element of warning. What is important is that this teaching and admonishing in song is the effect of being filled with the Spirit. This is the Spirit teaching in an indirect way, not through preachers or prophets, but through the congregational singing of God's people.

6:17

Take the helmet of salvation and the sword of the Spirit, which is the word of God.

In delineating the Christian armour Paul speaks of 'the sword of the Spirit, which is the word of God'. The thought seems to be that the word of God is used by the Spirit as his sword[38] in the spiritual warfare that Paul is speaking about. The Spirit is the power which is effective in enabling the Christian to stand in the evil day. This perhaps can be considered in various ways. As the battle is with the principalities and powers it may be that Paul is indicating that it is the Spirit through the word who silences the attacks of the principalities and so on, that is, the Spirit is actually operative in confronting the principalities (cf. Rev. 12:11: 'they overcame ... through the word of their testimony'). In addition it may be that the Spirit through the word is considered as effective in the mind of the believer himself. That, presumably, is where the battle rages and perhaps the thought is that the Spirit brings home the word which banishes fear and brings release and calm.[39] Thirdly, this warfare is also with people insofar as they are the instruments of the principalities, that is, those who persecute, who resist the gospel, etc. In confrontation with them the Spirit through the word is what believers are to rely on (cf. Matt. 10:17–20). The Spirit, then, is the dynamic of the word of God who works in the minds of opposers, silencing their opposition and in some cases convincing them of the truth, and on the other hand who also works in the minds of believers freeing them from fear.[40]

Summary

Ephesians is very clear in its description of the state of mind of those who have not believed. That state is one of spiritual death, darkness and ignorance. This has implications both for knowledge (God is not known), and for behaviour (the desires of the sinful nature are indulged).

The answer to this is the action of God himself through Christ. Involved in this is enlightenment, indeed in the Lord believers become light themselves. Any role of the Spirit in this is not spelled out, but there is a link in 1:17.

Included in what God has lavished upon believers are wisdom and insight which enable them to discern the mystery of God's will. Just as there is a revelation by the Spirit of the mystery to apostles and prophets to enable them to preach it to others, so there is also a revelation by the Spirit to those who hear the mystery through the preaching of others.

Although there is knowledge imparted at conversion, there is a continuing work of the Spirit in granting wisdom and revelation, and enabling God's people to grasp realities like the love of Christ. The renewal of the mind by the Spirit is one of the priorities of the Christian life. Out of the spiritual knowledge imparted by the Spirit flows a life of holiness.

The Spirit seals Christians and is given to them as a guarantee of their future inheritance. This involves a relationship between Christians and the Spirit which is of a sensitive nature so that the Spirit can be grieved and the relationship strained. This implies a consciousness of the Spirit's presence.

CHAPTER 9

PHILIPPIANS to 2 TIMOTHY

There are no relevant references in Titus and Philemon, and the rest of the Pauline letters do not have a great deal of material that needs to be examined. However, there are a few relevant passages in Philippians, Colossians, 1 and 2 Thessalonians, and 1 and 2 Timothy. It is to these passages that we now turn.

Philippians

Philippians 1:9–10

And this is my prayer: that your love may abound more and more in knowledge and depth of insight, so that you may be able to discern what is best and may be pure and blameless until the day of Christ.

This is another of Paul's prayers, and it is interesting to notice how Paul prayed for knowledge and insight for the members of the churches (Eph. 1:17–19; 3:16–19; Col. 1:9–10). He clearly believed that right understanding was very important and a key to living the Christian life. Two things are significant here.

Firstly, Paul prays that the Philippians' love might abound in knowledge and insight. The suggestion is that their love might have been blind, that is, that its expression would not have been guided by the knowledge and understanding which was necessary for the complicated task of living the Christian life in a pagan environment. More than that, however, here love is prior and so knowledge and insight are not ends in themselves, but enable love to be guided and expressed as it ought to be.

Secondly, the purpose of this is that they might be able to approve 'the things that really matter' (BAGD). A great deal of living consists of choices, and often great experience and insight is needed to make the right choice in a particular situation. What Paul is praying for then is a particular type of discernment that will enable the Philippians to distinguish between different courses of action and always choose what is best.[1] There is no reference to the Holy Spirit[2] here but Paul is praying to God for this discerning knowledge. Doubtless he expected it to be developed and refined by experience, but he also expects God to grant it.

Philippians 2:1–2

If you have any encouragement from being united with Christ, if any comfort from his love, if any fellowship with the Spirit, if any tenderness and compassion, then make my joy complete by being like-minded, having the same love, being one in spirit and purpose.

In verse 2 Paul is particularly concerned that the Philippians should be united in mind and heart, this is clear from the way in which he expresses the same basic thought in four different ways. What is of special interest is that in the first verse, as he urges various motives for such like-mindedness, he includes 'if there is any fellowship of the Spirit'.[3] However this phrase is understood, whether 'participation in the Spirit',[4] or 'fellowship produced by the Spirit',[5] its bearing on verse 2 is not much altered. According to Paul fellowship in the Spirit ought to be expressed in like-mindedness, and he urges the Philippians to make sure it does.[6]

Philippians 3:15

All of us who are mature should take such a view of things. And if on some point you think differently, that too God will make clear to you.

This verse can be linked with the verses just considered. Paul recognises that there may be differences of understanding and thought amongst the believers, but he also knows that God will reveal this to them. For the time being they must live up to what they have already attained (v. 16, NIV), but he wants a greater measure of unanimity in the future which he anticipates God will grant. 2:1 would suggest that such fellowship will arise from their mutual participation in the Spirit.[7]

Colossians

Colossians 1:9–10

For this reason, since the day we heard about you, we have not stopped praying for you and asking God to fill you with the knowledge of his will through all spiritual wisdom and understanding.

Here, in another prayer, Paul asks that wisdom and knowledge may be given to his readers. Here the petition differs in certain details from his prayers in Ephesians 1:17–18 and Philippians 1:9–10. The main prayer is for 'the knowledge of [God's] will'. Verse 10 indicates that the primary aim of this is so that the Colossians can live a life worthy of the Lord, pleasing to him, and fruitful in all good works. To that end, Paul includes a prayer that they might know God's will 'in all wisdom and spiritual understanding' – at least this is how it is often translated (e.g. REB, NKJV). This is similar to Paul's prayer in Philippians, only instead of love needing direction by discernment, here he asks for wisdom and understanding in the practical application and outworking of the will of God.

What, however, is to be made of πνευματικῇ which while it might only qualify συνέσει could easily belong to σοφίᾳ as well? Writers differ on how to translate, but most see at least an indirect reference to the Holy Spirit here (if not to the Spirit himself at least to a gift or working of the Spirit).[8] This is the more likely in view of Paul's reference to the Spirit in the previous verse. For Paul, spiritual understanding must in the last analysis be an understanding which comes from the Holy Spirit.

One further point is that knowledge of God's will is not just for the purpose of living a life which is good and pleasing to God, it also leads on to 'growing in the knowledge of God'. This is important as knowledge is an important theme in Colossians, possibly because of an emphasis on a false *gnosis* among the heretics at Colosse.[9]

Wisdom and understanding, bestowed ultimately by the Spirit, together with a knowledge of God's will, lead on to God's people growing in their personal knowledge of him.

Colossians 1:21

Once you were alienated from God and were enemies in your minds because of your evil behaviour.

In this verse Paul describes how the Colossians once were 'alienated and enemies' with respect to God, but Christ has now reconciled them. He says they were alienated and enemies *in mind* (τῇ διανοίᾳ)[10] by the evil deeds they did. They were hostile to God because they lived in ways which were evil to him, but the source of the trouble was the mind. This is not elaborated any more in this context, but it is a reminder of Paul's teaching elsewhere that the mind shares in human fallenness and sin.

Colossians 2:2–3

My purpose is that they may be encouraged in heart and united in love, so that they may have the full riches of complete understanding, in order that they may know the mystery of God, namely, Christ, in whom are hidden all the treasures of wisdom and knowledge.

This is, in effect, another prayer of Paul's; at least it expresses the urgent longing he felt for all Christians he had never met. Once more his concern is with knowledge, understanding and wisdom. In verse 3 he uses the word γνῶσις (rather than ἐπίγνωσις), which might suggest he is taking up a word used by the heretics and saying firmly that all γνῶσις is to be found in Christ and nowhere else.[11]

    There is considerable textual variation at the end of verse 2. The context would seem to support the reading τοῦ θεοῦ, Χριστοῦ which is probably best translated as NIV, 'the mystery of God, namely, Christ'.[12] Certainly the whole passage, and the letter itself, emphasizes the centrality of Christ. There is no reference here to the Holy Spirit and this is in line with the general emphasis of the letter which seems to keep such references to a minimum, presumably in order to keep the focus on Christ.[13] The contrast with Ephesians in this respect is very marked.

The progression of thought is this: Paul desires for his readers encouragement of heart and a uniting in love – the corporate element seems important here[14] – which will lead to (εἰς) the full riches of complete understanding, into (εἰς) the knowledge of the mystery of God. The last clause may be parallel and epexegetical rather than sequential. And the mystery of God is Christ, in whom all the treasures of wisdom and knowledge are hidden. A knowledge of Christ thus opens the treasure-house to all the wisdom and knowledge which are found in him. A knowledge of God and of his will, with all the practical implications of that for Christian life and witness, comes from knowing Christ. Other references in Paul (e.g. Rom. 8:9) indicate that knowing Christ comes by the Spirit, but to say this would be a diversion in this letter where it is the person and fullness of Christ which Paul finds necessary to stress.

Colossians 2:8–9

See to it that no-one takes you captive through hollow and deceptive philosophy, which depends on human tradition and the basic principles of this world rather than on Christ. For in Christ all the fulness of the Deity lives in bodily form.

Verse 8 indicates that part of the problem in Colosse was a type of philosophy which seems to have been attractive to the Colossians. Probably the words of the phrase τῆς φιλοσοφίας καὶ κενῆς ἀπάτης should all be taken together as, for example, in REB and NIV, the latter reading, 'hollow and deceptive philosophy'. This does not in the context of the verse seem to point to some esoteric *gnosis* so much as to a system of thought which was congenial to the Colossians because of their background and the type of thinking which was current in their world. The point to be noticed is that the Colossians must guard their minds from error, and the answer to this is Christ, because all the fullness of the Godhead, and thus all the treasures of wisdom and knowledge, resides in him bodily.

1 Thessalonians

1 Thessalonians 1:5

because our gospel came to you not simply with words, but also with power, with the Holy Spirit and with deep conviction. You know how we lived among you for your sake.

In this verse Paul refers to the way in which the gospel originally came to the Thessalonians through his preaching. As in Galatians 3:1–2 and 1 Corinthians 2:1–2 one of the most notable features was that the gospel was with power and with the Holy Spirit. REB links 'power' with the Holy Spirit ('in the power of the Holy Spirit') but it seems best to take all three phrases as independent. At the same time it is clear that 'power',[15] 'the Holy Spirit', and 'much assurance' (or 'deep conviction', NIV) all describe together the effects of the gospel, and all three belong together. 'Conviction' seems to mean that the gospel came to the Thessalonians in such a way that they were convinced of its truthfulness and their need of it, though it is possible to envisage Paul speaking of the conviction which he and his colleagues felt as they preached it.[16] Either way the presence and working in power of the Holy Spirit brought an assurance and certainty of the message of the gospel as it was preached.

1 Thessalonians 2:13

And we also thank God continually because, when you received the word of God, which you heard from us, you accepted it not as the word of men, but as it actually is, the word of God, which is at work in you who believe.

There is a similarity to 1:5 in this verse as Paul is also going back to the occasion when he first preached the gospel to the Thessalonians. But there is a different note here because Paul not only remembers how they *received* (aorist) the word of God, but that this word is *still* at work[17] within those who believe. There is no reference to the Holy Spirit here, and the emphasis is upon the nature and origin of

Paul's message, λόγον θεοῦ and οὐ λόγον ἀνθρώπων. It is because this is a divine message that it 'works' within those who believe it. Nevertheless 1:5 suggests what could be deduced from elsewhere in Paul that the ongoing power and conviction of the word of God in the lives of the Thessalonians is closely related to the work of the Spirit.[18]

2 Thessalonians

2 Thessalonians 2:9–12

The coming of the lawless one will be in accordance with the work of Satan displayed in all kinds of counterfeit miracles, signs and wonders, and in every sort of evil that deceives those who are perishing. They perish because they refused to love the truth and so be saved. For this reason God sends them a powerful delusion so that they will believe the lie and so that all will be condemned who have not believed the truth but have delighted in wickedness.

In these verses Paul speaks of the deception and delusion which will attend the revealing of the one he describes as 'the lawless one'. What is relevant from the point of view of this study is that he sees the deception of those days as a judgment of God, in similar terms to the giving up of Romans 1:18–32. The reason here for God sending (πέμπει, v. 11)[19] such deception is because they did not receive the love of the truth (v. 10)[20], nor did they believe the truth but made unrighteousness their choice (εὐδοκήσαντες, v. 12). There is no indication that this is a special group or class of people intended, rather they are 'those who are perishing' (v. 10a).[21] The situation is the same as that already seen in Paul that sin blinds and hardens people to the truth, and this in turn leads to judgment in which God confirms them in this condition.[22]

2 Thessalonians 2:13

But we ought always to thank God for you, brothers loved by the Lord, because from the beginning God chose you to be saved through the sanctifying work of the Spirit and through belief in the truth.

Here Paul thanks God because he chose the Thessalonians to salvation. This emphasizes the need for divine intervention if those who have sinful hearts which prefer unrighteousness are to be saved. This salvation comes to them by the sanctifying work of the Spirit and belief of the truth. These two phrases are closely linked.[23] 'Sanctification' here probably means 'setting apart'. Both sanctification by the Spirit and belief of the truth occur at the same time and it is difficult not to infer that belief of the truth takes place because of the Spirit's activity in the heart.[24] There is a hint here then that, against the background of those who did not welcome the truth, those chosen by God are set apart by the Spirit thus enabling them to believe the truth which otherwise they would reject. This work of the Spirit hints at an understanding and acceptance of the truth, that is, the truth of the gospel.

1 Timothy

1 Timothy 1:5–7

The goal of this command is love, which comes from a pure heart and a good conscience and a sincere faith. Some have wandered away from these and turned to meaningless talk. They want to be teachers of the law, but they do not know what they are talking about or what they so confidently affirm.

Against the background of heterodox teachers (v. 3. ἵνα παραγγείλῃς τισὶν μὴ ἑτεροδιδασκαλεῖν) Paul says that the purpose of the commandment – he has the law particularly in mind here – is love, love out of a pure heart, good conscience and sincere faith. Some, he says, have strayed from these and turned to empty speech. They want to be teachers of the law but they do not know what they are talking about! Here there is a linking of love and understanding such as has been seen already (e.g. in 1 Cor. 8:1–3; Eph. 3:17–20; Phil. 1:9–10). Without love one cannot understand the law and so cannot be a teacher of the law. Love, however, is the fruit of the Spirit, and this is recognized in 2 Timothy 1:7.

1 Timothy 3:9

They must keep hold of the deep truths of the faith with a clear conscience.

In talking of deacons Paul says that they must hold to the mystery (translated by NIV here as 'deep truths') of the faith. The word 'mystery' calls to mind the fact that the gospel has been revealed, and that it needs the Holy Spirit's enlightenment to understand and hold to this mystery (e.g. 1 Cor. 2:7–16).[25]

1 Timothy 3:16

Beyond all question, the mystery of godliness is great: He appeared in a body, was vindicated by the Spirit, was seen by angels, was preached among the nations, was believed on in the world, was taken up in glory.

In the second clause of what might well be a catechetical statement Paul says of Christ, 'he was vindicated in the Spirit'. There is considerable discussion about the exact meaning of this clause; is this 'spirit' or 'Spirit', and how was he vindicated? Many writers point to the resurrection as the vindication of Christ and if this is right then 'by the Spirit'[26] seems a legitimate translation, especially in view of Romans 1:4. It is also possible to point to the work of the Spirit in the ministry of Jesus (e.g. Matt. 12:28) as his vindication, a vindication which was completed by the resurrection.[27] This can then be seen as part of the Spirit's witness to Jesus, something which is taken up particularly by John (John 15:26; 16:14).

1 Timothy 4:1

The Spirit clearly says that in later times some will abandon the faith and follow deceiving spirits and things taught by demons.

Here the Spirit is spoken of as giving a clear warning (REB seems justified in translating 'warns' because of the content of what is said). We are not told how or where this warning is given – apart from, of course, at this point in the letter.[28] The word 'explicitly' (ῥητῶς) seems to indicate that this is something the Spirit particularly and urgently testifies to.[29] Perhaps this was the burden of the messages of a number of prophets at that time. Or perhaps the thought is more that the Spirit especially bears his witness to warnings that are given of these future apostates.[30] Either way this is a particular aspect of the teaching ministry of the Spirit.

1 Timothy 4:13–14

Until I come, devote yourself to the public reading of Scripture, to preaching and to teaching. Do not neglect your gift, which was given you through a prophetic message when the body of elders laid their hands on you.

In urging Timothy to give himself to the fulfilling of his ministry (v. 13) Paul also warns him not to neglect the gift which has been given to him. There seems to be a connection between the verses, in that if Timothy were to slacken off his ministry he would be neglecting his gift.[31] Gift is χάρισμα, which is presumably why REB translates by 'spiritual endowment'.[32] The laying on of the hands of the elders might suggest a symbolic act of equipping for service, and the mention of prophecy suggests the presence of the Holy Spirit. The Spirit was at times imparted through the laying on of hands in Acts (8:17–18; 9:17–18), but there are other occasions when no mention is made of such an impartation (e.g. 6:6; 13:3). Moreover the references that do speak of the Holy Spirit being given refer to the time of conversion and do not refer to any subsequent equipping for ministry. Nevertheless it is likely that Paul is referring here to a divine gift, either the Spirit himself, or perhaps a gift or working of the Spirit, which will accompany and give effectiveness to Timothy's ministry of reading, exhorting and teaching.

2 Timothy

2 Timothy 1:6–7

For this reason I remind you to fan into flame the gift of God, which is in you through the laying on of my hands. For God did not give us a spirit of timidity, but a spirit of power, of love and of self-discipline.

These verses may be related to the verses above in 1 Timothy. This depends on whether Paul joined with the elders in laying hands on Timothy at the time he was set apart for ministry. This may well have been the case. On the other hand, this might refer to the time of Timothy's conversion and perhaps baptism.[33] Certainly the gift here is not one which has any special bearing on the sort of ministry which is mentioned in 1 Timothy 4:13. The question rises once again over the word 'spirit'.[34] However, as this 'spirit' is a gift of God and not a natural disposition of Timothy, in the last analysis it seems that it must at least be the product of the working of the Holy Spirit.[35] As a minister Timothy should be composed and bold, though loving, because of God's gift to him. There is nothing here about the Spirit teaching or illuminating but again the fact that Christians and ministers of the gospel can only function as they should by the gift and grace of the Spirit is evident. However, 'self-discipline' (σωφρονισμοῦ) does indicate an effect of the Spirit upon the mind.[36]

2 Timothy 1:14

Guard the good deposit that was entrusted to you – guard it with the help of the Holy Spirit who lives in us.

In this verse Timothy is called upon to guard the good deposit – 'the treasure put into our charge', REB – by the Holy Spirit who dwells in us. It is not apparent what this treasure is which has been entrusted to Timothy. Presumably it is the pattern of sound words of which the previous verse speaks.[37] Timothy had heard this from Paul and it appears it was in this way that it was committed to him. It is not exactly clear how the Holy Spirit will enable him to guard this, or exactly in what way this guarding is to take place. Perhaps Paul is thinking of Timothy defending the pattern of sound words from heretics and opponents, but there is nothing about this in the immediate context.[38] Verse 13, on the other hand, urges Timothy to hold on to the pattern of teaching, so it may be that rather than thinking of the Holy Spirit's assistance in defence and apology, we should think of him testifying to Timothy of the truth of what Paul has passed on to him.

2 Timothy 2:16–17

Avoid godless chatter, because those who indulge in it will become more and more ungodly. Their teaching will spread like gangrene. Among them are Hymenaeus and Philetus.

In these verses profane and empty talk is spoken of as something which increases to more ungodliness and which spreads like gangrene.[39] This underlines the fact that there is a certain power and force to wrong and ungodly ideas. It is not that they can simply and easily be detected intellectually and then be rejected; they have a power of their own which causes them to grow and spread. It is because this is the nature and effect of falsehood that the work of the Holy Spirit is so important, both in bringing people to a knowledge of the truth and in guiding them into fulness of truth and keeping them from error.

2 Timothy 2:24–26

And the Lord's servant must not quarrel; instead, he must be kind to everyone, able to teach, not resentful. Those who oppose him he must gently instruct, in the hope that God will grant them repentance leading them to a knowledge of the truth, and that they will come to their senses and escape from the trap of the devil, who has taken them captive to do his will.

That this is so is brought out more explicitly in this passage.

In the first place, Paul says that it is God who gives to those ensnared in error 'repentance to the acknowledging of the truth'. He enjoins Timothy to be humble and gentle, not quarrelsome, in his dealings with such people, for browbeating cannot do any good, but through patient correction God may grant the 'change of mind' (REB) that is needful.

Secondly, Paul says that through this 'they will come to their senses and escape the snare of the devil'. On the one hand, their condition has been one of a sort of intoxication,[40] they have not been able to think straight, they have not been in their right mind. On the other, the devil has taken them captive so that they will do his will. For both these reasons, which are closely related, it is necessary for God to give them repentance. There is a spiritual and moral bondage from which they need to be delivered by divine power.

2 Timothy 3:7–9

always learning but never able to acknowledge the truth. Just as Jannes and Jambres opposed Moses, so also these men oppose the truth – men of depraved minds, who, as far as the faith is concerned, are rejected. But they will not get very far because, as in the case of those men, their folly will be clear to everyone.

These verses strengthen what has been seen in the two previous passages. Here are people[41] who, for all their learning, are 'never able to come to a knowledge of the truth'. They oppose the truth, their minds are corrupt, they have been tested and are rejected (ἀδόκιμοι) concerning the faith. In this case it appears that Paul is speaking about a type of heretic who has proceeded further along the road of error than in 2:24–26, because he does not seem to envisage these being granted repentance, rather their folly will be made plain to everyone. It may be that this is unjustified inference; what is clear is that by themselves, apart from an intervention by God, they cannot know the truth.

Summary

Negatively in these letters we see evidence that the human mind is hostile to God before reconciliation takes place; those who do not receive the truth are liable to deception. Heresy is like an infection, and behind it is the power of the devil; it takes God's gift of repentance to deliver someone from it.

Conversely God does do this; so it is by power of the Spirit that the gospel comes; the Spirit sets apart people for God, and the word continues to work effectively in those who have received it.

Christians need wisdom, knowledge and insight for living the Christian life. These are gifts from God, they are found in Christ, and there is evidence that they are related to the Spirit.

The Spirit fulfils a variety of functions:

• bringing God's people to unity of mind and purpose
• vindicating Jesus Christ
• warning against coming errors
• enabling ministers of the gospel to fulfil their tasks of teaching and preaching
• giving Christians the personal qualities they need in difficult circumstances
• enabling Christians to guard the truth of the gospel

All these are different facets of the teaching and illuminating work of the Spirit.

CHAPTER 10

GENERAL EPISTLES

Hebrews

There are probably seven references to the Holy Spirit[1] in the letter to the Hebrews. Three of these have some significance for this book, but there are no other themes which bear on it. The letter[2] quotes a great deal from the Old Testament and interprets these quotations from a Christian perspective. The three references that need to be considered are 3:7, 9:8 and 10:15.

The first feature to be noticed in these verses is the use of the present tense when referring to Old Testament texts, 'the Holy Spirit says' (3:7), 'showing' (9:8), 'bears witness' (10:15). This is characteristic of the writer's quotations from the Old Testament. While there is occasional use of the aorist and perfect tenses, the present is most frequently used.[3] On most occasions the subject of the verb is God[4] (the writer shows a distinct lack of interest in the human authors[5]) on other occasions it is Christ,[6] and on these three the subject is the Holy Spirit. However, where God and Christ are subjects this usually has to be determined from the context and is not explicitly stated, as is the case with the Holy Spirit. When the writer wishes to specify an author for scripture it is the Holy Spirit whom he mentions.

The use of the present tense gives a sense of the writer's understanding of the relevance of the Old Testament for the present generation of believers. It is not just truth from the past, it is the voice of God in the present. This is the more remarkable because the writer is not just asserting the continuing significance of the Old Testament, he is interpreting and applying it christologically in such a way that many of its provisions are actually shown to be done away by the coming of Christ. So the voice of the Spirit in Old Testament scripture does not simply reiterate the words of psalmists and prophets but speaks them afresh in the light of the climax of revelation with the coming of God's Son (1:1–2).

The vivid sense of the present speaking of God in scripture which is conveyed by the use of the present tense is encapsulated by the writer in 4:12.[7] Here the living power of what God says,[8] and the way in which it penetrates and searches the heart, is described as sharper than any two-edged sword. Although some have seen the phrase 'the word of God' here as referring to Christ,[9] in the context of this letter with its almost constant interaction with the Old Testament, it is the latter which seems to be intended.

In 3:7 the quotation from the Old Testament is introduced by the phrase, 'as the Holy Spirit says', but in 9:8 there is no direct quotation and the reference is to a summary of details about the Old Testament tabernacle. From this, the writer says, 'the Holy Spirit [is] showing[10] that the way into the holiest was not yet manifest while the first tabernacle was still standing'. This conclusion arises from the description of the structure of the tabernacle and the fact that the High Priest went only once a year into the holiest of all. Yet the writer clearly has in mind the thought that one day people will be able to go into the holiest, but this will be when the earthly tabernacle has become obsolete. This he takes up in verse 11ff. The important point, however, is that it is the description of the tabernacle and its procedures, *plus the implications of this*, which are shown by the Holy Spirit.[11]

In 10:15 the Holy Spirit 'witnesses to us'. This is a stronger expression than 'speaks' and there is also an emphasis on 'to us', which is based on 'after those days' in the quotation from Jeremiah 31. The writer's perspective is that through the Old Testament scriptures the Holy Spirit is bearing witness to his present day readers. The argument which the writer presents is not simply his argument; it arises out of scripture through which the Holy Spirit bears his witness.[12]

Certain points arise from an examination of these texts. The Holy Spirit is the active power of God still speaking the words of scripture to its readers and hearers. There is an element which goes beyond just speaking the text in which the Holy Spirit also brings out the implications, or aspects of the significance, of the content of scripture. This means that the word of God is living and powerful, and the writer doubtless expects that word to pierce the hearts of his readers so that any unbelief is revealed to them, and their allegiance to Jesus Christ is renewed. At the same time the scripture is the voice of the Spirit speaking to them whether a response is evoked or not.

1 Peter

1 Peter 1:2

who have been chosen according to the fore-knowledge of God the Father, through the sanctifying work of the Spirit, for obedience to Jesus Christ and sprinkling by his blood: Grace and peace be yours in abundance.

The first reference to the Holy Spirit in this letter comes here in the greeting. Peter describes those to whom he directs his letter as 'chosen in the foreknowledge of God the Father, by the consecrating work of the Holy Spirit, for obedience to Jesus Christ and sprinkling with his blood'.[13] The central phrases, 'by the consecrating work of the Holy Spirit, for obedience to Jesus Christ'[14] involve at least two main ideas. The first is a work of the Holy Spirit by which Peter's readers are being 'consecrated'.[15] The second is that they are to live in obedience to Jesus Christ. It may be that εἰς is dependent on ἁγιασμῷ,[16] in which case the text means that obedience springs out of the consecrating work of the Spirit. It is common to take the phrases in verse 2 as dependent on 'chosen' in verse 1, and translations either repeat the idea (as NIV 'God's elect ... chosen') or else save 'chosen' until verse 2 (REB, NKJV). However Grudem[17] has recently argued that these phrases do not modify 'chosen' but rather the whole situation described in verse 1. This leads him to comment in this way on 'in sanctification of the Spirit':[18]

> It is much easier, again, to see the phrase 'in sanctification of the Spirit' as referring to the entire present status of Peter's readers. This allows *en* to have its common sense 'in': Peter is saying that

his readers' *whole existence* as 'chosen sojourners of the Dispersion ...' is being lived 'in' the realm of the sanctifying work of the Spirit. The unseen, unheard activity of God's Holy Spirit surrounds them almost like a spiritual atmosphere 'in' which they live and breathe, turning every circumstance, every sorrow, every hardship into a tool for his patient sanctifying work ...[19]

Every activity of the Christian life thus takes place 'in sanctification of the Spirit'.

1 Peter 1:3ff.

Praise be to the God and Father of our Lord Jesus Christ! In his great mercy he has given us new birth into a living hope through the resurrection of Jesus Christ from the dead.

In the third verse Peter gives thanks that God has begotten Christians ('us') to a 'living hope',[20] a hope which is defined in terms of 'an inheritance reserved in heaven' in the next verse. The hope is thus, first of all, an objective hope. It is based on the objective resurrection of Jesus Christ and consists of a heavenly inheritance. However, it is difficult to think that there is no subjective element also on the part of those who have been given new birth. Indeed the fact that they have experienced such a radical renewal seems almost inevitably to involve it. A change has taken place in them which gives a living hope[21] (ἀναγεννήσας ... εἰς); it would be surprising indeed if there were no sense of hope within them.

Along with this verse 8 needs to be considered. Peter acknowledges that his readers have not seen Jesus Christ,[22] but he maintains that through believing they both love him and rejoice with joy that is inexpressible and full of glory.[23] It appears then that the new birth brings with it a sense of hope, while faith enables those who have it to be so sure of the reality of the Jesus they have never actually seen that it fills them with overwhelming joy,[24] even though they may be passing through very difficult circumstances (v. 6). There is therefore a spiritual knowledge which comes by faith which brings great assurance leading to joy. There is, however, no mention of the Spirit in this connection here.

1 Peter 1:10–12

Concerning this salvation, the prophets, who spoke of the grace that was to come to you, searched intently and with the greatest care, trying to find out the time and circumstances to which the Spirit of Christ in them was pointing when he predicted the sufferings of Christ and the glories that would follow. It was revealed to them that they were not serving themselves but you, when they spoke of the things that have now been told you by those who have preached the gospel to you by the Holy Spirit sent from heaven. Even angels long to look into these things.

These verses are of particular importance. The following are crucial points:

According to Peter the Spirit[25] of Christ was in the prophets and enabled them to speak beforehand of the sufferings of Christ and the glories to follow, and of the grace which would come to Peter's generation. It is because the Spirit is the Spirit of Christ that the prophets spoke specifically of him.

It was revealed to the prophets that they were ministering not to themselves, but to a future generation, so they inquired and searched diligently (ἐξεζήτησαν καὶ ἐξηραύνησαν), searching what or what time (ἐραυνῶντες εἰς τίνα ἢ ποῖον καιρὸν) the Spirit of Christ was pointing to.

The things the prophets spoke of had been preached to Peter's readers by those whose preaching was accompanied by 'the Holy Spirit sent down from heaven.'[26]

Several conclusions can be drawn from these considerations:

Firstly, the prophets were aware to some extent that what they said by the Spirit of Christ referred to things that would take place in the future. But there were aspects that they did not know about,[27] though they desired to know. This indicates that at least some Old Testament prophecy has a *sensus plenior* which is apparent only when considered in the light of the actual coming of Jesus and the events that his coming initiated.[28]

Secondly, when the things which the prophets had spoken of were preached after their fulfilment, this preaching took place with the Holy Spirit sent down from heaven. This assistance of the Holy Spirit was presumably not so much for the preacher's benefit, but for the benefit of the hearers; so that the preaching would be believed, appropriated and evoke a response.

Thirdly, there is no direct mention here of the need for any work of the Holy Spirit in understanding the prophetic portions of the Old Testament, nor in understanding the preaching, though this seems to be implied. However the twofold reference to the Spirit is significant and is certainly congruent with, and may hint at, such a work of the Spirit. However, the fact that no mention is made indicates that we are not to assume such a work would be of the same nature as that work of the Spirit in prophets or preachers.

1 Peter 3:15

But in your hearts set apart Christ as Lord. Always be prepared to give an answer to everyone who asks you to give the reason for the hope that you have. But do this with gentleness and respect ...

Whether this verse is relevant depends on the connection of thought between the opening statement and the rest of the verse. The verb that belongs to ἕτοιμοι (ἔχειν) is understood and the exact sense is difficult to ascertain. While translations generally express the two clauses as co-ordinates: 'Sanctify Christ as lord[29] in your hearts' 'be ready to give an answer ...', it may be better to translate 'being ready'. The thought may be that setting apart Christ in the heart is a means to being ready to give an answer. In the Gospels the promise of special help from the Holy Spirit is given for those who are being brought before the authorities (Matt. 10:19–20; Mark 13:11; Luke 12:11–12; 21:15), and this may be an allusion to the same thing.[30] Those who set Christ apart in their hearts will be prepared to give an answer, because he will enable them to do so. This is through the Spirit, though there is no reference here to this factor.

2 Peter

In this letter there are several references to 'knowledge'. In 1:2 grace and peace come 'through knowledge of God and Jesus our Lord'. In verse 3 God's power has given Christians everything needed for life and godliness 'through the knowledge of him who called us'. These references speak of a knowledge which is already received. In 1:5–6 knowledge is to be added to other graces.[31] In 1:8 the addition of grace upon grace leads to Christians being 'neither barren nor unfruitful in the knowledge of our Lord Jesus Christ'; while in the last verse of the letter the exhortation is given, 'Grow in the grace and knowledge of our Lord and Saviour Jesus Christ.' Perhaps unexpectedly, false teachers are described in 2:20 as having 'escaped the pollutions of the world through the knowledge of our Lord and Saviour Jesus Christ'.[32] Knowledge is clearly an important concept in this letter.

This knowledge is primarily a knowledge of God and Jesus Christ. Legal terminology may be reflected in 1:2 (BAGD), and 2:20 may suggest that the reference is more to an historical knowledge and external allegiance. Nevertheless it is a knowledge which is productive of spiritual benefits, and which is to grow and increase. At the heart of the Christian faith in 2 Peter lies a new knowledge which belongs to Christians, one which can become barren; in which case the person reverts to a condition of blindness and forgetfulness (1:9), but which is capable of development. Such knowledge is crucial for the Christian as the soil out of which the whole Christian life grows (1:3–2:12; 1:8; 3:18).

2 Peter 1:20–21

Above all, you must understand that no prophecy of Scripture came about by the prophet's own interpretation. For prophecy never had its origin in the will of man, but men spoke from God as they were carried along by the Holy Spirit.

These verses speak of interpretation in the context of the prophecies in the Old Testament. But there is considerable disagreement about their meaning. Many writers see here, in the words of James

Moffatt, a warning 'against the danger of unauthorized interpretations of the OT'.[33] 'The guarantee against that spiritual anarchy is the recognition that the Holy Scripture must be interpreted by those who are properly qualified, who have been called of God and prompted by the Spirit, which is true of the apostles and their legitimate successors.'[34]

Although this view would support the need for Spirit-guided interpreters of the Old Testament, it is very doubtful whether it can be sustained. Bauckham's very thorough discussion comes out in favour of the view which takes verse 20 to mean 'no prophecy of Scripture derives from the prophet's own interpretation'. As a result he says, 'If interpretation (2) is correct, this verse says nothing about the *interpretation* of Scripture, and therefore nothing about an authoritative teaching office in the Church to which all interpretation must be subject (Käsemann, 'Apologia' 189-90) or about the charism of teaching (Curran, TS4 [1943] 364-67).'[35] These verses are almost certainly about the *origin* of prophecy and they cannot therefore be used to answer the question whether the Holy Spirit can be considered to assist in the *interpretation* of Scripture.

Summary

In Hebrews the emphasis is on Scripture as the voice of the Holy Spirit; through the Old Testament texts the Spirit speaks, shows and witnesses.

In 1 Peter part of what it means to be a Christian is being consecrated by the Spirit; every aspect of the Christian life involves the work of the Spirit. There is hope and a spiritual knowledge which leads to great joy given to believers, though this is not attributed directly to the Spirit. The Old Testament prophets spoke by the Spirit of Christ about things yet to come which they earnestly enquired after, suggesting that there is a deeper meaning to some of their words than they were aware of. The gospel was also preached with the Holy Spirit, presumably for the benefit of the hearers.

Peter's second letter emphasizes the importance of a knowledge which is given at conversion but which has to grow; but there is no reference to the Spirit in this connection. Although many writers have considered that 1:20–21 show the need for Spirit-guided interpreters (though this itself is an inference), it is almost certain that these verses are speaking about the origin of prophecy rather than its interpretation.

CHAPTER 11

THE LETTERS OF JOHN

In 5:13 of his first letter John tells his readers he has written the things in this letter that they may know that they have eternal life. In accordance with this purpose John frequently speaks of knowledge in the sense of assurance and certainty. It is also in this connection that he speaks of the Holy Spirit; he is the one who bears witness because he is the truth (5:6–8) whose presence brings assurance (3:24; 4:13). But the thought is complex, or perhaps many-faceted, and each facet needs to be looked at in turn.

1 John 1:1–3

That which was from the beginning, which we have heard, which we have seen with our eyes, which we have looked at and our hands have touched – this we proclaim concerning the Word of life. The life appeared; we have seen it and testify to it, and we proclaim to you the eternal life, which was with the Father and has appeared to us. We proclaim to you what we have seen and heard, so that you also may have fellowship with us. And our fellowship is with the Father and with his Son, Jesus Christ.

In the opening verses John emphasizes the historical manifestation of the Word of life[1] in the person of Jesus Christ, and the testimony which he, and others like him, can give to the Word as eye-witnesses.[2] This means that whatever John is going to say to give assurance to his readers, and whatever subjective factors may be involved in this, he lays the foundation in an objective, clearly witnessed incarnation of the Son of God (4:2, 3; 9, 10, 14; 5:6–9). Moreover reassurance is mediated by the letter John writes (cf. 2:1, 7–8, 12–14, 21, 26; 5:13) in which he declares this witness to his readers (1:2, 3, 5).

1 John 2:3–5

We know that we have come to know him if we obey his commands. The man who says, 'I know him,' but does not do what he commands is a liar, and the truth is not in him. But if anyone obeys his word, God's love is truly made complete in him. This is how we know we are in him.

In verse 3 John states that we – here meaning 'we Christians' – know that we know him, if we keep his commandments. This is reminiscent of the words of Jesus in John's Gospel, 7:17. John is using keeping the commandments as evidence that a person is now different from those who do not keep the commandments. Those who keep the commandments, or word (v. 5), have the love of God perfected in them. By this fact Christians know that they are in Christ. On the other hand those who do not keep the commandments do not have the truth in them, and if one of them says, 'I know him', he is a liar.[3] While in one sense assurance is inferential here (from keeping the commandments), it is deeper than that, because keeping the commandments is an expression of God's love being perfected within a person.[4] The stress is as much on verse 4 as it is on the other verses, where what is clear is that disobedience to the commandments is clear evidence that the truth is not in a person, whatever he may say.

1 John 2:13–14

I write to you, fathers, because you have known him who is from the beginning. I write to you, young men, because you have overcome the evil one. I write to you, dear children, because you have known the Father. I write to you, fathers, because you have known him who is from the beginning. I write to you, young men, because you are strong, and the word of God lives in you, and you have overcome the evil one.

In these verses which describe various groups – little children, fathers and young men – John speaks three times of knowledge; the fathers have known him who is from the beginning, and the little children have known the Father. These references suggest that knowledge of God belongs to Christians from the beginning of their Christian lives and continues throughout them.[5] In the context of this letter this suggests that John's purpose is to remind his readers of the knowledge that is theirs, and clarify it for them.

1 John 2:20–27

But you have an anointing from the Holy One, and all of you know the truth. I do not write to you because you do not know the truth, but because you do know it and because no lie comes from the truth. Who is the liar? It is the man who denies that Jesus is the Christ. Such a man is the antichrist – he denies the Father and the Son. No-one who denies the Son has the Father; whoever acknowledges the Son has the Father also. See that what you have heard from the beginning remains in you. If it does, you also will remain in the Son and in the Father. And this is what he promised us – even eternal life. I am writing these things to you about those who are trying to lead you astray. As for you, the anointing you received from him remains in you, and you do not need anyone to teach you. But as his anointing teaches you about all things and as that anointing is real, not counterfeit – just as it has taught you, remain in him.

This is a crucial passage in this letter. There are three references to 'the anointing' (χρῖσμα) which Christians have and which remains in them, and through which they have a knowledge of the truth. Several points need to be mentioned.

Firstly, there is little doubt that by the anointing John means the Holy Spirit.[6]

Secondly, it is not clear why he uses the term 'anointing', nor is its significance clear.[7] Presumably this term was understood by the first readers and was adequate to express to them all that John intended.[8]

Thirdly, there is a textual variation in verse 20.[9] Both readings fit the context and the evidence is not conclusive either way. Fortunately the difference does not seriously affect the sense of the whole passage.

Fourthly, verse 21 suggests what we have also seen at verses 13 and 14. John writes, not because his readers do not have knowledge (here a knowledge given by the anointing), but in order to clarify the truth *which they do have*.[10] Verse 27 is difficult because of the way in which it says that the readers do not need teaching.[11] Yet John is not so much teaching in this letter as helping them to distinguish their experience and knowledge from the false claims of others which had inevitably confused them and undermined their own sense of assurance. John calls them back to the knowledge which they have by virtue of the anointing they had received.

Fifthly, this knowledge is not just a knowledge of God, or of their own relationship to God, it also includes truths about God and Christ (διδάσκει ὑμας περὶ πάντων). John does not set any limits to this knowledge and it obviously includes truths like that of the incarnation (4:2–3). Not that they received a knowledge of the incarnation via the anointing, this had come through the apostles and those who had been taught by them (v. 24), but that the anointing assured them when they heard of the incarnation that this was true.[12]

1 John 3:14

We know that we have passed from death to life, because we love our brothers. Anyone who does not love remains in death.

This verse is similar to 2:3, though, in contrast with the world in the previous verse, there is an emphasis on 'we': '*We* know[13] *we* have crossed over from death to life.' In 2:3 the reason given for such knowledge was keeping God's commandments, here it is love for Christian brothers. The flow of thought seems to derive from verse 9 via verse 10. The one who does not 'love his fellow-Christians is not a child of God' (v. 10, REB), but the divine seed remains in the man who is born from God so that he both does what is right and loves his brother. Love for brothers is thus an evidence of divine birth, and so carries assurance with it.[14]

1 John 3:19–20

This then is how we know that we belong to the truth, and how we set our hearts at rest in his presence whenever our hearts condemn us. For God is greater than our hearts, and he knows everything.

These verses should be taken in conjunction with verse 14. The sequence of thought seems to follow from the previous verses. Once again it is love, here practical love, which assures the hearts of believers before God, and makes them know they are of the truth. The connection between verse 19 and verse 20 is not absolutely clear; however, John envisages the possibility that a believer's heart may condemn him, in which case he can fall back on the fact that God is greater than the heart and knows everything.

1 John 3:24

Those who obey his commands live in him, and he in them. And this is how we know that he lives in us: We know it by the Spirit he gave us.

This is the first explicit reference to the Spirit in this letter.[15] The assurance that Jesus Christ dwells in 'us' believers comes from the Spirit who has been given to us. Exactly how this assurance comes depends on our understanding of the relationship between this verse and the verses that follow.[16] The operative words ἐκ τοῦ πνεύματος οὗ ἡμῖν ἔδωκεν are almost identical with 4:13: ἐκ τοῦ πνεύματος αὐτοῦ δέδωκεν ἡμῖν. Later 4:14 goes on to speak of the witness of the apostles and those who saw Jesus in the days of his flesh, so the knowledge brought by the Spirit here does not replace historical testimony.

1 John 4:1–6

Dear friends, do not believe every spirit, but test the spirits to see whether they are from God, because many false prophets have gone out into the world. This is how you can recognise the Spirit of God:

Every spirit that acknowledges that Jesus Christ has come in the flesh is from God, but every spirit that does not acknowledge Jesus is not from God. This is the spirit of the antichrist, which you have heard is coming and even now is already in the world. You, dear children, are from God and have overcome them, because the one who is in you is greater than the one who is in the world. They are from the world and therefore speak from the viewpoint of the world, and the world listens to them. We are from God, and whoever knows God listens to us; but whoever is not from God does not listen to us. This is how we recognise the Spirit of truth and the spirit of falsehood.

The opening words seem to take up the reference to the Spirit in 3:24[17] and indicate a complicating factor: there are other spirits[18] and they must not be believed. This passage indicates that the Spirit who has been given is active in the community of believers, and part of this activity is prophecy. It is not just that he indwells believers; rather it is the indwelling of Jesus to which he bears testimony (3:24), though the one implies the other. Two tests are given for distinguishing the Spirit of God from other spirits. The first is doctrinal: the confession that Jesus Christ has come in the flesh.[19] The second is that those who know God hear[20] 'us' – once again apparently referring to the witness of the apostles and others who knew the historical Jesus.[21] It is because of the 'anointing' (2:20, 27) that those who know God listen to 'us'.[22] The Spirit of truth thus bears witness to the same truth to which the eye-witnesses of Jesus also give their testimony. There is a consistency between the word spoken by true prophets in the Spirit and the word of the eye-witnesses.

1 John 4:7–8, 16

Dear friends, let us love one another, for love comes from God. Everyone who loves has been born of God and knows God. Whoever does not love does not know God, because God is love. And so we know and rely on the love God has for us. God is love. Whoever lives in love lives in God, and God in him.

In verse 7 love is described as the result of being born of God and existing along with the knowledge of God. In the next verse the negative is expressed: 'he who does not love does not know God, for God is love'. The thought is the same as that in 3:14. Those who are born of God both love and know, but there seems to be a nuance indicating that love testifies to and assures knowledge. Verse 16 is slightly different in content, but the basic thought is the same. This knowledge arising from love actually gives boldness on the day of judgment and casts out fear (vv. 17, 18).

1 John 5:6–12

This is the one who came by water and blood – Jesus Christ. He did not come by water only, but by water and blood. And it is the Spirit who testifies, because the Spirit is the truth. For there are three that testify: the Spirit, the water and the blood; and the three are in agreement. We accept man's testimony, but God's testimony is greater because it is the testimony of God, which he has given about his Son. Anyone who believes in the Son of God has this testimony in his heart. Anyone who does not believe God has made him out to be a liar, because he has not believed the testimony God has given about his Son. And this is the testimony; God has given us eternal life, and this life is in his Son. He who has the Son has life; he who does not have the Son of God does not have life.

The Spirit is described as the one who bears witness, because the Spirit is the truth (v. 6b).[23] This witness is to Jesus Christ, but it is likely that it includes the idea of witnessing to the fact that he came by water and blood. Water and blood appear to refer to the baptism and death of Jesus,[24] and perhaps the baptism testifies to the divine Sonship of Jesus and his death to the reality of his humanity – the final assurance that he has come in the flesh (4:2).

The Spirit is probably referred to because of his descent upon Jesus at his baptism.[25] John in his Gospel particularly records that it was the Spirit coming and remaining upon Jesus that assured John the Baptist that Jesus was the Son of God (John 1:32–34). There are three witnesses to Jesus Christ, the Spirit, the water and the blood, and they are united in their testimony. However, there appears to be a difference in the witness they bear. The water and the blood are purely historical factors pointing to the truth about Jesus; the Spirit is the truth. This seems to indicate that the reference to the Spirit is more than to the event of the descent upon Jesus at his baptism. The same Spirit who came upon Jesus is also present in the community of believers as the truth; testifying to the truth about Jesus.[26]

In verse 10a John asserts that those who believe on the Son of God have the witness within themselves (ἔχει τὴν μαρτυρίαν ἐν αὐτῷ). This is not explained any further, but as the Spirit bears witness (v. 6) it seems that an inward witness of the Spirit is intended.[27] This is a witness to objective truth about Christ's person, and agrees with the historical evidence supplied by the baptism and death of Jesus.[28]

Verse 9 speaks of the witness of God. This is not a separate witness.[29] The voice of God was heard at the baptism of Jesus, and the implication of the descent of the Spirit from heaven is that the Spirit has come from God (so also John 3:34, '... for God does not give the Spirit by measure'). It is also God who has given the Spirit to believers (3:24; 4:13), so the witness the Spirit bears is the witness of God.

1 John 5:19–20

We know that we are children of God, and that the whole world is under the control of the evil one. We know also that the Son of God has come and has given us understanding, so that we may know him who is true. And we are in him who is true – even in his Son Jesus Christ. He is the true God and eternal life.

In accordance with John's purpose (5:13) these final verses (apart from a concluding warning in verse 21) are also about assurance and certainty. Speaking of Christians, John says, 'We know we are of God ... we know that the Son of God has come and given us an understanding, that we may know him who is true ...'[30] What this understanding consists of is not explained. The concept seems close to that of the 'anointing'[31] in 2:20, 27, because that also gives knowledge. The understanding is given by the Son of God. John does not give any indication that he has the Spirit, or the work of the Spirit, in mind, but in the context of this letter it would seem inappropriate to conclude that the understanding has no relation to the Spirit at all.

2 John 9

Anyone who runs ahead and does not continue in the teaching of Christ does not have God; whoever continues in the teaching has both the Father and the Son.

A note on this verse also needs to be added. Here John indicates that there is a relationship between knowing truth about Christ and having God. Those who 'go beyond' (REB) the teaching about Christ do not have God. Those who continue in the teaching have both the Father and the Son. Possession of God, a bold way to express the relationship between Christians and God, is prior and gives a knowledge of teaching, so that those who depart from the teaching show that they do not possess God.

Summary
First John emphasizes knowledge and assurance. In the first place knowledge depends on the testimony of eye-witnesses, but those who have a personal knowledge of the truth are those who keep Christ's commandments and who love their Christian brothers and sisters. Those who do love have been born of God. Knowledge and assurance do not simply result from teaching, but from a transforming work in the believer.

Christians also have received an anointing, which almost certainly refers to the Holy Spirit. The anointing teaches them, gives knowledge of 'all things', so that those who have it do not need teaching. This anointing seems to have been given along with the apostolic teaching at conversion, bringing an assurance of its truth. In the face of other teachings John recalls his readers to the assured truth given by the anointing.

The Holy Spirit has been given to believers and by this they know that Jesus Christ dwells in them. He also enables prophets to confess the truth that Jesus Christ has come in the flesh. He bears witness to the divine Sonship and true humanity of Jesus Christ. This is the witness of God; a witness within those who believe on the Son of God.

CHAPTER 12

THE BOOK OF REVELATION

There are 18 references to the Spirit in the book of Revelation and one use of the adverb πνευματικῶς (11:8). According to R. J. Bauckham, whose recent book on Revelation contains a study of the Spirit, these references can be divided into three categories: four occurrences of the phrase 'in the Spirit' (ἐν πνεύματι:1:10; 4:2; 17:3; 21:10); four references to the seven Spirits (1:4; 3:1; 4:5; 5:6) and ten other references to the Spirit (2:7, 11, 17, 29; 3:6, 13, 22; 14:13; 19:10; 22:17).[1]

The references to the seven Spirits, based on Zechariah 3:9 to 4:14,[2] do not relate the Spirit to any of the themes relevant to our present study but comment will be made on the other references. Bauckham considers the phrase ἐν πνεύματι under the heading 'The Spirit of Vision'.[3] He says, 'For the purpose of passing on the revelation John needed only to indicate that the whole revelation came to him ἐν πνεύματι – which was a theological claim as much as a psychological statement.'[4] It was while he was ἐν πνεύματι that John received the revelation and heard the voice (1:10), and it was ἐν πνεύματι that he came up and saw heavenly realities (4:1–2).[5] The other two references, according to Bauckham, 'are strategically placed for literary effect and theological significance, rather than to show that the Spirit played a special role at those points and not others.'[6] This emphasis on the whole revelation being given while John was ἐν πνεύματι is particularly important if we bear in mind that John was in exile for the faith, and that he was writing to Christians who were either suffering persecution, or faced with the threat of it, to encourage them and to interpret their experiences and circumstances in the light of the purposes of God.

Bauckham groups the other ten references to the Spirit together under the heading 'The Spirit of Prophecy'.[7] Perhaps the key reference here is 19:10, 'For the testimony of Jesus is the Spirit of prophecy.' Also the first seven references occur in each of the letters to the seven churches, indicating that they are prophetic messages to the churches and doubtless reflecting the role of Christian prophets in the churches at that time. These references serve to stress the status of the revelation as prophecy (1:3; 22:18).

In commenting on πνευματικῶς (11:8) Bauckham speaks of 'The Spirit and the eschatological perspective'. He maintains that the word 'refers to Spirit-given perception'.[8] He says, 'The story of the witnesses is to be read neither as a simple prediction (history written in advance) nor as allegory (history or future history written in code symbols). Rather it is a story through which the churches are to perceive imaginatively, through the perspective granted them by the Spirit, their vocation and duty.'[9] Thus he goes on to say,

Any and every city in whose streets the corpses of the witnesses lie is *thereby* identified, its character seen in the Spirit, as Sodom and Egypt. The value of this identification as part of the Spirit's message to the churches is that it enables them to characterize situations of conflict in their true perspective, to distinguish appearances from underlying reality, to see through the apparent success of the hostile world and the apparent failure of faithful witness. This example of the function of one passage in Revelation may serve to illustrate how the apocalyptic imagery functions as a vehicle of the eschatological perception which the Spirit imparts through the prophets.[10]

One apparent implication of the last point is that the churches will continue to need 'Spirit-given perception'. If they are going to apply the apocalyptic imagery to their own circumstances, they appear to need a sensitivity both to the text of Revelation and the spiritual realities of their own day. This actually points to the greater hermeneutical question of applying the whole of Scripture to the horizon of its readers. The emphasis of Revelation on the Spirit as the Spirit of vision, as the Spirit of prophecy, as well as the Spirit who gives perception of the eschatological perspective, all point to a continuing need of the Spirit for its readers. It would seem the antithesis of John's own experience and understanding for him to anticipate that his readers would by their own intellectual powers be able to read off their situation in the light of his words in Revelation.

Another feature of Revelation is the extensive allusion to the Old Testament which is found throughout. Bauckham refers to 'a pattern of disciplined and deliberate *allusion* to specific Old Testament texts. Reference to and interpretation of these texts is an extremely important part of the meaning of the text of the Apocalypse. It is a book designed to be read in constant intertextual relationship with the Old Testament. John was writing what he understood to be a work of prophetic scripture, the climax of prophetic revelation, which gathered up the prophetic meaning of the Old Testament and disclosed the way in which it was being and was to be fulfilled in the last days.'[11] There are two features which emerge here. The first is that as a prophetic revelation the book is a Spirit-given interpretation of the Old Testament. It is both 'in the Spirit' and, as one through whom the Spirit of prophecy speaks, John weaves the Old Testament into the warp and woof of his book. Secondly this points to a continuing need for illumination by the Spirit in reading the Old Testament, but also in reading the New in the light of its intertextual relationship with the Old.

It is perhaps significant that the emphasis of the last book of the New Testament upon the Spirit involves necessary implications for a continuing work of the Spirit in its readers, and the readers of the Old Testament, if they are to understand these books aright and be able to relate them sensitively to their own days and needs.

CONCLUSION

In this last section I intend to summarize the New Testament evidence and briefly relate it to the area of biblical hermeneutics.

Summary of the New Testament evidence

The first clearly discerned emphasis is that people are unable and unwilling to grasp and appreciate truth about God[1] by themselves. This is because of the effects of sin, conceived of as an inner power of evil, in their minds and understanding, not because such truth is necessarily beyond the intellectual grasp of human beings. This emphasis is described in the Synoptic Gospels and is manifested most clearly in the Jewish religious leaders and their attitude towards Jesus Christ and his teaching. The emphasis is not taken up directly in Acts, but it is especially prominent in the writings of Paul who introduces the further thought of hardening as a judicial confirmation of human refusal to listen or respond to God's word. It is also strongly marked in John's writings, particularly the Fourth Gospel with its contrast between light and darkness and its predestinarian emphasis.

Correlative to the problem of sin is the need for light and understanding, both of which are given directly by God, especially in the experience which brings a person to faith in Jesus Christ, described by the broad term 'conversion'. In the Synoptic Gospels, things which are hidden from the wise and prudent are revealed to babes, the secrets of the kingdom are made known to disciples, the messiahship and divine sonship of Jesus are revealed to Peter by the Father. In Luke/Acts the Spirit shows Simeon the significance of the babe brought to the temple by Joseph and Mary, and Jesus opens the minds of his disciples to understand the christological significance of the Old Testament. The Lord also opens Lydia's heart to listen to the word Paul brings.

The renewing of the mind is an important theme in the writings of Paul. It is God who bestows wisdom and knowledge; but the wisdom of this world does not lead to a knowledge of God. God shines into

167

the darkened hearts of unbelievers to give the light of the knowledge of the glory of God in the face of Jesus Christ, an experience which Paul himself received on the road to Damascus and which became definitive for him in understanding his mission and the nature of conversion. Prayer for wisdom and understanding was a priority for Paul in his concern for the churches; these things were vital to deliver Christians from fear, to foster their growth and development in holy living, as well as in knowing God and his love.

In John, in addition to the contrast of light over against darkness, there is a marked emphasis on knowledge and truth. Spiritual knowledge of the truth is not obtainable by reasoning or natural insight, rather it is received from God through Jesus Christ. The essence of eternal life is to know the only true God and Jesus Christ. Knowledge is also an important emphasis in 2 Peter. Christians have received knowledge; but such knowledge needs to grow, and is also crucial for living a godly life.

The New Testament does not claim anywhere that rational argument and the use of the human mind are dispensable. The mind is important: truth, the word of the gospel, preaching, letters, Scripture – all are addressed to the mind. Indeed people are held responsible for not responding to the truth which is so presented. The problem is not an intellectual blockage which has to be solved by approaching people by another route (by direct intuition or immediate effect upon the emotions or will). The problem is a deeper moral and spiritual one, and it requires a solution enabling the mind, and all the inner faculties of what the Bible calls the heart, to function as it should when presented with the word of God. See, for example, 1 Thessalonians 1:5; 2:13.

The giving of light, understanding and knowledge is often linked to the work of the Holy Spirit, and this leads to a consideration of the material which deals with this subject. The main conclusions are as follows.

In the Gospels the Holy Spirit comes upon Jesus Christ. All the gifts which he needed for his ministry were bestowed on him by the Holy Spirit; this equipping of Jesus by the Spirit was understood in terms of various prophecies of the Spirit in the Old Testament. As the One upon whom the fullness of the Spirit rested he also bestowed the same Spirit upon his disciples. In Acts this takes place climactically on the day of Pentecost, though Peter makes it clear that those who repent and are baptized in the name of Jesus Christ will also receive the gift of the Holy Spirit. In John's Gospel Jesus is presented as the baptizer in the Spirit; the Spirit effects the new birth, but the coming of the Spirit in fullness nevertheless awaits the glorification of Jesus. Just as the Spirit came upon Jesus to enable him to fulfil his ministry, so whatever is needed by his disciples for their lives and ministries is supplied by the Spirit.

The Spirit also gives knowledge and understanding at conversion. This is especially apparent in 1 Corinthians 2. God reveals things that surpass the imagination; even the depths of God are revealed by the Spirit to those who believe, thus constituting them spiritual people who have the mind of Christ. It is also implied in 2 Corinthians 3, for the gospel ministry is the ministry of the Spirit, and the glory of the new covenant is made known to the one who turns to the Lord, who is the Spirit. In 1 John believers have received an anointing which teaches them concerning 'all things' so that they know the truth. This anointing almost certainly refers to the Holy Spirit.

However, the Spirit does not bestow complete spiritual knowledge and understanding at the time of conversion. While certain truths may be made plain at that time, there still needs to be continual development in understanding. For this reason, Paul often prays that this might be given, sometimes linking it with the Spirit, most noticeably in Ephesians 1:18–19, where he desires for his readers the Spirit of wisdom and revelation in the knowledge of God.

In John's Gospel the Holy Spirit as the Paraclete is also *the Spirit of truth who teaches and leads into truth, bringing to the memories of his disciples the things which Jesus had spoken to them.* While aspects of this ministry appear to belong particularly to the apostles in their task of bearing the first witness to Jesus, including the production of written testimony, in the context it is difficult to restrict all that is said to them. All disciples now live in the period following the return of Jesus to his Father, and therefore it is appropriate to see an ongoing ministry of the Spirit in the church. In the Paraclete passages *the Spirit is also the one who convicts the world.* As the disciples of Christ bear their testimony in a hostile world it is the Spirit who brings conviction concerning sin, righteousness and judgment, to the minds of those who belong to the world. Such a work is also illustrated in the Acts account of Peter's preaching on the day of Pentecost, and in Paul's references to preaching with the power of the Spirit.

As in the Old Testament, *the Spirit is looked upon as the Spirit of prophecy,* but there is another closely related element in the New Testament. The Spirit also gives insight into the meaning and relevance of the Old Testament. This is seen in Zechariah's song in Luke 1; it is particularly marked in Acts, and is also illustrated by the way the New Testament writers handle Old Testament texts.

It is also made quite clear that *the whole Christian life is one lived in the Spirit, and that the Holy Spirit grants the grace and energy for fulfilling all the responsibilities of that life.* This is clear from the emphasis in Acts on believers receiving the Holy Spirit, and is especially marked in Paul's thought, particularly Romans 8. While this is mainly oriented towards Christian living and growth in holiness, it is impossible to restrict it to the ethical sphere. Whatever responsibilities lie upon Christians, and whatever the activity, especially in relation to witness and the growth of the churches, the work of the Spirit is indispensable.

Relevance for biblical hermeneutics

What bearing does this pervasive New Testament teaching concerning the Spirit's role in teaching have on biblical hermeneutics? The evidence suggests that there is a specifically Christian way of reading and understanding the Bible. But what is that way, and how does it differ, if at all, from usual hermeneutical approaches? Is it possible to correlate the practice of biblical hermeneutics with the teaching ministry of the Holy Spirit? This final section seeks to probe some of the areas of hermeneutical interest and discover what bearing the ministry of the Spirit may have on them.

At the most basic level, hermeneutics includes exegesis based on grammatical study and historical criticism. In seeking to relate such study to the ministry of the Holy Spirit six points will be considered.

First, it is quite clear that whatever stress may be placed on the ministry of the Spirit in relation to hermeneutics, *this cannot abrogate or replace exegetical and historical criticism.* The actual text of Scripture remains of fundamental importance for understanding, just as the teaching of Christ, or the preaching of the apostles, or the written letters were of fundamental importance for hearers and readers in the days of the New Testament. Such basic tools of understanding need to remain because it is the written, objective text which is to be understood.

Furthermore, a recognition of the ministry of the Spirit actually demands close attention to the text and its background. The perversity which some of Jesus' hearers showed to his words manifested itself in careless listening, evoking the words, 'he who has ears, let him hear'. Those who did not treat his words seriously could not expect to understand what he meant. They also exposed themselves to the possibility of losing whatever understanding they might have gained (Matt. 13:12), and eventually of a mind hardened against the truth. The work of the Spirit we are considering is one which enables people to understand an inscripturated message, and therefore necessarily indicates that the enlightenment of the Spirit comes not as an alternative to study, but through the active use of the mind and the proper use of the appropriate tools.

Third, a recognition of the illuminating work of the Spirit also means that the text must be approached with the intention of allowing it to speak in its own terms, and with an effort to distance oneself from one's own presuppositions.[2] In discussing the hermeneutics of Calvin, Thomas Torrance points out that faith 'by its very nature involves us in a relationship toward God in which the emphasis is laid, not on our own powers or resources, but on Christ'. To lay the emphasis on Christ involves also laying the emphasis on his Spirit. As Torrance continues, 'We know him therefore in Spirit and in Truth as he reveals himself to us in his Word and not by trying to form our thoughts of him in accordance with our own presuppositions.'[3] At this point it is possible to bring in the idea of the hermeneutical spiral. As one comes again and again to the text so presuppositions become altered and one approaches more closely to an understanding of the text.[4] The point being emphasized here is that this must be done in dependence upon the Spirit.

Fourthly, the need for the ministry of the Holy Spirit indicates that exegesis and historical study alone will not be adequate by themselves for a real understanding of the text.

Fifthly, the ministry of the Spirit also suggests that study of the historical background ought to take full cognizance of what might be called the spiritual dimension of the text. The text has a spiritual milieu which it is essential to explore if there is to be as full an understanding as possible. This is of particular importance because the Bible was written from what might be called a spiritual perspective. The historical books are classified by the Jews as prophetic books because they are written from a particular perspective which highlights and illustrates the attitude of God towards Israel. Even more than the other historical books, the books of Chronicles (classified among the Writings) exemplify this type of approach. The same is true of the New Testament. The study of the Gospels currently concentrates upon the situations in which, and to which, the Gospels were addressed. Insofar as this reflects a genuine study of the text, as opposed to hypothesizing possible redactional purposes, it helps to earth such study in both the actual situation described in the text and the use to which the writers are putting their narratives.

Finally, the ministry of the Spirit raises an expectation of understanding; that is to say, the study of exegesis and historical background in dependence upon the Spirit will not be a vain enterprise. Torrance speaks of the way in which Calvin created a theology relying upon its own foundations in the Word of God. He comments, 'for as we cannot know God except in accordance with the way in which he has revealed himself to us, so we cannot interpret the means which he has provided as the medium of that revelation except in the light of its actual content in the knowledge of God. Interpretation and understanding go hand in hand together – that is the contribution of Calvin to hermeneutics which we must seek to elucidate.'[5] This also implies that real interpretation is possible, leading to increasing understanding and knowledge of God.

This section seeks *to relate the teaching ministry of the Spirit to the purposes and functions of Scripture*. *Purpose* is not precisely the same as what is usually meant by authorial *intention*. Intention refers to the meaning the author intended by what he wrote, while purpose refers to the reason for writing, and so extends to the intended function of what was written. Generally there will be several purposes and the writing will function in various ways. A writer will usually choose a genre which is suitable for his purpose for the whole work, but will often use a different genre to make a point in a particular place. From the viewpoint of the New Testament writers the holy Scriptures, though authored by men, were nevertheless produced under the guiding influence of the Holy Spirit.[6]

If purpose is important in the way that is being suggested, it follows that it is only possible to understand the biblical writings properly if the purpose(s) of the text are identified and kept in mind. Biblical study has sometimes suffered from an inadequate appreciation of the genre of a particular text, and a failure to consider how the writer intended his writing to affect his readers. The isolation of biblical studies from other literary studies[7] appears to have had the effect, perhaps with other influences, of allowing biblical study to follow a scientific methodology which emphasizes detached, objective, empirical study. Such a methodology is very congenial to grammatical study and historical criticism; it helps in determining precisely what a writer wrote, but not necessarily why he wrote and what he intended by doing so.

Genre interpretation is now widely recognized, so the flattening effect of a generalized scientific methodology is much less common in biblical studies than appears to have been the case earlier in the twentieth century. This naturally arouses an interest in the purposes of the text. Of course authorial purpose is only discernible from the actual text, but what is being argued is that considering the purposes provides a way in to discovering the meaning; if it can be seen why the work was produced, that is itself part of its meaning.

A way of considering the purposes of a text is to see how it functions, or to consider how it was intended to function among its original readers, bearing in mind that it may well have been intended to function in different ways among different readers. It is superficially evident that some parts of the Bible were intended to function in certain ways. Some of the Psalms were intended to evoke praise; others to supply hope or encouragement. Paul's letters are not simply to instruct; in places he rebukes, in others he comforts, in others he breaks out into doxology and clearly expects his readers to be moved to do the same. Real understanding must include sensitivity to these functions, and often an entering into the states of mind and feelings which the text is intended to evoke. A commentary on a text which leaves a reader with an apprehension opposite to that which the text was intended to evoke, for example, does not appear to have given real understanding.

Sensitivity to the functions of a writing is something which would certainly come within the sphere of the ministry of the Holy Spirit as this is described in the New Testament. As the Holy Spirit is conceived of as guiding the authors, so he is also conceived of as guiding disciples into all truth, and this in their reading of Scripture and listening to it, as well as when it is preached. It is perhaps in this respect that the Holy Spirit is particularly needed. The meaning of words and historical background can be discovered by study, but a sympathetic insight into the purpose of a writing may require qualities like perceptiveness and imagination.

In some ways such an understanding may go beyond the purposes and functions envisaged by the author. A writing may legitimately function in ways he has not fully foreseen, or in circumstances which did not come within his purview. Comment must be made on reader-response later on, but there is an anticipation here that the Holy Spirit may enable the biblical writings to function in contemporary application, in ways that are fully in accord with what the author wrote but which go beyond what he was able to foresee.

Some comment should also be made *linking the ministry of the Spirit in hermeneutics to the church*.[8] The Bible belongs to the church; it creates and sustains the church, but also the church interprets and uses the Bible in its ministry in the world.

Just as the biblical writings have their own functions, so the church has its functions also. In the New Testament perspective the Bible functions both towards the world in terms of apologetics with a view to conversion, and towards the church in terms of spiritual nurture. In fact the church functions in exactly the same twofold way and has the Bible as its primary resource in doing so. This means that interpretation must take place within the framework of the functions of the Bible and the church. This has not always been the case. The Bible has sometimes been used to erect teachings which are quite outside such a framework, e.g. of a scientific nature; at other times to develop esoteric understanding of things like numbers; and sometimes hermeneutics appears to be an academic discipline with no purpose beyond itself. But the nature of the Bible and the calling of the church mean that interpretation is for certain purposes, and if these are not pursued then interpretation itself becomes skewed and results in a distortion of the Bible.[9]

It is also clear that in the New Testament the Holy Spirit has been given to the church in order for it to fulfil all its functions, both towards those outside and to its own members. It is, for example, part of the ministry of the Spirit to convict the world, and therefore it can rely on the help of the Spirit in the application of the Bible to its apologetics; the same is also true in respect of its nurture of its own members.[10] There is a correlation between the Bible, the church, and the Holy Spirit in what might be termed practical hermeneutics. All three belong together, and right understanding depends on this.

There are some indications in the New Testament that understanding is received in a corporate way. This has doubtless to be held in tension with the fact that within the church pastors and teachers are appointed whose obvious responsibility is to teach others. Nevertheless, this brings together again the Bible, the church and the Holy Spirit, for the church is the body which is made up of Christians and is the locus of the Holy Spirit, though a number of qualifications need to be made. It is also true that the Holy Spirit indwells individuals. It is true, again, that in the New Testament the word 'church' usually refers to the local congregation, and it is in the inter-personal Christian relationships that take place in such a setting that corporate understanding and mutual edification are most likely to arise. This may seem a far cry from the individual scholar jealously working at his personal project, though the fact that he is likely to check his work by, and almost certainly use, other scholars does indicate a corporateness. The fraternity of scholars, however, may not be quite the same as the fellowship of the Spirit in the church.

In post-Reformation Protestant writers there has been a tendency to contrast the church and the Holy Spirit. This is the premise on which John Owen's 'The Causes, Ways, and Means of Understanding the Mind of God as Revealed in his Word' proceeds. Of course the contrast is primarily with the church of Rome (later in the treatise he allows the use of what he calls 'ecclesiastical helps'), but he is very much concerned with the individual believer. 'My principal design is, to manifest that every believer may, in due use of the means appointed of God for that end, attain unto such a full assurance of understanding in the truth, or all that knowledge of the mind and will of God revealed in the Scripture, which is sufficient to direct him in the life of God, to deliver him from the dangers of ignorance, darkness, and error, and to conduct him unto blessedness.' The principal efficient cause for coming to such an understanding, he says, 'is an especial work of the Spirit of God on the minds of men, communicating spiritual wisdom, light, and understanding unto them, necessary unto their discerning and apprehending aright the mind of God in his word, and the understanding of the mysteries of heavenly truth contained therein'.[11]

It could be suggested that Owen was particularly concerned with how an individual could come to a knowledge of the truth in a confused situation where many heresies and errors might be prevalent. What he says in this respect seems fully justified by the Bible. Yet he also acknowledges 'many who are *truly enlightened* and sanctified by him [i.e. the Spirit] do yet fall into sundry *errors* and mistakes, which the differences and divisions among themselves do openly proclaim.'[12] In the continuing growth in understanding necessary for Christian maturity he would undoubtedly place an emphasis on the fellowship of the church, as well as the use of the writings of what he calls *'persons holy and learned* who have gone before us in the investigation of the truth, ... whether of *old* or of *late'*.[13]

In the twentieth century *the focus shifted from the author on to the readers*, sometimes almost exclusively so. It is surprising that in biblical hermeneutics little attention was paid to readers in the past. If I am justified in including understanding the Bible under the rubric of the ministry of the Holy Spirit then it is specifically at this point that integration between the work of the Spirit and hermeneutics occurs.

It is evident that people read the Bible for a variety of reasons and purposes. Books on hermeneutics appear to assume that hermeneutics is the province of students; even at the popular level, understanding the Bible is thought of in terms of Bible study. It is of course recognized that a large number of those studying the Bible will be ministers preparing sermons and addresses, but it still seems to be assumed that there is only one way of approaching the Bible and that is the way of the student. This, of course, is closely linked to the dominance of grammatical/historical study and the perceived need to begin with the historical locus of the author and his writing. On the other hand, most people reading the Bible, and probably those reading it with the greatest seriousness, neither approach it in that way nor think of themselves as students in any academic sense.

On the surface all this seems remarkably strange. It is both possible and legitimate to study the plays of Shakespeare as an exercise in literary criticism, and presumably to become quite an expert without ever having seen one of them on stage. Still, as Shakespeare wrote them as *plays* this must mean that a whole dimension of understanding is bound to be missed, and the real power and character of his work not appreciated. Many people who have never studied literary criticism in their lives nevertheless have an understanding and appreciation of these plays according to the purpose for which they were written. For an all-round understanding doubtless attendance at the theatre and literary criticism are both necessary.

One of the recent gains in hermeneutical study is canonical criticism which sees the biblical writings as the canon of religious writings which function to express and guide the religious thinking first of the Jewish nation and then the Christian church. Applying the illustration about Shakespeare it seems evident that if the writings brought together as the Bible have been brought together because of the way they function in religious community then, at the least, study of the Bible ought not to overlook this fact. Most of the letters of Paul were written to churches, and the reason they have been preserved is because they have continued to function within churches as sources of truth, guidance, devotion, warning and so on. It is at least possible to argue that a better understanding of one of Paul's letters might be reached by studying how it ought to function today within the churches, than by trying to reconstruct the situation to which it was originally written.[14]

The point that is being made here is that the Bible is read for a whole variety of reasons, personal and corporate, but naturally most of these reasons are religious. It continues to have the place that it does because it is found to be a resource for people with a whole range of religious questions and needs, and because it functions as it has always done as the primary resource for the faith and devotion of the churches. Any study of the Bible and attempt to understand it which does not give a large place to the consideration of how it actually functions in the lives of people and the churches is bound to be one-sided and inadequate. And it is supremely this area that in the New Testament is the province of the ministry of the Holy Spirit.

At this point it is possible to pick up the earlier discussion about the purposes and functions of the biblical writings. The New Testament writers looked upon the scriptures as being written for the learning of those who came after as well as the immediate addressees.[15] Paul considered the scripture as profitable for teaching, reproof, correction, instruction in righteousness so that God's people might be complete and fully equipped for every good work.[16] Moreover the writers considered that the scriptures could function in this way because they were written by men of God who were guided and helped by the Holy Spirit. Thus there was a presumption in their minds that they would find religious, spiritual help in those writings. For the same reason, following their example, Christian people have always turned to the Bible for the same purpose. So the purposes of scripture are matched by the spiritual needs of those who read it most avidly. In the process of understanding, which such people need supremely, there is the promise of the Holy Spirit's help. In this respect the work of the Holy Spirit can legitimately be thought of as creating a spiritual awareness and sensitivity to the suitability of the appropriate text for the particular need and enabling a believing appropriation of it.

This leads on to a note about reader-response theories and the work of the Spirit in hermeneutics. Firstly, it can be suggested that the emergence of reader-response views came at a time when a genre of literature was being produced which required the reader to interact with the text in a creative way, the leaders in this respect being James Joyce and T. S. Eliot.[17] This suggests the possibility that some of the biblical writings may require an imaginative involvement on the part of the reader that goes beyond a simple concern to establish the original meaning of the text. It is possible to suggest that this may be the case with a book like Job, or with some of the parables.

This can also be linked with some of the emphases that belong more to a literary approach to hermeneutics. The idea of the text drawing the reader into its world and enabling him imaginatively to experience the dramatic situation being described is very similar to what has been described above. Such approaches to the Bible, or more accurately to certain genres within the biblical writings, are important for gaining a full understanding of the text. They are also approaches which have a close affinity with the ministry of the Spirit, depending as they do on sensitivity to the text, to the artistry and spiritual insight of the author, and the power of the written word to evoke images and feeling.

Finally, *the work of the Spirit can be considered in relation to discussion of the fusing of the two horizons.* Especially since the publication of Thiselton's book, it has been customary to think of understanding in terms of the merging, or fusing, of the horizons of author and reader; though this is not construed as something final, but rather leading to an ongoing, ever more refined understanding, sometimes understood in terms of a hermeneutical spiral.[18]

A hermeneutic which emphasizes the ministry of the Holy Spirit in understanding appears to present certain ways in which the sense of distantiation between the author and readers is at least lessened, and which tend to bring the horizons together. For example, the writers of Scripture are described as spiritual people, that is those indwelt and guided by the Spirit. But then the same is true of Christian readers also; they too are indwelt by the Spirit, and receive guidance and help in understanding by the Spirit; not that the latter is being considered as directly comparable to the guidance of the Spirit in the writing of Scripture. In such a case the possibility of understanding is enhanced. The scriptures were also written from a spiritual perspective. For most readers it is this that they are concerned to know. From the point of view of the content of the Bible there is an affinity between the authors and the readers.

The model of the two horizons ought not to be over-stressed. Looked at from a time perspective, the horizons of modern readers are very far apart from those of all the biblical writers and especially those of the earliest. However it may well be that in an age of great specialization and the fragmentation of knowledge, there are greater 'distances' of understanding to overcome between people within our contemporary culture, than there are over time, and between different cultures, for those with a shared experience, even if the settings of that experience are very different.

How far the 'settings' referred to are important for understanding depends on a number of factors, and may often be relatively unimportant. The command 'You shall not steal' was given in a particular cultural setting, and maybe had specific applications in that setting which time has rendered obsolete, but the command itself is still as clear and relevant to the setting of the present day. It can be argued then that the idea of horizons is at least liable to confuse and complicate. A sensitive understanding of the content may be possible without any real understanding of the setting at all. It is even possible to envisage that there could be a truer insight into the meaning of scripture on the part of someone who was quite mistaken about many matters of grammar and history,[19] than someone who had extensive background knowledge but who was not spiritually attuned to the message being conveyed. The Gospels appear to present a precedent for this also in the picture which they present of the Jewish teachers of the law. It would be possible to argue some of these points even apart from envisaging any ministry of the Holy Spirit. Such a ministry, however, only emphasizes them more and gives a greater reason to stress their importance for biblical hermeneutics.

Conclusion

In a recent book,[20] David Dockery argues that the way forward in biblical hermeneutics is a synthesis of the three perspectives which he calls 'author-oriented', 'reader-oriented' and 'text-oriented'.[21] He also adds, 'We are suggesting that discovering Scripture's meaning involves not only examining the author's result in the written text, but also the Holy Spirit's work of illuminating the reader's mind to interpret the text. With the enablement of the Spirit, discerning a text's meaning and significance is not only possible but plausible.'[22] It is my contention that an examination of the New Testament itself provides the justification for such a position. The corollary is that the work of the Holy Spirit needs to be given a far greater prominence in hermeneutical discussion and that an exploration of biblical hermeneutics from the perspective of what might be called a hermeneutic of the Holy Spirit is likely to prove particularly fruitful.

REFERENCES

Introduction

[1] These words are taken from John 14:15–17, 25–26; 15:25–26; 16:7–15; 1 Corinthians 2:6-16; Ephesians 1:17–19; 1 John 2:20, 21, 27.

[2] In 'Recent Trends in Pneumatology' (*Evangel,* Spring 1989, pp 13-15) Dr Gerald Bray says, 'However, a glance at scholarly publishing will soon show that although it is probably no longer correct to say that the Holy Spirit is "forgotten", he is still a long way from receiving the kind of attention devoted to the Son, or even to the Father, if books on theism in general can be said to relate in some special way to the First Person of the Godhead. Leaving aside works on spiritual gifts, which usually concentrate more on the gifts themselves than the giver, there are only about 20 serious theological studies of the Holy Spirit which have appeared in the 1980s...' (p.13). In his bibliography Bray lists 13 books and 10 articles. Since then, Gordon D. Fee's massive, nearly 1,000 page study in the Holy Spirit in Paul's letters has appeared (*God's Empowering Presence*, Peabody: Hendricksen, 1994).

[3] For example, Wayne Grudem, *The Gift of Prophecy in 1 Corinthians* (Washington DC: University Press of America, 1982; followed by his popularisation *The Gift of Prophecy*, Eastbourne: Kingsway, 1988); David Hill, *New Testament Prophecy* (Atlanta: John Knox Press, 1979); David Aune, *Prophecy in Early Christianity and the Ancient Mediterranean World* (Grand Rapids: Eerdmans, 1983); Max Turner and David MacKinder, 'Prophecy and Spiritual Gifts Then and Now' in I. H. Marshall (ed.), *Christian Experience in Theology and Life* (Edinburgh: Rutherford House Books, 1988). Two more general recent books are Tom Smail's *The Giving Gift* (Hodder and Stoughton, 1988), in which he concentrates on 'the distinct personhood of the Spirit', and Stanley M. Burgess' *The Spirit and the Church: Antiquity* (Volume 1 in a trilogy devoted to the history of Christian pneumatology, Peabody: Hendrickson Publishers, Inc., 1984) in which the author recounts Christian efforts to understand the person and work of the Holy Spirit up to the end of the fifth century. Quotations are so extensive that the book is almost an anthology of writing on the Holy Spirit.

[4] There does not appear to be any book or article of any length which concentrates on this theme. Aspects of it are covered in Gary M. Burge's *The Anointed Community, The Holy Spirit in the Johannine Tradition* (Grand Rapids: Eerdmans, 1987).

⁵ H. B. Swete in his book *The Holy Spirit in the New Testament* (Macmillan, London, 1910) is able to survey all the references to the Holy Spirit adequately, though not of course at great depth, in 400 pages.

⁶ For example, Matthew 16:17; John 6:45; 1 Corinthians 2:14; Ephesians 2:1–3; 4:17–19. Berkouwer writes: 'It is not difficult to see why, in connection with salvation and certainty, the church's reflection and discussion always centered on the Holy Spirit. From the Word of God it increasingly learned to understand better that certainty of faith was by no means a self-evident human correlate of revelation by natural rational insight. The biblical-pneumatological aspect of faith, knowledge, trust and certainty is clearly seen in the fact that faith and knowledge do not come from "flesh and blood" (see Matt.16:17), and in the radical and revealing statement that "no-one comprehends the thoughts of God except the Spirit of God" (1 Cor.2:11). According to the New Testament, certainty can never be explained in terms of the receptivity of the human heart or its capacity to reassure itself and convince itself of the truth. In the words of Paul, it is God himself who has revealed it to us through the Spirit, who "searches everything, even the depths of God" (1 Cor.2:10). The Spirit is given "that we might understand the gifts bestowed on us by God" (v.12). We need to be "taught by the Spirit" (v.13), since "the unspiritual man does not receive the gift of the Spirit of God" and is thus unable to understand them (vv.14,15)' (G.C. Berkouwer; 'The Testimony of the Spirit' in Donald McKim (ed.), *The Authoritative Word* [Grand Rapids: Eerdmans, 1983,] p.164).

⁷ Bray, *op.cit.*, says, 'A curious feature of recent writing is that much of the traditional understanding of the Holy Spirit has given way to new concerns and emphases. However, there are some articles which continue to examine more classical themes, such as G.C. Berkouwer's *The Testimony of the Spirit*, a discussion of the role of the Holy Spirit in Biblical interpretation' (p.15). An older book like George S. Hendry's *The Holy Spirit in Christian Theology* (London: SCM Press), has a chapter on 'The Holy Spirit and the Word'.

⁸ 'Calvin replaced the voice of the Church, which supposedly tells us with great assurance that the Scriptures are the Word of God, with the *internal witness of the Holy Spirit*' (Bernard Ramm, *The Witness of the Spirit* [Grand Rapids: Eerdmans, 1960] p.12; italics in original). John Calvin, *Institutes of the Christian Religion*, Book 1:VII. Anthony N.S. Lane, 'John Calvin: The Witness of the Holy

Spirit', in *Faith and Ferment* (Papers read at the Westminster Conference, 1982).

[9] Ramm (*op. cit.* p.7) writes, 'The impulse to write this book comes directly from writing "*The Pattern of Religious Authority*". In working through the materials for that book it became apparent that the doctrine of the internal witness of the Holy Spirit had almost disappeared from evangelical literature and theology, and that this disappearance was unfortunate for both the spirit and methodology of that theology.'

[10] Burgess' book referred to in fn.3 above describes itself as 'a study of the order/prophecy tension – a struggle between major and minor traditions' (p.7), though it is more than that. G.F. Nuttall in *The Holy Spirit in Puritan Faith and Experience* (Oxford: Basil Blackwell, 1946; reprinted University of Chicago Press, 1992) covers the ground in a specific historical context.

[11] John Owen, *The Causes, Ways, and Means of Understanding the Mind of God as Revealed in His Word*, in *Works* (Edinburgh: Banner of Truth, 1974) vol.4, pp.121–234.

[12] 'As God, the Holy Spirit is a unique person. But He is not an independent divinity side by side with the unique Word of God. He is simply the Teacher of the Word: of that Word which is never without its Teacher. When it is a matter of instructing and instruction by the Word, that instructing and instruction are the work of the Holy Spirit' (Karl Barth, *Church Dogmatics*, Vol.1 *The Doctrine of the Word of God*, 2nd half-volume [Edinburgh: T.&T. Clark, 1956], p.243).

[13] 'Rather the absolute, no, God was present in His Word as the Lord, as the One who commands and the One who shows mercy, as in the human word of the Bible' (*ibid*, p.499). Also T. E. Provence, 'The Sovereign Subject Matter: Hermeneutics in the Church Dogmatics', in D. McKim (ed.), *A Guide to Contemporary Hermeneutics* (Grand Rapids: Eerdmans, 1986).

[14] See Anthony C. Thiselton, *The Two Horizons* (Exeter: Paternoster Press, 1980), pp. 88–90. In Barth's thinking the Bible becomes the Word of God as it mediates the presence of Christ: 'the human side of its life with the Bible can consist only in the fact that it prays that the Bible may be the Word of God here and now, that there may take place that work of the Holy Spirit.... the fulfilment of this prayer, that the Bible is the Word of God here and now in virtue of the eternal, hidden, heavenly presence of Christ' (Barth, *op. cit.* p.514).

[15] Referring to two earlier standard works on biblical interpretation,

Klein, Blomberg and Hubbard Jr. say, 'developments since the 1960s have been so profuse and so pervasive that current students find those volumes out of date in many ways. Today a serious student of biblical interpretation faces an imposing quantity and range of books and articles'. (W.W. Klein, C.L. Blomberg, R.L. Hubbard Jr., *Introduction to Biblical Interpretation* [Dallas: Word Publishing, 1993], p.xix).

[16] This was the way in which hermeneutics was understood in the protestant tradition. So, for example, Milton S. Terry's *Biblical Hermeneutics*, which appears to have been published around the turn of the century (reprinted Grand Rapids: Zondervan, 1983).

[17] 'hermeneutics concerns not only the interpretation of texts, but the interpretation and understanding of any act of communication, whether written or oral, verbal or non-verbal (such as symbols or symbolic acts). Biblical hermeneutics is a specific area which concerns the interpretation, understanding and appropriation of biblical texts. Second, theorists are no longer content to speak of rules for the interpretation of texts, as if to imply that understanding can be generated merely by the mechanical application of purely scientific principles. Hermeneutics raises prior and more fundamental questions about the very nature of language, meaning, communication and understanding. The subject thus involves an examination of the whole interpretative process' (A.C. Thiselton, 'Hermeneutics' in Ferguson and Wright (eds.), *New Dictionary of Theology* [Leicester: IVP, 1988], p.293).

[18] There has been a recent concentration on literary approaches to understanding the Bible; for example: Robert Alter and Frank Kermode (eds.), *The Literary Guide to the Bible* (London: Fontana, 1989); T.R. Wright, *Theology and Literature* (Oxford: Blackwell, 1988); Stephen Prickett, *Words and the Word* (Cambridge: Cambridge University Press, 1988); Patrick Grant, *Reading the New Testament* (London: Macmillan, 1989); Tremper Longman III, *Literary Approaches to Biblical Interpretation* (Leicester: Apollos, 1987). A new direction in hermeneutics has been taken by Peter Cotterell and Max Turner in *Linguistics and Biblical Interpretation* (London: SPCK, 1989). A trend towards linking hermeneutics and preaching is seen in Sidney Greidanus, *The Modern Preacher and the Ancient Text* (Leicester: IVP/Eerdmans, 1988) and Elliott E. Johnson, *Expository Hermeneutics* (Grand Rapids: Academie/Zondervan, 1990).

[19] E.g. John Painter, *Theology as Hermeneutics: Rudolf Bultmann's Interpretation of the History of Jesus* (The Almond Press, 1987).

[20] Jose Miguez Bonino, 'Hermeneutics, Truth and Praxis', in D. McKim (ed.) *A Guide to Contemporary Hermeneutics* (Grand Rapids: Eerdmans, 1986). In the same volume Elisabeth Schussler Fiorenza in her section entitled 'Towards a Feminist Biblical Hermeneutic: Biblical Interpretation and Liberation Theology' writes, 'In conclusion, liberation theologians must abandon the hermeneutic-contextual paradigm of biblical interpretation, and construct within the context of a critical theology of liberation, a new interpretative paradigm that has as its aim emancipatory praxis' (p.381).

[21] Patrick R. Keifert, 'Mind Reader and Maestro: Models for Understanding Biblical Interpreters', *op.cit*. Robert Morgan has also recently emphasized the importance of the aims of interpreters and the uses of the Bible in his book with John Barton, *Biblical Interpretation* (Oxford: Oxford University Press, 1989).

[22] 'Hermeneutics, therefore is never *only* a matter of understanding, but also of *hearing* and of *appropriation*' (A.C. Thiselton, *The Two Horizons*, p.287).

[23] 'As the Lord's own Baptism had been followed by His ministry in Galilee, so the Baptism of the Church was to be preparatory to a world-wide ministry: a ministry, not like His own, creative of a new order, but one of simple testimony; yet only to be fulfilled in the power of the Spirit of God' (H.B. Swete, *op. cit.* p.66).

[24] 'Infallible Scripture and the Role of Hermeneutics' in D.A. Carson and John D. Woodbridge (eds.), *Scripture and Truth* (Leicester: IVP, 1983), p.347.

[25] Romans 8:13-14; Galatians 5:16–25; Ephesians.5:18; 1 Thessalonians.4:7–8; James 4:5; 1 Peter1:2. 'The presence and working of the Spirit of God are no longer conceived of as rare and isolated phenomena, but as entering into all Christian thought and work, an element in life so universal, so constantly meeting the observer, that the briefest of names (the Spirit) was sufficient to indicate it' (Swete, *op. cit.* p.287).

[26] Thiselton, *The Two Horizons*, p.92.

[27] Francis Watson, *Text, Church and World* (Edinburgh: T & T Clark, 1994), p.17.

[28] Swete, *op. cit.* From the Preface.

[29] See, for example, J.N.D. Kelly, *A Commentary on the Pastoral Epistles*, BNTC (London: A. & C. Black, 1963); T.C. Oden, *First and Second Timothy and Titus*, Interpretation (Louisville: John Knox Press, 1989); Oden says, 'Now I am convinced that many in my own generation prematurely accepted the premise of non-Pauline authorship of the Pastorals without adequately examining the evidence for Pauline authorship' (p.10).

[30] See Ralph P. Martin, *Ephesians, Colossians, and Philemon*, Interpretation (Louisville: John Knox Press, 1992); also Andrew T. Lincoln, *Ephesians*, WBC (Dallas: Word Books, 1990).

[31] 'Another solution to the problem of the differences in vocabulary and style between the PE and the other Paulines is that a secretary or amanuensis wrote the letters under Paul's authority but did so in such a way as to have an impact upon the language and style of the letters' (George W. Knight III, *The Pastoral Epistles*, NIGTC [Grand Rapids and Carlisle: Eerdmans/Paternoster, 1992], p.48). Knight himself concludes in favour of Pauline authorship.

[32] Arthur G. Patzia, 'The Deutero-Pauline Hypothesis: An Attempt at Clarification', in *Evangelical Quarterly 52* (Exeter: Paternoster Press,1980), pp.27-42,.

[33] A. Thiselton, *New Horizons in Hermeneutics* (London: Harper/Collins, 1992), p.619.

Chapter 1: The Synoptic Gospels

[1] This, of course, raises the question of the Synoptic problem. Although the two-source theory (Mark and Q, the latter sometimes called the 'double tradition') is still widely held and is the more customary way of understanding the evidence, there is a note of caution sounded today: 'Now a great many scholars would prefer to talk of Q material rather than Q ... the contradictions in which we land ourselves as soon as we try to draw up more exactly the contents of this hypothetical document warn us that it is better to leave the matter a little vague rather than to seek for certainty where certainty is not to be had' (Stephen Neill and Tom Wright, *The Interpretation of the New Testament* 1861–1986 [Oxford: Oxford University Press, 1988], pp. 145–146). 'Especially important is the need to be open to the possibility that, in a given pericope, an explanation based on the two-source hypothesis may not fit the facts. For a given text we thus may conclude that Matthew is more primitive than Mark, or that Luke has

followed a special eye-witness source rather than Mark, or that Matthew has relied on his own remembrance or written notes rather than Q' (D.A. Carson, D.J. Moo and L. Morris, *An Introduction to the New Testament* [Grand Rapids: Apollos, 1992], p. 38).

[2] 'Christian truth' is used as a broad description of the content of the revelation of God and his will, especially as it relates to the person and mission of Jesus Christ.

[3] The *Revised English Bible* (Oxford University Press and Cambridge University Press, 1989).

[4] Bauer, Arndt, Gingrich and Danker, *A Greek-English Lexicon of the New Testament* (Chicago and London: University of Chicago Press, 1979).

[5] H. N. Ridderbos, *Matthew*, trans. Ray Togtman (Grand Rapids: Regency/Zondervan, 1987), p. 138. So also Suzanne de Dietrich, *Saint Matthew*, LBC (London: SCM Press, 1961), p. 44. R. V. G. Tasker (*The Gospel according to St. Matthew*, TNTC[London: Tyndale Press, 1961], speaks of 'their spiritual sense', (p. 75). It may seem too bald a statement to say that 'the eye is an analogue for the heart' (W. C. Allen (*Matthew*, ICC [Edinburgh: T. & T. Clark, 1907]) says: 'The idea here is the naive one that the eye is the organ through which light has access to the whole body, and that there is a spiritual eye through which spiritual light enters and illuminates the whole personality. This spiritual eye must be kept sound, or else light cannot enter, and the inner man dwells in darkness' (p. 62). However, there is no actual spiritual eye which allows light to illuminate the inner man and we are forced to concentrate upon the heart which is either good or bad.

[6] *The Holy Bible, New King James Version.*

[7] 'In the Jewish context, to "see God" is to appear in his presence, to enjoy unbroken communion with him' (F. W. Beare, *The Gospel according to Matthew* [London: Basil Blackwell, 1981], p. 133). Is 'seeing God', then, to be understood in an eschatological sense here? The setting of this saying in the Beatitudes, which are themselves an introduction to a discourse whose leading theme is the kingdom of heaven, suggests that the answer is 'yes' in the sense that the kingdom has come in Jesus, and yet has not come as it will yet come. 'We should rather consider the characteristic and peculiar nature of Jesus' preaching to be his proclamation of the kingdom in its consummative eschatological significance both as a present and as a future reality. The fulfilment is there, and yet the kingdom is still to come. The

kingdom has come, and yet the fulfilment is in abeyance' (H.
Ridderbos, *The Coming of the Kingdom*, trans. H. de Jongste
[Philadelphia: Presbyterian and Reformed Pub. Assn., 1962], p. 106).
'Seeing God' includes then the present experience of those to whom
the kingdom has come.
      [8] *Holy Bible, New International Version* (London: Hodder and
Stoughton, 1986).
      [9] 'In the Gospels the term *Holy Spirit* (along with "the Spirit",
"Spirit of God", "Paraclete", etc.) is a referring expression for the
power and presence of God in action, especially as the means of
God's self-revelation' (M. B. B. Turner, 'Holy Spirit' in J. B. Green,
S. McKnight and I. H. Marshall (eds.), *Dictionary of Jesus and the
Gospels* [Leicester: IVP, 1992], p. 341). 'St Luke tells us that Jesus
returned from the Jordan "in the power of the Spirit" into Galilee
(4:14) and St Peter in Acts (10:38f.) tells how God anointed Him (in
the Baptism) "with the holy spirit and power"; and it is under these
conditions that the Evangelists conceive this whole ministry to be
fulfilled. If they do not mention the Spirit at every step, it is because
they think of Him as in full possession of it continually' (James Denney,
'Holy Spirit' in J. Hastings (ed.), *Dictionary of Christ and the
Gospels* [Edinburgh: T. & T. Clark, 1906], Vol. 1, p. 732).
      [10] N. Geldenhuys, *Commentary on the Gospel of Luke* (London:
Marshall, Morgan & Scott, 1956), pp. 306–307. Against this Beare
says, 'The contrast "wise and prudent" as against "babes" can only
mean the contrast between the schooled and the unschooled' (*op.
cit.*, p. 265). This, however, is a matter of judgment and there seems
no reason in the text to understand the contrast in this way. Calvin
notes 'brilliant minds are often so hindered that they cannot allow
themselves to be taught' (Calvin's Commentaries, *A Harmony of
the Gospels, Matthew, Mark, Luke*, Vol. II, trans. by T. H. L. Parker
[Edinburgh: St Andrew Press, 1972], p. 22).
      [11] 'That Jesus included in his thanksgiving the Father's hiding things
from the wise should not shock us. This hiding is the dark side of
grace, a foil to God's revelation to the infants' (R. H. Gundry, *Matthew,
A Commentary on His Literary and Theological Art* [Grand Rapids:
Eerdmans, 1982], p. 216).
      [12] S. de Dietrich, *op. cit.,* pp. 72–73. So also Gundry (*op. cit.,* p.
217) comments, 'All in all, knowledge of personal identity – knowledge
that is intimate and personal identity that includes character – best

fits the requirement of the text, especially the exclusiveness and reciprocal nature of the knowledge and the more-than-common usage of the term "Father" with which the passage begins.'

[13] BAGD, p. 291.

[14] Calvin, *op. cit.*, pp. 23–24.

[15] 'A mystery in the New Testament is not something hard to understand, but something hidden, revealed only to the initiated' (E. P. Gould, *Mark*, ICC [Edinburgh: T. & T. Clark, 1901], p. 71).

[16] J. A. Alexander, *Mark* (reprinted Banner of Truth Trust, 1960), p. 71.

[17] L. Morris, *Luke*, TNTC (London: Inter-Varsity Press, 1974), p.152.

[18] Calvin, *op. cit.,* p. 67.

[19] R. T. France, *Matthew*, TNTC (Leicester/Grand Rapids: IVP/ Eerdmans, 1985), p. 224.

[20] W. C. Allen, *op. cit.*, p. 147.

[21] Vincent Taylor's comments are interesting at this point: 'What Mark does is to distinguish revelation to the disciples and concealment from the crowd, and for this view he has warrant in the Q sayings in Luke 10:21 = Matt. 11:25f. and Luke 10:23f. = Matt. 13:16f.' Taylor is particularly explaining 'Mark's meaning ... that ... the purpose of the parables is to conceal the truth and to prevent repentance and forgiveness' (Vincent Taylor, *The Gospel according to St Mark, the Greek Text with Introduction, Notes and Indexes* [London: Macmillan, 1952], p. 257).

[22] Calvin, *op. cit.*, p. 185.

[23] de Dietrich, *op. cit.*, p. 93. Mark 8:13–21 shows how the disciples often failed to understand the words of Jesus and to interpret his acts aright.

[24] Daniel Patte writes: 'But being a disciple is not sufficient; one still needs to receive a revelation from the Father' (*The Gospel according to Matthew: A Structural Commentary on Matthew's Faith* [Philadelphia: Fortress Press, 1987], p. 232).

[25] Ridderbos, *op. cit.*, p. 311.

[26] Beare says, 'The verb φρονέω (φρονειτε, "you are set on") is used of the inward disposition, the whole cast of mind and feeling – a "visceral" rather than a mental attitude.... It is not the mind as the seat of conscious thought that is intended, but the heart and will. The accusation is not that Peter has some wrong ideas, but that his outlook

is governed by ambitions and desires which belong to the realm of Satan, not by whole-hearted acceptance of the will of God' (Beare, *op. cit.*, p. 259). There is some truth here, though it is doubtful if the use of the verb φρονέω allows for such a clear-cut contrast between the mind and the heart and will.

[27] France, *op. cit.*, p. 264.

[28] Vernon C. Grounds states: 'In Christianity, as I see it, paradox is not a concession: it is an indispensable category, a sheer necessity – a logical necessity' ('The Postulate of Paradox' in *Bulletin of the Evangelical Theological Society*, No. 1 [Winter 1964], p. 5), quoted in A. A. Hoekema *Saved by Grace* (Grand Rapids and Exeter: Eerdmans/Paternoster, 1989), p. 7. From a different perspective, I. H. Marshall, discussing perseverance and falling away, says, 'The New Testament is content to hold together the facts of perseverance and apostasy in paradox' *(Kept by the Power of God* [London: Epworth Press, 1969], p. 207). See also D.A. Carson, *Divine Sovereignty and Human Responsibility* (Marshall Pickering, 1994).

[29] 'the references in none of the four gospels can be said to be prolific. Indeed, in view of the multiplicity of references in the Acts and epistles, it is surprising that the gospels contain so few references' (Donald Guthrie, *New Testament Theology* [Leicester: IVP, 1981], p. 514).

[30] James D. G. Dunn, *Jesus and the Spirit* (London: SCM, 1975).

[31] 'All four accounts directly link with baptism the anointing of Jesus with the Spirit and the declaration of his sonship. It is this anointing that inaugurates the ministry of Jesus which will be characterized by the power of the Spirit of the new age (Matt. 12:18, 28; Luke 4:18; 11:20; Acts 10:28)' (D. Dockery, 'Baptism', in J. B .Green, S. McKnight, I. H. Marshall (eds.), *Dictionary of Jesus and the Gospels* [Leicester: IVP, 1992], p. 57).

[32] J. Dunn, *op. cit.*, p. 54.

[33] 'A major strand of Judaism anticipated a Messiah mightily endowed with the Spirit as both the Spirit of prophecy (affording unique wisdom and knowledge of the Lord on the basis of dynamic righteousness) and the Spirit of power. The model is first David, then more especially the Davidic figure of Isaiah 11:1–4, endowed with the Spirit of wisdom, knowledge and power' (M. B. B. Turner, 'Holy Spirit' in *Dictionary of Jesus and the Gospels*, p. 342).

[34] Plummer, on Luke 3:16 says, 'The passage is one of many, the

exact meaning of which must remain doubtful' (*Luke*, ICC, [Edinburgh: T. & T. Clark, 1901], p. 95). So also Guthrie, 'It is difficult to be sure what John the Baptist had in mind, but at least the importance of the Spirit's role is indisputable' (*op. cit.*, p. 516).

[35] So Dockery (*op. cit.*, p. 55) and Turner (*op. cit.*, p. 344); others refer to Malachi 3:2f., so de Dietrich (*op. cit.*, p. 22); France (*op. cit.*, p. 93); Taylor (*op. cit.*, p. 157); Alexander Jones, *The Gospel according to Matthew* (London: Geoffrey Chapman, 1965), p. 61. Denney (*op. cit.*, p. 731) thinks that later evangelists have added the words 'with fire' in the light of the post-Pentecostal experiences.

[36] Denney, *op. cit.*, p. 731.

[37] D. G. Miller, *St Luke*, LBC (London: SCM Press, 1966), p. 49.

[38] Dunn, *op. cit.*, p. 47–48.

[39] Denney, *op. cit.*, p. 733.

[40] Turner, *op. cit.*, p. 347.

[41] Patte, *op. cit.*, p. 150.

[42] Miller, *op. cit.*, p. 107

[43] 'By far the most widespread understanding of the Spirit in Judaism is as "the Spirit of Prophecy" (a regular term for the Spirit, especially in the Targums), in other words, the Spirit acting as the organ of communication between God and a person' (Turner, *op. cit.*, p. 342).

[44] Guthrie says, 'In his teaching Jesus prepared his disciples for the age of the Spirit ... there is some indication in the synoptics of exciting possibilities: *provision is made for guidance in apologetic, for a right approach to the OT*, for ability to overcome adverse spiritual forces for power in witness' (*op. cit.*, p. 525; *my italics*).

Chapter 2: Luke and Acts

[1] This excludes possible references in 1:17 (*cf.* 2 Kings 2:9, 15) and 1:80.

[2] Joseph A. Fitzmyer, *The Gospel according to Luke I-IX*, AB (New York: S. J. Doubleday & Company Inc., 1981), p. 228.

[3] 'There are fifty-seven occasions when πνεῦμα almost certainly refers to the Divine Spirit' (J. H. E. Hull, *The Holy Spirit in Acts of the Apostles* [London: Lutterworth Press, 1967], p. 189). The figure omits the possible addition of 18:25; 19:21. So also Fitzmyer, *op. cit.*, p. 227.

[4] I. H. Marshall, *The Gospel of Luke*, NIGTC (Exeter: Paternoster Press, 1978), p. 58.

[5] 'The idiom Πιμπλάναι πνεύματος ἁγίου (with or without the article and without regard for word order) is found three times in the infancy narratives, five times in Acts, and not in the rest of the NT or LXX' (John Nolland, *Luke 1–9:20*, WBC, 35A [Dallas: Word Books, 1989], p. 30). The references are 1:15, 41, 67; Acts 2:4; 4:8, 31; 7:55; 13:9. 7:55 is commented on later. The continuous sense of the verb in Ephesians 5:18 makes it significantly different.

[6] Nolland, *op. cit.*, p. 66.

[7] Marshall, *op. cit.*, p. 70.

[8] William F. Arndt, *The Gospel according to Luke* (St Louis: Concordia Publishing House, 1956), p. 66. So also Nolland, *op. cit.*, p. 84, Geldenhuys, *op. cit.*, p. 93, Miller, *op. cit.*, p. 33.

[9] Nolland, *op. cit.*, p. 119–120.

[10] Fitzmyer, *op. cit.*, p. 437.

[11] Turner, *op. cit.*, p. 344. So also Swete, p. 37: 'Thus the Spirit in the Boy is seen at once illuminating thought and prompting to duty, opening the mind to the mysteries of God, and at the same time, urging the regular discharge of the responsibilities of an obscure and monotonous life.' James Dunn calls this 'quite probable, though not certain' (*Baptism in the Holy Spirit* [London: SCM Press, 1970], p. 24).

[12] Fitzmyer, *Luke X-XXIV*, AB (New York: Doubleday, 1985), p. 1580.

[13] F. Godet, *The Gospel of St Luke* ([Edinburgh: T. & T. Clark, 1870], Vol.2, p. 259–260).

[14] Plummer, *Luke*, ICC (Edinburgh: T. & T. Clark, 1901), p. 562; Arndt, *op. cit.*, p. 497.

[15] Fitzmyer, *op. cit.*, p.1580. Swete makes a similar point, 'As the Lord's own baptism had been followed by His Ministry in Galilee, so the Baptism of the Church was to be preparatory to a world-wide ministry, a ministry not, like his own, creative of a new order but one of simple testimony; yet only to be fulfilled in the power of the Spirit of God' (*op. cit.*, p. 66).

[16] J. Denney, 'Holy Spirit' in J. Hastings (ed.), *Dictionary of Christ and the Gospels* (Edinburgh: T. & T. Clark, 1906), Vol. 1, p. 738. Swete also comments, 'The chrism which followed baptism in the ancient church bore witness to the belief that every Christian receives from the Head of the Church the same Divine Unction that descended on the Christ' (*op. cit.*, p. 49); and Dunn, *op. cit.*, p. 96,

'To become a Christian, in short, is to receive the Spirit of Christ, the Holy Spirit.'

[17] I. H. Marshall (*Acts*, TNTC [Leicester: Inter-Varsity Press, 1980]) takes 'through the Holy Spirit' with 'whom he had chosen' (p. 57, footnote). However, Lenski (*The Acts of the Apostles* [Minneapolis: Augsburg Publishing House, 1961) points out, 'We do not read that the election of the apostles was connected with the Spirit' (p. 22).

[18] Denney, *op. cit.*, p. 736–737: 'It [Acts 1:2] seems to suggest that with the Resurrection the dispensation of the Holy Spirit began, and that the disciples were conscious, as they listened to the new and final charge of their Lord that they were in contact, as they had never been before, with the powers of the world to come (Heb. 6:5), the Divine inspiration of the Messianic Age.'

[19] 'And in order that what Christ commanded them might receive the greater reverence, he adds that this was done by the direction of the Holy Spirit. And this, not because the Son of God, who is eternal Wisdom, required to be guided by any other, but because He was also man, that no one should think that what He delivered to the apostles came forth from a human spirit, He recalls us expressly to the authority of God. Just as the Lord Himself so often affirmed, that He taught nothing except what He received from the Father, and therefore declared that His teaching was not His own. He makes clear therefore that in the preaching of the Gospel there is nothing which derives from man, but it is a divine ordinance of the Spirit to which the whole world must be subject' (Calvin, *The Acts 1-13* [Edinburgh: Saint Andrew Press, 1965], p. 23–24).

[20] D. J. Williams, *Acts*, NIBC (Peabody: Hendrickson, 1985), pp. 23–24. So also Lenski, 'In the sense in which the apostles were witnesses no others were or could be' (*op. cit.*, p. 31).

[21] Williams says, 'What happened at this Pentecost marked the beginning of the church. There were, of course, many believers before this, but only now were they constituted as the "body of Christ" ' (*op. cit.*, p. 44). 'In the full sense of the Church in vigorous life, redeemed by the cross of Christ, invigorated by the divine power, set forth on the path of work and worship, the Church certainly did not come into existence until the day of Pentecost' (L. Morris, *Spirit of the Living God* [London: Inter-Varsity, 1960], pp. 54f.). R. B. Rackham distinguishes between the birth of the church and its second birth, or baptism. This distinction is doubtful and makes no essential difference

to understanding the Pentecost narrative (*The Acts of the Apostles* [London: Methuen, 1901], p. 15).

[22] Swete, *op. cit.*, p.79: 'The Pentecostal outpouring of the Holy Spirit was far more than a miraculous display of spiritual power, intended to arrest attention and invite inquiry into the new faith. It was the beginning of a new era; an advent of the Spirit, as the Incarnation was the advent of the Son.' James Dunn, speaking of Paul's teaching says, 'The Corinthians knew they were members of one body because the metaphors of "being baptised in one Spirit" and of being "drenched in one Spirit" were living realities in their common experience and memory ("all").... In Paul's development of the metaphor [body], however, it becomes an expression not simply of community but specifically of charismatic community' (*Jesus and the Spirit*, p. 261–262).

[23] Denney (*op. cit.*, p. 737): 'St Peter's sermon in Acts 2 is a specimen of Christian prophecy' and Lenski (*op. cit.*, p. 74): 'The chief effect of the Spirit's activity is always prophesying, not in the narrow sense of fore-telling future events, but in the broad and far more important sense of voicing the saving and blessed will of God for men everywhere.'

[24] Denney's words in the previous footnote continue: 'The Spirit enables him to read the OT (Joel and the Psalms) in a Christian sense, and to find in it Jesus and the Messianic age' (*ibid.*). Swete, in commenting on Acts 1:16, says, 'But it is new to find one of the Eleven interpreting the Psalms as prophetic of events in the life of Jesus; that he could do so even before the coming of the Spirit seems to be due to the impression left upon his mind by the teaching of the risen Lord. In the sequel we shall see to what purpose the same apostle uses this new key to the understanding of the Psalms and the Prophets when the Spirit of Christ has opened his mind yet further to see the ultimate purpose of OT prophecy' (*op. cit.*, p. 67).

[25] Williams, *op. cit.*, p. 110.

[26] Rackham (*op. cit.*, p. 83) quotes from Chrysostom here, 'It needed great philosophy to bear the complaints of the widows.'

[27] Williams, *op. cit.*, p. 122. So also Calvin, 'Therefore interpret those words like this: they were not able to withstand the wisdom with which the Spirit of God supplied him' (*op. cit.*, I. p.166). REB actually translates by 'inspired wisdom'.

[28] Hull, *op. cit.*, p. 147.

[29] Hull says, 'It is even more significant that for "filled with" here Luke does not use πλησθείς, a word we have previously encountered connoting a "special filling" with the Spirit, but ὑπάρχων (lit. "being constantly full of"), which signifies a permanent state' (*op. cit.*, p. 166). This links with what is said of Stephen in 6:5.

[30] Williams, *op. cit.*, p. 146.

[31] Jesus himself also referred to the Son of Man prophecy, Luke 22:69 (par.). In the case of both Jesus and Stephen this was the final straw that led to their deaths.

[32] Swete, *op. cit.*, p. 93.

[33] Marshall: 'These are two features that one might expect in a divine revelation. The bright light is to be understood as an expression of divine glory' (*op. cit.*, p. 169). Williams: 'Light is often associated in Scripture with the revelation of God (*cf.* 12:7), and this was clearly the case here' (*op. cit.*, p. 168).

[34] Rackham: 'the spiritual experience which this denotes was symbolised by St. Paul's own bodily experience, when sight was restored to his bodily eyes' (*op. cit.*, p. 409). Williams: 'There may be some play intended on the idea of his spiritual blindness before and his physical blindness after his conversion' (*op. cit.*, p. 419).

[35] Calvin, *op. cit.*, II, p. 276.

[36] Rackham, *op. cit.*, p. 283.

[37] The same word διανοίγειν is used.

[38] Calvin, *op. cit.*, II, p. 101.

[39] Hull, *op. cit.*, p. 132–133.

Chapter 3: John's Gospel

[1] As with the Synoptics and Pauline literature it is not possible to discuss critical questions concerning authorship and provenance. G. R. Beasley-Murray reflects widespread opinion when he writes, 'As the authority figure to which the Johannine communities looked, the Beloved Disciple appears to have had a group of teachers about him. The existence of a Johannine literature alongside the Gospel, including the three epistles and the Book of Revelation, points to a group of teachers having a common centre of loyalty, with a diversity not too great to be contained within the unity' (G. R. Beasley-Murray, *John*, Word Biblical Commentary 36, Dallas: Word, 1991; p.lxxiv). However, the view is largely speculative and the most convincing position remains the traditional one that the Gospel was written by John son of Zebedee,

who also wrote the epistles and the book of Revelation (see the discussion in Carson, Moo and Morris, op. cit., especially pp. 138–57).

² *op.cit.* p.221.

³ Bultmann says, 'it is only because the Logos is constantly present as the light of men that the world of men can be σκοτια at all' (Rudolf Bultmann, *The Gospel of John*, A Commentary, [trans. G.R. Beasley-Murray, Basil Blackwell, Oxford, 1991], p.47). But as Carson points out: 'The "darkness" in John is not only absence of light, but positive evil...' He speaks of the verse being 'a masterpiece of planned ambiguity', combining the themes both of creation and salvation (D.A. Carson, *The Gospel according to John*, [Inter-Varsity Press, Leicester, 1991], p.119).

⁴ Bultmann: 'Since the οὐ κατέλαβεν has its parallels in οὐκ ἔγνω, οὐ παρέλαβον vv. 10ff. καταλαμβανειν cannot have the meaning of 'attack (cf. on 12:35), 'seize' in a hostile sense, 'overwhelm', although Orig. and the majority of Gr. exegetes took it in this sense, but can only mean 'grasp' = to make one's own, as in Romans 9:30, 1 Corinthians 9:24, Philippians 3:12;...' *op cit.* p.48 footnote 1. This understanding is supported by Beasley-Murray, *ibid*, and, more cautiously, by Carson, *ibid*. Sanders and Mastin say: 'John is fond of using words with two meanings, both of which are applicable. Of this characteristic of his style master (κατέλαβεν) is an example. The verb καταλαμβάνω means both 'overcome, overtake' (as in 12:35...) and 'understand, comprehend'. Here 'overcome' is the primary meaning, with 'understand' as an overtone – the darkness failed to overcome the light, and would not have attempted to do so if it had understood it' (J.N. Sanders & B.A. Mastin, *The Gospel according to St John,* Black's New Testament Commentaries [A & C Black, London, 1968], p.72). However, the context seems against this.

⁵ 'Yet led by their reason they do not reach or even approach God; and so all their intelligence is in the end nothing but vanity. Whence it follows that there is no hope for men's salvation unless God shall help them with a new help' (John Calvin, *The Gospel according to St John 1–10*, translated by T.H.L. Parker [The St Andrew Press, Edinburgh, 1972], p.12).

⁶ REB has 'live by'. William Hendriksen translates by 'doing what is true' (William Hendriksen, *The Gospel of John* [Banner of

Truth Trust, London, 1959], p.144). Carson says that 'to do the truth' is a Semitic expression which means 'to act faithfully', 'to act honourably' (*op. cit.* p.207).

[7] Hendriksen, following Calvin, understands 'done in God' to mean 'wrought with God's approval' (*op. cit.* p.144). However Lindars says, 'wrought in God: i.e. done in fellowship with God' (Barnabas Lindars, *The Gospel of John,* New Century Bible [Oliphants, London, 1977], p.161).

[8] 'The theme of Jesus the Light of the World, developed in the healing of the blind man, as is made clear in the explanatory sayings at the beginning (v.5) and the end (v.39), stands in relation to the word of revelation at 8:12.' 'The chapter is a masterpiece of narrative which combines theological and historical strands with dramatic skill' (Rudolf Schnackenburg, *The Gospel according to St John,* Vol. 2 [Burns & Oates, London, 1971], pp. 238, 239). Beasley-Murray entitles this chapter in his commentary, 'Jesus the Light of the World That Brings Judgment to the World' (*op. cit.* p.149).

[9] 'In one sense they have the faculty of 'sight', they are scribes, theologically educated and used to argument. If they nevertheless close themselves to the realisation that Jesus comes from God (9:29–33) that is bad faith, sin...the answer gives specific content to the blindness Jesus is talking about: it is a fundamental refusal on the part of human beings to expose themselves to God's revelation, and has its origin in human arrogance and false self-images...' (Schnackenburg, *op. cit.* p.256).

[10] D.A. Carson, *Divine Sovereignty and Human Responsibility* [Marshall Pickering, London, 1994 ed.], p.196. Both Augustine and Chrysostom understand this in terms of hardening: Augustine: 'But I answer, that they well deserved this. For God hardens and blinds a man, by forsaking and not supporting him; and this by a secret sentence; by an unjust one He cannot.' Chrysostom: 'Whereby it is plain that we begin to forsake first, and are the cause of our own perdition. For it is not the fault of the sun, that it hurts weak eyes, so neither is God to blame for punishing those who do not attend to His words' (Quoted in John Henry Parker, *Catena Aurea, Commentary on John* [Oxford, J.G.F. & J. Rivington, London, 1845], p.414).

[11] Raymond Brown, in a long discussion, links this passage with Deuteronomy 29:2-4; 'In vs. 37 the writer introduces his evaluation by echoing the last part of Deuteronomy (xxix 2-4). There Moses

begins his third and final address by reminding the people that, although the Lord had *performed signs before them* in Egypt, the Lord has still not given them the mind to comprehend or the eyes to see, or the ears to hear. (This primitive thought shows no theoretical awareness of secondary causality or divine permissiveness as regards what is related to salvation. The Lord causes these things directly; and so if they did not see or hear, it was because the Lord had caused them not to see or hear.) In exactly the same way, the Gospel tells us, Jesus has performed signs, and yet they had refused to believe' (Raymond Brown, *The Gospel according to John (1-12)*, The Anchor Bible [Doubleday and Company Inc. Garden City, New York, 1966], pp.484-5). Calvin, commenting on verse 38, says: 'The word *arm* as is well-known, denotes power. The prophet declares that God's arm, which is contained in the teaching of the Gospel, is hidden until it is revealed; and at the same time he says that not all are partakers of this revelation indiscriminately. Hence it follows that many are left in their blindness without inward light, because hearing they do not hear.' However, on verse 39 he adds: 'But in this passage he speaks of the hardness with which God punished the malice of an ungrateful people. Those who do not notice these degrees confound Scriptural passages of varying meaning' (John Calvin, *The Gospel according to St John 11-21* [translated by T.H.L. Parker, The Saint Andrew Press, Edinburgh, 1972], p.46). Calvin thus appears to agree with Carson who concludes that this passage does not show that 'reprobation is the symmetrical antithesis of election' (idem. p.196).

[12]   Tasker points out that 'Different words are used in this verse for *know*. The Pharisees have not "come to know" God for what He really is. Jesus does not have to "come to know" the Father for He has immediate knowledge of Him. The former sense is expressed by *ginosko* and the latter by *oida*'. RGV Tasker, *The Gospel according to St John*, TNTC,, Tyndale Press, London, 1960; p.122. This distinction, which follows classical Greek, is disputed for koine.

[13]   'Failure to believe in Jesus is therefore compelling evidence that, however exacting the scholarship that was studying that revelation, the revelation itself had not been absorbed, understood, obeyed' (Carson, *Gospel*, p.263).

[14]   Brown comments that the 'love of God' is probably possessive, God's love for men, as in the rest of the Gospel, though he does admit that the phrase might be ambiguous (*op.cit.* p. 226). Others disagree,

but Beasley-Murray points out: 'The Jews addressed by Jesus have neither the word of God in them (v38) nor the life of God (v40), nor the love of God (v42)' (*op. cit.* p.79).

[15] 'The life-communicating function of the word of God preserved in Scripture is transferred to the one whose words are spirit and life (6:63b,68). Hence it is not possible for God's life to *abide* in those who, though they open themselves to the word of Scripture, are shut fast against the living, personal Word of God' (Schnackenburg, *op. cit.* p.125).

[16] Calvin says: 'He is not only speaking of the evil that men bring on themselves, but of the state of human nature. The philosophers thought that any man by his own choice becomes a slave and returns to freedom. But here Christ declares that all who are not freed by Him are in slavery, and that all who derive the contagion of sin from corrupted nature are slaves from birth. We must grasp this comparison between grace and nature which Christ emphasizes here, and from which we can easily see that men are despoiled of freedom unless they recover it from elsewhere. Yet this slavery is voluntary, so that those who sin of necessity are not forced to sin' (*op. cit.* p. 223).

[17] Raymond Brown says that the background here may be the LXX of Jeremiah 31:3. He adds: 'This teaching has its external aspect in the sense that it is embodied in Jesus who walks among them, but it is also internal in the sense that God acts in their hearts. It is a fulfilment of what Jer.xxxi 33 has promised; 'I will put my law within them, and on their hearts will write it.' (John Bright, The Anchor Bible, vol.21). This internal moving of the heart by the Father will enable them to believe in the Son and thus possess eternal life' (Vol I, p.277).

[18] 'As far as the manner of drawing goes, it is not violent so as to compel men by an external force; but yet it is an effectual movement of the Holy Spirit, turning men from being unwilling and reluctant into willing' (Calvin, Vol. 1, p.164). 'When he compels belief, it is not by the savage constraint of a rapist, but by the wonderful wooing of a lover. Otherwise put, it is by an insight, a teaching, an illumination implanted within the individual, in fulfilment of the Old Testament promise, *They will all be taught by God*' (Carson, *Gospel*, p.293).

[19] Carson says, 'it is clear that the giving by the Father of certain men to the Son *precedes* their reception of eternal life, and governs the purpose of the Son's mission. There is no way to escape the

implicit election' (*Divine Sovereignty*, p.187).

[20] 'To tell the truth, the entire allegory (*sic*) runs like this: the sheep recognise their shepherd as soon as he presents himself to them, because even before that moment they already belong to him. Jesus recognises them, because they had been given to him by the Father to be his disciples, and they recognise Jesus because he had been sent to them by the Father to be their shepherd' (A. Vanhoye, 'Notre foi, oeuvre divine, d'apres le quatrieme evangile', *Nouvelle Revue Theologique*, Vol lxxxvi (1964), p.343, quoted in Carson, idem, p.190). Schnackenburg says, 'A predestination of those who belong to Jesus and his community of faith is unmistakable' (*op. cit.* p.264), *Excursus on Personal commitment, Personal responsibility, Predestination and Hardening.*

[21] However the crucial position of 3:1–8 coming in the Gospel with the first representative of the Jews coming to Jesus indicates the importance of the work of the Spirit for John. Burge comments on this section in this way, 'The reader is introduced to John's first characteristic discourse wherein the person of Jesus, his work, and his call upon the convert's life are fully explicated' (*op. cit.* p.159).

[22] 'The connection with Jesus is essential to the idea of truth as we see it in this Gospel. It starts from the essential nature of God, it finds its expression in the gospel whereby God saves men and it issues in lives founded on truth and showing forth truth' (Leon Morris, *The Gospel according to John*, New International Commentary on the New Testament [Eerdmans, Grand Rapids, 1995], Additional note D: *Truth*, p.262). Because the Holy Spirit is considered as a separate section no link is made at this point between the concepts of Knowledge and Truth and the work of the Spirit. However, the work of the Spirit is essential for John's understanding of truth as de la Potterie indicates, 'These two verses [John's Gospel 14:6; 1 John 5:6] do not mean that there are actually two revealers, but that there are two times of revelation as in the revelations of the Apocalypses: the first is the time of Christ, who brings revelation objectively and historically, the second the time of the Spirit, who illuminates the truth of Christ and renders it subjectively present in us. These two definitions are to be taken together if we want to have a complete idea of the Johannine truth: the truth is not simply the revelation of Jesus: it is that revelation illuminated by the Holy Spirit. Without the action of the Spirit there is no interior awareness of the truth' (Ignace de la Potterie, 'The Truth

in Saint John', in *The Interpretation of John*, ed. John Ashton, SPCK, London, 1986; p.63).

[23] So Carson, *Gospel*, p.135.

[24] Schnackenburg, *Excursus on Truth*; 'Nevertheless, because Jesus not only reveals the truth in his words and actions, but also embodies it in his person, God's reality becomes manifest in him, manifest as will and power to save' (*op. cit.* p.228).

[25] Hence ὁ διδάσκαλος.

[26] Carson is more specific; 'The 'heavenly things' are then the splendours of the consummated kingdom, and what it means to live under such glorious, ineffable rule' (*Gospel*, p.199).

[27] 'Nicodemus is manifestly addressed as representative of his people (λεγω σοι...εἰπον ὑμιν)...' (Beasley-Murray, *op. cit.* p.49).

[28] Lindars says, 'the repetition of will (verb and noun in the Greek) is reminiscent of the repetition of the noun in 5:30, and the sentence is to be understood in the light of that verse. It means, then, anyone whose intentions are the same as Jesus' own intentions, in which there is no self-seeking, but entire submission to God' (*op. cit.* p.288).

[29] 'Μεινητε signifies a settled determination to *live* in the word of Christ and by it, and so entails a perpetual listening to it, reflection on it, holding fast to it, carrying out its bidding' (Beasley-Murray, *op. cit.* p.133).

[30] Calvin understands this as taking place in a continuing sense, 'It is the same unvarying truth which Christ teaches His own from first to last; but first He enlightens them with small sparks, as it were, and finally pours out a full light upon them' (Vol. 1. p.221).

[31] 'Here *words* renders the Greek *rhemata,* neither Jesus' teaching as a whole nor his itemized precepts, but his actual "words" or his utterances' (Carson, *Gospel,* p.560).

[32] Calvin says, 'He therefore received the Spirit on that occasion not so much for Himself as for His people. And the Spirit descended visibly that we may know that in Christ dwells the abundance of all gifts of which we are destitute and empty' (Vol. 1. p.35). Burge emphasizes the word μενειν and says, 'Till then, no-one but Jesus had received a full measure of the Spirit that would remain, and by virtue of that endowment he was equipped to baptize in the Spirit. Hence this anointing made him more than a super-endowed prophet. He could now be the distributor of the Spirit' (*op. cit.* p.55).

[33] 'The exact significance of the expression is not easy to discern'

(Leon Morris, *Jesus is the Christ, Studies in the Theology of John* [Inter Varsity Press, Leicester 1989], p.149). He adds, 'But it is usually accepted that in the present passage the parallelism with baptism 'in water' shows that we should take 'Spirit' as the means or agency of the baptism in question,' ibid. footnote 7.

[34] Turner says, 'It would seem then that John portrays the gift of the Spirit to Jesus at his baptism as the gift of full revelation and the power to impart it to others' (art. 'Holy Spirit' in *A Dictionary of Jesus and the Gospels*; p.347). Morris goes beyond this when he says, 'But Jesus does what the Baptist could never do; he brings the gift of the Holy Spirit with all that that means in terms of newness of life' (*Studies*, p.148).

[35] It is noteworthy that Morris does this when he heads a section in *Studies*, Baptism in the Spirit, and goes straight on from the verses we have just considered to 3:5-8.

[36] This would be particularly likely if 'born from water and Spirit' referred to the baptism of John and of Jesus. Burge argues that though 'water' in this phrase has Old Testament and Jewish antecedents, 'it is evident that the most significant contemporary usage of lustrations for the Johannine setting (and we might add, the most relevant one for the Evangelist) is the work of John the Baptist. The Baptist stands at the end of the Palestinian Jewish development outlined above. Therefore it does not seem extraordinary to conclude that the initial point of reference for ὕδωρ in John 3:5 is John's baptism' (*op. cit.* p.162).

It also seems that this would be the most likely way Nicodemus would understand the reference to water; he would undoubtedly be aware of the ministry of John and might also have heard of the words of John about Jesus baptizing in the Holy Spirit.

Burge considers several other references and comes to this conclusion. 'Therefore the added allusion to baptism in John 4 (on a very secondary level), when joined to the references in 3:22ff, and 4:1-2, strengthens the case for a baptismal reference in John 3:5. But in John 4 itself the theological orientation we are about to discover in John 3 is evident: baptism introduces the Samaritan pericope but is soon neglected, and Jesus' reference to water quickly becomes a metaphor for the Spirit. The same Jesus who was baptizing in water now offers water in a new context and symbolically portrays the Spirit through it.

Therefore in both John 3 and 4 the surface meaning of "water" is transcended by the higher gift that Christ himself will give: the Spirit' (*op. cit.* p.165).

[37] This suggests a very different pattern of thought, where the emphasis is on the freeness and sovereignty of the Spirit rather than the ministry of Jesus.

[38] 'This means "to experience, encounter, participate in", as, eg., in "see death" (8:51), "see life", (3:36). Notice the synonymous, parallel expression "enter" in vs. 5; perhaps "see" brings out more clearly the relationship of the kingdom to the revelation brought by Jesus, revelation that has to be seen, accepted, believed' (Brown, vol. 1, p.130).

[39] Schnackenburg says, 'It is possible to say that the only person who will understand the words about the Spirit is one who has already experienced the presence of the Spirit' (Vol.III, p.153). Quoted in Morris, *Studies*, p.145.

[40] Augustine said, 'To men, therefore, it is by measure.... But Christ, who gives, received not by measure' (*Lectures or Tractates on the Gospel according to St John*, Vol. I, translated by John Gibb, T & T Clark, Edinburgh, 1873; p.207). Carson says, 'this almost certainly is the correct rendering' (*Gospel*; p.213.

[41] Augustine bases this on the phrase 'gift of God' (*op. cit.* p.216). Beasley-Murray says, 'It is evident that "living water" has a variety of nuances that must be taken into account; chiefly it appears to denote the *life mediated by the Spirit sent from the (crucified and exalted) Revealer-Redeemer'* (*op. cit.* p.60). Carson says, 'In this chapter, the water is the satisfying eternal life mediated by the Spirit that only Jesus, the Messiah and Saviour of the world, can provide' (*Gospel*, p.219).

[42] 'To say to a human being that God is Spirit is to say that their relationship must be a spiritual relationship. Because God is Spirit, human beings must possess the Spirit' (Burge, *op. cit.* p.192). 'Worship must be in spirit and in truth, and this can hardly be intelligible if it is not an indirect allusion to the Spirit of truth, who would lead the believers in Christ into true worship' (Guthrie, *New Testament Theology*, p.528).

[43] 'One must be joined with "the above" – be born of the Spirit – in order to share in the discipleship of Jesus, who has descended from this place. The entire orientation of worship in Spirit and truth should point away from personal efforts and ambitions and focus on the power of God at work' (Burge, *op. cit.* p.192).

⁴⁴ In discussing these verses Johnston says, 'The need of the Church could be summarized in one phrase: "the energy of Jesus" or "the spirit of Jesus"; so they had to be *baptized with holy spirit!* (1:33; 20:22)' (George Johnston, *The Spirit-Paraclete in the Gospel of John* [Cambridge University Press, Cambridge, 1970], p.46).

⁴⁵ Burge goes further than this when he says, 'Therefore truth and Spirit must function as a unity especially in their dependence on Jesus. John's use of a single preposition governing both substantives confirms this interpretation. The sphere of Christian worship is delineated by the power brought by the resurrected Christ (πνεῦμα) and the single basis of this supernatural life, Jesus Christ (ἀλήθεια). Therefore worship in Spirit and truth is worship that is focussed on and empowered by Jesus' (*op. cit.* p.194). John Rea comments, 'Genuine worship that pleases God operates in the realm of truth – the true knowledge of God.' He does also add, 'Worship in Spirit and truth is worship that is focussed on the risen, exalted Christ and empowered by his Spirit' (John Rea, *The Holy Spirit in the Bible* [Marshall Pickering, London, 1990], pp.147-8).

⁴⁶ The repetition of ἐστιν is important in this verse; 'they are spirit and they are life'. REB has 'both spirit and life' but this does not adequately reflect the Greek. It is possible to understand the sentence in this way, 'they are Spirit and so they are also life.' Morris says, 'He is saying that his teaching is not to be interpreted in a wooden, literalistic manner, but as the Holy Spirit enlightens. There is a strong emphasis on the connection with real life and the Holy Spirit' (*Studies*, p.152).

⁴⁷ Lindars says, 'John is speaking of the disciples' capacity to perceive the truth. It is one of his principles that only the spiritual man can perceive spiritual things...flesh here is the earthly part of man, man as he is by nature, his intellect remaining unilluminated by the revelation of God. It is only if he is open to the influence of God, that he can perceive divine things...the words...are spirit and life: the reference may be simply to the preceding discourse or (as Barrett suggests) to the teaching of Jesus as a whole. This seems preferable, for this is a general statement on the disciples' capacity to perceive the truth. Just as a man can only receive spiritual things when illuminated by the Spirit, so it must be clearly understood that all Jesus' teaching belongs to the category of spiritual things' (*op. cit.* p.273-4).

⁴⁸ It is not necessary for the purposes of this thesis to discuss the

exact syntax of verses 37, 38 or whether 'him' in verse 38 refers to Jesus or the believer.

[49] 'What the evangelist means is that the Spirit of the dawning kingdom comes as the result – indeed, the entailment – of the Son's completed work, and up to that point the Holy Spirit was *not* given in the full, Christian sense of the term' (Carson, *Gospel*, p.329). 'John is explaining then, that the death of Jesus is the necessary preliminary to the full work of the Spirit... There could be preliminary manifestations of the Spirit, but the full working of the Spirit of God depended on the accomplishing of the atoning work of Christ' (Morris, *Studies*, p.154).

[50] *op. cit.* p.116.

[51] *op. cit.* p.149. Brown, 'we recognize that for John this is the high point of the post-resurrectional activity of Jesus and that already in several ways the earlier part of this chapter has prepared us for this dramatic moment' (*op. cit.* Vol.II, p.1037).

[52] *op. cit.* p.649 ff.

[53] 'There is no doubt from the context that the reference is to forgiving sins, or withholding forgiveness. But though this sounds stern and harsh, it is simply the result of the preaching of the gospel, which either brings men to repent as they hear of the ready and costly forgiveness of God, or leaves them unresponsive to the offer of forgiveness which is the gospel, and so they are left in their sins' (John Marsh, *The Gospel of St John* [Harmondsworth, 1968], pp.641-42; quoted in Morris, *Studies*, p.169).

[54] It does not seem adequate simply to transliterate the word as Paraclete, at least not in translations, but it is almost impossible to come up with one word which is suitable for English versions, hence the difficulties which all translations seem to have. Burge explains the root of the problem, 'Therefore John's usage departs from the standard understanding of the Greek term. John has given a special forensic title to a figure which barely fits the customary pattern.' He thus concludes, 'In order to preserve the uniqueness of this title and not obliterate the manifold functions of the Johannine Spirit, perhaps no translation should be adopted. Jerome faced this same quandry when he worked on the Latin Vulgate. Rather than choose *advocatus* or *consolator*, he simply and wisely employed the transliteration *paracletus* throughout the Farewell Discourses' (*op. cit.* pp.7, 9-10).

[55] 'The meaning of παρακλητος in John is best arrived at by considering the use of παρακαλειν and other cognates in the N.T.

This is two-fold. (a) παρακαλειν and παρακλησις both refer to prophetic Christian preaching (and to the same preaching communicated by apostolic letter); e.g. Acts 2:40; 1 Cor.14:3. This corresponds to a normal Greek usage in which παρακαλειν means 'to exhort'. (b) Both words are used in another sense which seems to have little or no basis in Greek that is independent of the Hebrew Bible; they refer to consolation, and in particular to the consolation to be expected in the messianic age. This usage is common in the Old Testament (e.g. Isa.40:1), recurs in the N.T. (e.g. Matt.5:4; Luke 2:25) and is paralleled in the rabbinic נחמה (nehameh, e.g. Makhoth 5b). The two usages, (a) and (b), though distinct, are closely combined: the main burden of the παρακλησις (prophetic exhortation) is that men should enter, or accept, the παρακλησις (messianic salvation), which has been brought into being through the work of Jesus; cf. 1 Cor. 14:24,31' (C.K Barrett, *The Gospel according to John* [S.P.C.K., 1972], pp. 385-6). Johnston's approach is different: 'So the words that unfold the wealth of Johannine teaching about the spirit of truth and the paraclete are *comforter, interpreter* or exegete, *teacher, prophet, legal counsel*: and the right method of study is to begin from them, not from any non-Christian etymology and not with the non-Johannine use of paraclete in its Greek or Hebrew form.' He provides this working definition: 'the spirit of truth, as paraclete, acts on behalf of Christ and for the advantage of the disciples. The most useful word in English to cover all the meanings of the Greek παρακλητος is the word "representative" ' (*op. cit.* p. 87).

[56] Note the ascription of διδάσκαλος to Jesus, 1:38; 3:2; (8:4), 11:28; 13:13,14; 20:16; Rabbi 4:31; 9:2; 11:8; (20:16); and the verb διδασκω 6:59; 7:14,28,35; (8:2); 18:20. And of course also extensively in the Synoptics.

[57] 'However, the masculine pronouns ἐκεῖνος and αὐτός are used of the Spirit/Paraclete in 15:26; 16:7,8,13,14. As the Paraclete, the Spirit takes on a more personal role than in many other sections of the NT' (Brown, Vol.II; p.639).

[58] 'John does not tell us why the Holy Spirit is called "the Spirit of truth" in these passages, but it is not unlikely that he means that the Spirit characteristically bears witness to the truth' (Morris, *Studies*; p.156).

[59] Hendriksen argues against this saying, 'Hence, one is not justified in making any sharp distinction between the present *by your*

side relationship and the future *in the midst of* and *within* relationship.'
He takes μενει to have a future sense, 'This reading of a present
tense as if it were future is fully justified in such a context' (*op. cit.*
p.278). Others follow an alternative reading and understand both verbs
as present.

⁶⁰ 'the coming of Christ is in the coming of the Paraclete and the
mutual indwelling of Christ and Paraclete which this implies is no
more difficult to comprehend than that of Christ and the Father
emphasized in the chapter (cf.14:10, 20)' (Sanders and Mastin, *op.cit.*
p.330). Carson, following Beasley-Murray denies that this is a coming
in the Spirit: 'Indeed, it is not clear at all that John ever speaks of the
coming of Jesus *in* the Spirit' (*Gospel*; p.501). He refers these verses
to post-resurrection appearances of Jesus to his disciples. However
vv. 22, 23 seem to confirm the interpretation suggested. Carson himself
on verse 23 says: 'Presumably this manifestation of the Father and
the Son in the life of the believer is through the Spirit although the text
does not explicitly say so' (*Gospel,* p.504).

⁶¹ This indicates that the δὲ at the beginning of verse 26 is to be
understood adversatively, and REB, NIV and NKJV etc. are right to
translate by 'But...'

⁶² 'John has made it clear that the disciples did not grasp the
significance of a good deal that their Master taught them. It seems
likely that they let slip some of the things they did not understand.
Jesus is now saying that the Holy Spirit will supply their lack. Notice
that the things of which He will remind them are the things that Jesus
has spoken to them. In other words the Spirit will not dispense with
the teaching of Jesus. The teaching to be recalled is His' (Morris,
Gospel; p.657).

⁶³ Swete says, 'not universal knowledge, but all that belongs to
the sphere of spiritual truth; nothing that is essential to the knowledge
of God or the guidance of life shall be wanting' (*op. cit.* p.153).

⁶⁴ Beasley-Murray comments, 'The term "remind" (ὑπο-
μιμνησκω) occurs here alone in the Gospel, but the simpler μιμνησκω
is used in the passive with the sense of "remember"; it occurs in two
significant passages in the Gospel: first in 2:17,22 it is said after Easter
the disciples *remembered* the enigmatic saying regarding the
destruction of the temple and the formation of a new one (2:19), together
with the relevance of Psalm 69:9 concerning the cleansing of the
temple and the saying itself, and so the meaning of the whole event;

the second is in 12:16, where it is stated that "after Jesus was glorified" the disciples *remembered* the triumphal entry of Jesus into Jerusalem and the scriptures which illuminated the meaning of the event. These two occasions of 'remembering' in the time following Easter and the coming of the Spirit provide illustrations of what is meant by the Spirit "reminding" the disciples of what Jesus said: he not only enables them to *recall* these things but to perceive their significance, and so he *teaches* the disciples to grasp the revelation of God brought by Jesus in its richness and profundity' (*op. cit.* p.261).

[65] Many writers stress that this is not new revelation. Burge quotes from Kothgasser, 'With few exceptions the author never tires of saying repeatedly that the Holy Spirit brings nothing basically new, has not "supplemented" the revelation, nor ever shall substitute through something new and better a rival to this revelation. Rather the author stresses far more that the Spirit enables the revelation of Christ to be recalled, interpreted, and experienced ever anew, Christ is *the* Revealer and the Holy Spirit is the teacher, not alongside Christ, but after Christ and subordinate to him' (Kothgasser A.M., *'Die Lehr-, Erinnerungs-Bezeugungs-, und Einfurhungs-funktion des Johanneischen Geist-Parakleten gegenuber der Christus-Offenbarung'*, *Salesianum* 33 (1971) 557-98; 34(1972) 2-51; in Burge, p.213). While this is true the emphasis must be on the word 'basically' cf. 16:12,13.

[66] 'But the "reminding" went of course much further than a mere recovery of the Lord's sayings; it enabled those who had been present to live through the Ministry again with a new appreciation of its meaning; logion and parable, question and answer, command and promise returned to them in new light, and formed, it cannot be doubted, the basis of the Apostles' own teaching, and ultimately the nucleus of that great stream of Christian tradition which has moulded Christian belief and practice from their time to our own' (Swete, *op. cit.* p.154).

[67] 'But the traditional belief in the inspiration of the NT finds its justification in the promises of Divine assistance made by our Lord to the apostles and their company, and the special gifts of the Spirit possessed by the Apostolic age. If the first age was specially guided by the Spirit into a knowledge of all essential truth, its writings have rightly been gathered by the church into a sacred canon' (Swete, *op. cit.* p.389). Also Carson, 'Granted the prominence of this theme, the promise of v.26 has in view the Spirit's role to the first generation of

disciples, not to all subsequent Christians. John's purpose in including this theme and this verse is not to explain how readers at the end of the first century may be taught by the Spirit, but to explain to readers at the end of the first century how the first witnesses, the first disciples, came to an accurate and full understanding of the truth of Jesus Christ. The Spirit's ministry in this respect was not to bring qualitatively new revelation, but to complete, fill out, the revelation brought by Jesus himself' (*Gospel*. p.505).

[68] 'Jesus is promising the assistance of the Spirit, to inspire the disciples to defend the faith in time of persecution. It probably means legal testimony in a court of law, as in Matt.10:20' (Lindars, *op. cit.* p.496).

[69] 'Superficially this gives the impression of a witness in addition to that of the Paraclete/Spirit; but, as Hoskyns, p.481, indicates, the idea is: "And, moreover, it is you who must do and bear the witness (of the Spirit)." A similar co-ordination in Johannine writing about the Spirit is found in 1 John 4:13-14: "He has given us of his own Spirit, and we...can testify" (cf. also III John 12)' (Brown, *op. cit.* Vol.II, p.689).

[70] 'The world will persecute the disciples because of Jesus' name, and to counter this the Paraclete will be sent in Jesus' name (14:26). In this persecution the Christian disciple is not to be a passive victim; the Paraclete dwells within him (14:17), and he is to give voice to the Paraclete's witness against the world. This aggressive witness-bearing will produce further hostility on the world's part (16:1-4a).' Brown, op. cit. Vol. II; p.698. Many scholars see the idea of the Paraclete developing out of the background of persecution and trial. Burge says of what he calls the 'trial motif', 'When this motif is extended by John beyond the earthly life of Jesus and into the era of the church, then we may have located the exact forensic context which have rise (sic) to a juridical Spirit (the Paraclete) whose evidence before the world consisted in unique revelations. As Christ was on trial and revealed the Father, so too the disciples (and the Paraclete) were on trial, and in their witness they glorified and revealed Christ' (*op. cit.* p.41).

[71] 'Their witness is linked with that of the Holy Spirit. It is the same Christ to whom they bear witness, and it is the same salvation of which they bear witness. At the same time it is *their* witness... But the really significant witness is that of the Holy Spirit, for he alone

can bring home to the hearts of men the truth and the significance of all this' (Morris, *Gospel*; p.684).

[72] Its usage in John 8:46 might be translated, 'Which of you convinces me of sin'; but the sense could be 'which of you can honestly and successfully convict me of sin', and this seems to fit the context better. John 8:9 definitely bears the subjective sense, but there is a double textual problem and does not help us in understanding 16:8.

[73] So NIV, NKJV, NASB, RV; AV has 'reprove', which is much the same, but RSV has 'convince'. REB's 'will prove the world wrong' is nicely ambiguous.

[74] 'The effect of God's Word is thus to intensify the work of conscience. It is accordingly natural in the present passage to see in the work of the Paraclete an operation upon the conscience of the world, though John does not say in what way this operation will be effected' (Barrett, p. 405).

[75] Calvin explains it in this way, 'For the Spirit convicts men in the preaching of the Gospel in two ways. Some are touched seriously and humble themselves of their own accord and assent willingly to the judgment which condemns them. Others, although they are convinced of guilt and cannot escape, do not yield in sincerity or submit themselves to the authority and control of the Holy Spirit; on the contrary, when they are subdued they groan inwardly and, although confounded, still do not cease to cherish an inward obstinacy' (*op. cit.* Vol.II; p.116).

[76] Morris says, 'The Spirit convicts the world in two senses. In the first place he 'shows the world to be guilty' i.e. he secures a verdict of 'Guilty' against the world. But in the second place we should take the words to mean also that the Spirit brings the world's guilt home to itself. The Spirit convicts the individual sinner's conscience. Otherwise men would never be convicted of their sin' (*Gospel*; p.698).

[77] 'This convicting work of the Paraclete is therefore gracious: it is designed to bring men and women of the world to recognize their need, and so turn to Jesus, and thus stop being "the world" ' (Carson, *Gospel,* p.537).

[78] 'In common with other New Testament usages, *elencho* means 'to convict (the world)' in the personal sense, *i.e.* not arguing the case for the world's objective guilt before God at the final Great Assize,

but shaming the world and convincing it of its own guilt, thus calling it to repentance' (Carson, *Gospel,* p.537).

[79] Morris comments on this: 'It may mean that their experience thus far sets a limit to their ability to perceive. There are vistas of truth set before them which they cannot as yet enter, but they will enter when the Spirit comes. More probably it refers to their inability, until the Spirit should come, to live out the implications of the revelation' (*Gospel,* p.699). It is difficult to know why the second option should be more probable.

[80] 'It is clearly presupposed in the first half of this verse that what the spirit will teach will go beyond the message of the earthly Jesus... The Evangelist is clearly aware that there is a break between what the earthly Jesus said and did and the messsage of the Spirit' (Ernst Haenchen, *A Commentary on the Gospel of John*, vol 2 (chapters 7-21) [trans. Robert W. Funk, Fortress Press, Philadelphia, 1984] p.144).

[81] BAGD; cf. Acts 8:31. Dunn notes, 'What this interpretative work of the Spirit meant for John becomes clear as soon as we realize that *John would undoubtedly regard his own gospel as the product of the inspiring Spirit*; his own work was a fulfilment of these very promises; indeed these promises may constitute an implicit apologia for his gospel; the way in which John handles the words and deeds of the historical Jesus is typically the way in which the Spirit interprets Jesus to a new generation, guides them into the truth of Jesus' (*Jesus and the Spirit*, p.352).

[82] Carson, *Gospel*, p.539. Morris sees a continous sense here, 'As the days go by the Spirit will lead them deeper and deeper into a knowledge of the truth' (*Gospel*, p.700).

[83] 'The Spirit not only recalled our Lord's words, but revealed heights and depths in Him hitherto unsounded, declaring that which is His, and thereby (since whatsoever the Father has is His) declaring also that which is the Father's' (Swete, p.313).

[84] 'The statement that the Paraclete "will disclose to you the things that are coming" has caused no little discussion' (Beasley-Murray, *op. cit.* p.283).

[85] Carson comments, 'The Spirit tells the disciples *what is yet to come.* This has often been understood to refer to revelation about the later stages of the kingdom, perhaps in apocalyptic form and exemplified in the book of Revelation (so Schlatter, p.314; Bernard,

2.511; Johnston, pp.38-39). But there is nothing in the context that demands an essentially futurist eschatalogy, and the theme, though present in John, is scarcely central.' Later he says, 'These features square best with the view that *what is yet to come* refers to all that transpires *in consequence* of the pivotal revelation bound up with Jesus' person, ministry, death, resurrection and exaltation. This includes the Paraclete's own witness to Jesus, his ministry to the world (16:6-11) primarily through the church (15:26,27), the pattern of life and obedience under the inbreaking kingdom, up to and including the consummation' (*Gospel*, p.540).

[86] 'we note that John does not specify from whom the Paraclete hears what he speaks. But it is not a meaningful question to ask whether the Paraclete hears from Jesus or from the Father. If the implication is that he hears from Jesus (see 14), all that Jesus has is from the Father (15)' (Brown, vol.II, p.708). Johnston says, 'thus it is Jesus, the Logos incarnate, who has more to say; and it is therefore into his truth that the interpreter spirit is to guide disciples. Accordingly, "all the truth" may be paraphrased by "all the truth there is to know about me" or "all the truth I have come to reveal" ' (*op. cit.* p.37).

[87] 'It is important to recognize that the disciples who will directly benefit from these ministrations of the Spirit are *primarily* the apostles... Derivatively, we may speak of the Spirit's continued work in the disciples of Jesus today. But that is not the primary emphasis of these verses' (Carson, *Gospel*, p.541).

Chapter 4: Romans
[1] So e.g. C. E. B. Cranfield, *The Epistle to the Romans*, ICC (Edinburgh: T. & T. Clark, 1977, 1979), Vol. 1, p. 105; John Murray, *The Epistle to the Romans* (Edinburgh: Marshall, Morgan & Scott, 1967), p. 34; Leon Morris (*The Epistle to the Romans* [Leicester: IVP, 1988]), says, 'It is usually held that throughout this section Paul has the Gentile world in mind,' but he goes on to add, 'by keeping this section general Paul is really indicating all mankind' (p. 74).

[2] Following Blass, Debrunner and Funk, *A Greek Grammar of the New Testament and other early Christian literature* (Chicago: University of Chicago Press, 1975), p. 118 ('for' or 'to' is better than 'among') in contradistinction from e.g. Käsemann, *Commentary on Romans* (London: SCM Press, 1980), p. 38 '... ἐν αὐτοῖς means "among them".' However Calvin says, 'The force of the passage is

increased by the preposition in' and goes on to add '... since undoubtedly every one of us feels it engraved on his own heart' (*The Epistles of Paul the Apostle to the Romans and to the Thessalonians*, trans. Ross Mackenzie [Edinburgh: Saint Andrew Press, 1972], p. 31).

[3] Morris (*op. cit.*, p. 78), thinks that 'suppress' is 'too strong', and prefers a word like 'hinder'. Cranfield, like a number of writers, points out that the present participle here has a conative force and speaks of 'the attempt to suppress [the truth], to bury it out of sight, obliterate it from the memory' (*op. cit.*, p. 112).

[4] REB. Karl Barth says rather finely, 'The whole world is the footprint of God' (*The Epistle to the Romans*, trans. E. C. Hoskyns [London: Oxford University Press, 1933], p. 43).

[5] Käsemann, *op. cit.*, p. 44. Cranfield notes, 'it is a sober acknowledgment of the fact that the καρδια as the inner self of man shares fully in the fallenness of the whole man, that the intellect is not a part of human nature somehow exempted from the general corruption, not something which can be appealed to as an impartial arbiter capable of standing outside the influence of the ego and returning a perfectly objective standard' (*op. cit.*, p. 118).

[6] NKJV.

[7] BAGD, p. 544.

[8] REB. Murray says, 'A reprobate mind is therefore one abandoned or rejected of God and therefore not fit for any activity worthy of approbation or esteem. The judgment of God falls upon the seat of thought and action. "To do those things which are not fitting" is explanatory of what a reprobate mind entails and shows that "the mind" as conceived of by the apostle is concerned with action as well as thought' (*op. cit.*, p. 49, 50).

[9] NKJV. Cranfield comments on καρδια: 'Paul uses καρδια to denote a man's inward, hidden self as a thinking, willing and feeling subject' (*op. cit.*, p. 118).

[10] NKJV.

[11] REB.

[12] REB.

[13] NKJV. Brunner writes, 'It is just those who know so well how to talk about God who make his name hateful among men, because their lives darken the picture of God and turn it into a caricature' (*The Letter to the Romans* [London: Lutterworth Press, 1959], p. 23).

[14] So Luther says: 'the Apostle ... shows that also the Jews live in sin, above all because they obey the Law only outwardly, that is, according to the letter and not according to the spirit' (*Commentary on Romans*, trans. J. Theodore Mueller [Grand Rapids: Kregel Publications, 1976], p. 61).

[15] Dunn makes the point in a slightly different way when he says, 'To highlight the plight of humankind the singular (sin) is deliberately set over against the plural (Jews and Greeks): for all the differences of race, culture and religion which distinguish and divide human beings, they are all alike under the same domination – the power of a force which binds them to their creatureliness in forgetfulness of their creatureliness' (*Romans 1–8*, WBC, 38A [Dallas: Word Books, 1988], pp. 156–157).

[16] Murray comments on verse 11: 'Verse 10 had been a statement in general terms; this verse is more specific and particularizes respects in which universal sinfulness appears. In the noetic sphere there is no understanding; in the conative there is no movement towards God. With reference to God all men are noetically blind and in respect of Godward movement they are dead' (*op. cit.*, p. 103).

[17] Morris maintains that, 'Fear in this Psalm (Ps. 36 quoted in v. 18) is not to be understood in the sense of "reverence" but of terror. Evildoers would do well to have a healthy fear of him who will determine their eternal destiny' (*op. cit.*, p. 169).

[18] 'The prepositional formula "under sin" (as in 7:14 and Gal. 3:22) and the personification subsequently (most clearly 5:12, 21; 6:6,12–23; 7:8–11) indicate that Paul understands "sin" as a force (or power) within the world, which functions in and upon men to negative effect' (Dunn, *op. cit.*, p. 148).

[19] Looking at things from the opposite point of view, Morris says, 'His hardening always presupposes sin and is always part of the punishment of sin. God could kill the sinner immediately when he sinned, but he usually does not. But he shuts him up to the effect of his sin, so that the person who hardens himself is condemned to live as a hardened person' (*op. cit.*, p. 361).

[20] Barrett points out, 'If they were hardened, it was because someone hardened them, and there is no doubt who is the subject of the active verb in the next verse' (*The Epistle to the Romans*, BNTC, [London: A. & C. Black, 1975], p. 210).

[21] REB.

[22] '"In part" does not refer to the degree of hardening but to the fact that not all were hardened' (Murray, *op. cit.*, vol. 2, p. 92, footnote 45). 'Goodspeed translates "only partial insensibility", but most agree that it is not partial hardening but part of Israel that is meant. ... This is a temporary hardening, taking place while God's purpose is worked out among the Gentiles' (Morris, *op. cit.*, p. 420).

[23] Käsemann says, 'Paul stands here in an apocalyptic-enthusiast tradition.... Pneumatics know about what is hidden from the world because God has revealed his will and way to them' (*op. cit.*, p. 320). Both he and Murray link with 1 Corinthians 2:9ff. Calvin says, 'As, therefore, we are quite unable by our own powers to investigate the secrets of God, so we come to clear and certain knowledge of them by the grace of the Holy Spirit. Now if it is our duty to follow the guidance of the Spirit we must stop and take our stand where He has left us. If anyone affects to know more than the Spirit has revealed, he will be overwhelmed with the immeasurable brightness of that unapproachable light' (*op. cit.*, p. 260).

[24] Speaking of the verb Murray says, 'It is to approve ... But it has this meaning with a distinct shade of thought, namely to discover, to find out or learn by experience what the will of God is and therefore to learn how approved the will of God is' (*op cit.*, vol. 2, p.115). BAGD mentions both aspects.

[25] 'It is by the power of the indwelling Spirit, the pledge of their inheritance in the coming age, that they can resist the tendency to live on the level of "this age" ' (F. F. Bruce, *The Epistle of Paul to the Romans* TNTC [Tyndale Press, 1963], p. 226). Morris points out that the only other place in the New Testament where the word ἀνακαίνωσις occurs is Titus 3:5, 'the renewal of the Holy Spirit' (p. 435, fn. 17).

[26] It is not possible to be certain in every case that πνεῦμα is a definite reference to the Holy Spirit. This figure excludes 8:1 on textual grounds, though the attestation for inclusion is fairly strong. It is assumed that there is only one reference to the Holy Spirit in 8:15. 12:11 is included. The references are: 1:4; 2:29; 5:5; 7:6; 8:2, 4, 5(x2), 9(x3), 10, 11(x2), 13, 14, 15, 16, 23, 26(x2), 27; 9:1; 12:11; 14:17; 15:13, 16, 19, 30.

There are some 23 references in 1 Corinthians. This is assuming that 'my spirit' in 14:14 determines the use of the word 'spirit' in verses 15–16. There would be 4 more if πνευματικά / πνεύματα are included: 12:1; 14:1, 2, 12.

[27] G. Kittel and G. Friedrich, *Theological Dictionary of the New Testament*, abridged in one volume by G. W. Bromiley (Grand Rapids and Exeter: Eerdmans/Pasternoster, 1985), p. 728.

[28] On the phrase 'Spirit of holiness' Bruce says, 'The Spirit of holiness is the regular Hebrew way of saying "the Holy Spirit"; and Paul here reproduces the Hebrew idiom in Greek.' He goes on to add, 'The outpouring and ministry of the Spirit attest the enthronement of Jesus as "Son of God with power" ' (*op. cit.*, p. 73).

[29] Dunn says, 'ὁρισθεντος (only here in Paul) is quite frequently taken in the sense "designated" (RSV), "declared to be" (BAGD, NEB, NIV). This would be acceptable so long as it is recognized that the verb denotes an act of God which brought Jesus to his designated status ("Son of God with power")' (*op. cit.*, p. 13). Morris is more cautious and says, 'It would seem that declared is the better way to understand the expression, but that "appointed" is possible in a sense which safeguards the truth that Jesus was Son of God before as well as after the resurrection' (*op. cit.*, p. 45).

[30] Calvin takes the view that the reference to the Holy Spirit is not only to his activity in the historical resurrection, but also to the work of the Spirit in bringing home the truth of this to the heart. 'This power is laid hold of when it is sealed by the same Spirit in our hearts.' 'This glory, however, is not made known unto us until the same Spirit imprints it on our hearts' (*op. cit.*, p. 16).

[31] 'By this he most probably intends to indicate that the circumcision of the heart is not accomplished by the mere fulfilment of the letter of the law's requirement, but is a miracle, the work of God's Spirit' (Cranfield, *op. cit.*, p. 175). So also Murray.

[32] So for example Calvin, Cranfield, Morris, Murray. No-one has written more eloquently about this than Anders Nygren, 'When we realise that he never uses agape to express man's love to God, we shall not think that it is of man's love that Paul speaks in this verse. Agape, the love which God showed us in Christ, is for Paul so tremendous a fact that he regularly refrained from using the same word to express love to God' (*Commentary on Romans* [Philadelphia: Muhlenburg Press, 1949], p. 199).

[33] 'the meaning is that God's love has been lavished upon us (as will be spelled out in verses 6–8), and actually brought home to our hearts (so that we have recognized it and rejoice in it) by the Holy Spirit who has been given to us' (Cranfield, *op. cit.*, p. 263).

[34] The word order is significant here; the verb coming first in the sentence, 'Demonstrates his own love to us does God ...'

[35] This is developed further in Brown, 'Receiving the Holy Spirit' (*Foundations*, Issue 33, Autumn 1994).

[36] The use of the word in verses 2 and 4, establishes its use for this chapter. In verses 9, 11, 14, 16 we have clear references to the Holy Spirit. Fee says, 'Over one-third of the anarthrous instances [i.e. of "spirit" in Paul] occur in the three major discussions of the role of the Spirit in Christian life in 1 Corinthians 12–14, Galatians 5 and Romans 8. Since in each case they are surrounded by other references to the Spirit, mostly articular, it is simply not possible that Paul in these contexts means other than the Holy Spirit when using this formula as well' (*God's Empowering Presence,* p. 23).

[37] Dunn introduces the use of the word 'mind-set'; 'The modern composite "mind-set" probably comes closest to the sense, including both a fixed and resolute way of thinking' (*op. cit.*, p. 426). Cranfield, when speaking of φρόνημα refers to 'outlook, assumptions, values, desires and purposes' (*op. cit.*, p. 386).

[38] 'He is called "the Spirit of adoption", not because he is the agent of adoption but because it is he who creates in the children of God the filial love and confidence by which they are able to cry, "Abba, Father" and exercise the rights and privileges of God's children' (Murray, *op. cit.*, vol. 1, p. 296).

[39] So BAGD; also REB 'The Holy Spirit affirms to our spirit.' Morris discusses whether the translation should be witness 'with' or 'to', coming down for the latter. 'Unaided, we cannot testify to the reality of our standing before God. But we are not unaided; the Spirit of God testifies to our Spirit (sic) and gives us the assurance of our membership in the heavenly family. There is a direct operation of the Holy Spirit on our spirit' (*op. cit.*, p. 317).

[40] The distinction is a very fine one as the 'groanings' of the previous verse are surely uttered by the person concerned. Also God is described as the One who searches the hearts indicating that the mind of the Spirit for the individual is somehow located in the heart. Morris says, 'Perhaps we should say that as God searches the hearts he finds the "unutterable groanings" which are the intercession of the Spirit. He knows the Spirit's mind, and the implication is that he answers prayer' (*op. cit.*, p. 329).

[41] 'It is only as we are indwelt by the Spirit and live in the Spirit,

only as our minds are governed by the Spirit may we be assured that the voice of conscience is informed with truth and right' (Murray, *op. cit.*, vol. 2, p. 2).

Chapter 5: 1 Corinthians

[1] 'Both terms occur far more often in 1 and 2 Corinthians than in all the other Pauline letters, and in contexts that make it clear that they are Corinthian terms' (Gordon D. Fee, *The First Epistle to the Corinthians*, NICNT [Grand Rapids: Eerdmans, 1987], p. 39).

[2] '[God] is the implied subject of all the passive verbs in this paragraph' (*ibid.*, p.38, fn. 11).

[3] C. K. Barrett, *A Commentary on the First Epistle to the Corinthians*, BNTC (London: A. & C. Black, 1968), p. 37.

[4] Grosheide says, '*Knowledge* as it is used here may be the fruit of intuition, even of a mystic feeling. At least it is not exclusively the result of research or thinking, but is an insight into things' (*The First Epistle to the Corinthians*, NICNT [Grand Rapids: Eerdmans, 1953], p. 28).

[5] 'In your experience' (REB); so also Barrett, *op. cit.,* p. 38.

[6] *Ibid.*

[7] Nigel Watson (*The First Epistle to the Corinthians*, EC [London: Epworth Press, 1992]), concludes, 'Clearly, wisdom rather than signs represents the characteristic preoccupation of the Corinthian community.' He says that '"Wisdom" has a range of meanings in Paul', but that in 1:20–21 'it appears to denote a means by which people aspire to the knowledge of God, that is, a philosophy, but one which stands in sharp contrast to the true way to the knowledge of God, which is by revelation' (p. 12).

[8] Fee, 'the absolute use of γέγραπται in Paul is always a reference to the OT Scripture' (*op. cit.*, p. 69, fn. 10). The reference is to Isaiah 29:14.

[9] Fee says, 'this is an assertion based on what for Paul is a self-evident reality' (*op. cit.*, p. 72). Watson says, 'The world, for all its wisdom, has not known God. Indeed, it cannot, for God, the living God of the Bible, is not to be known by scaling Everests of metaphysical speculation' (*op. cit.*, p. 13).

[10] Anticipating Paul's use of the word 'spiritual' at the end of Chapter 2.

[11] Fee remarks, 'in saying that Christ is the "wisdom of God", he is

not using philosophical categories, nor is he personifying wisdom in Christ; rather, this is an evangelical statement, i.e., a statement about the effectual working of the Christian evangel. Christ is the "wisdom of God" precisely because he is "the power of God for the salvation of everyone who believes" (Rom. 1:16; cf. v. 30 below)' (*op. cit.*, p. 77). Or as Grosheide says, 'There is a wisdom of God which works and saves in Christ' (*op. cit.*, p. 49).

[12] Fee says, 'For them [i.e. the Corinthians] "Spirit" meant the gift of tongues; it meant to have arrived in the "excellence of wisdom" (v. 1; *cf.* 4:8, 10), to have entered into a new existence that raised them above mere earthly existence, quite unrelated to genuine ethical behaviour. For Paul, on the other hand, "Spirit" *included* inspired utterances – as long as they edified – but for him the emphasis lay on the Spirit's *power*, power to transform lives (as here), to reveal God's secret wisdom (2:6–16), to minister in weakness (4:9–13), and to effect holiness in the believing community (5:3–5)' (*op. cit.*, p. 96).

[13] This point is not sufficiently noted. Paul is showing the Corinthians that they must not go back to human wisdom, nor, for that matter, go on beyond their initial experience to human wisdom, but remember that they began in the Spirit and must continue in him.

[14] Watson, *op. cit.*, p. 21. Calvin comments that most interpreters understand 'demonstration' of miracles, 'But I understand it in a wider sense, viz. as the hand of God stretching itself out to act powerfully through the apostle in every way' (*The First Epistle to the Corinthians*, trans. John W. Fraser [Edinburgh: Oliver & Boyd, 1960], p. 51). Many commentators take 'Spirit and power' as a *hendiadys*. REB's translation is interesting, 'it [the gospel] carried conviction by spiritual power.'

[15] The quotation appears to be from Isaiah 64:4 with the addition of 65:17, and perhaps even 52:15 (so Robertson and Plummer, *1 Corinthians*, ICC [Edinburgh: T. & T. Clark, 1911], p. 40). Watson comments, 'Paul appears to be going out of his way to emphasize that the witness of Scripture to the truth he is asserting is not confined to a single passage' (*op. cit.*, p. 23–24).

[16] It is difficult to be quite sure why Paul switches to the plural 'we' at this point. Fee speaks of Paul's 'common editorial "we"' (p.101, fn. 13), and it is presumably because they take the same view that the REB translators feel free to continue in the first person singular. However, it seems better to follow Tasker at this point when he writes,

'The plural *we* links Paul's teaching with that of other Christian teachers. There was no division among them' (*The First Epistle to the Corinthians*, TNTC [London: Tyndale Press, 1958], p. 53).

[17] Paul is probably picking up a word used by the Corinthians when he uses τελείοις. As Fee argues this actually includes them all as Christians, 'Those "in Christ" (1:30) are "the mature", and thus the Corinthians are included' (*op. cit.*, p. 103). There is an irony here. Because the Corinthians are in Christ and have received the Spirit therefore they are mature and can understand the wisdom of God, but because they have become entranced with the wisdom of the world Paul cannot speak to them as spiritual, but has to treat them as infants in Christ (3:1).

[18] A very good case can be made out for the former position, as e.g. by Charles Hodge in *The First Epistle to the Corinthians* (reprinted London: The Banner of Truth Trust, 1958). He says, '*Unto us*, i.e. unto those to whom this revelation was made, viz. "the holy apostles and prophets", Ephesians 3:5' (p. 39). In this case verse 13a becomes important, 'These things we also speak;' the sense being, God has revealed them to us, and we speak them to others. However in addition to Fee's point it is very difficult to restrict verse 12 just to the apostles. 'The things which have been freely given to us by God' ('lavished on us' REB) looks very much like another way of saying 'the things which God has prepared for those who love him', in which case that 'us' must be 'us Christians' and this determines the usage throughout the passage.

[19] Robertson and Plummer take the aorist to mean 'a definite time when the revelation took place, viz. to the entry of the Gospel into the world' (*op. cit.*, p. 43). This seems very unlikely, and even more so any reference to Pentecost.

[20] So, for example, Acts 2:38–39; John 7:39; Romans 8:15; Ephesians 1:13; Galatians 3:2–3.

[21] This links with, e.g. Romans 5:5 and the love of God being shed abroad in the heart, and Romans 8:15–16 and the witness of the Spirit to sonship.

[22] Fee, *op. cit.*, p. 115. Barrett agrees with this (*op. cit.*, p. 76). However, as Fee acknowledges, the use of ψυχικὸς at the beginning of verse 14 tends to suggest that πνευματικοῖς refers to people, though he thinks the grammar is against this.

[23] Watson, *op. cit.*, p. 26.

[24] William F. Orr and James Arthur Walther in *1 Corinthians*, AB (New York: Doubleday & Co. Inc., 1976) have an interesting comment at this point, '*The affairs of God's Spirit* include the insights about the meaning of the gospel and, as the sequel seems to indicate, the application of the spirit of the gospel to all problematic areas of life. These things are *investigated in a spiritual manner*. Only by the agency of the Spirit can one carry out the kind of research, systematic examination, or questioning that enables one to discover or understand these things' (p. 166).

[25] So Fee, *op. cit.,* p. 119, fn. 87.

[26] Watson, *op. cit.*, p. 35.

[27] 'If a man conceives himself to be wise in such terms he cannot advance from human to divine wisdom by becoming wiser, he must negate the old wisdom in order to acquire the new' (Barrett, *op. cit.,* p. 94).

[28] Grosheide says, '*Knowledge* in Paul's vocabulary is not something purely intellectual, it is a knowledge which has results and leads to action, especially religious action' (*op. cit.*, p. 189). Barrett also commenting on γνῶσις says, 'The term was probably (at this stage) a wide one, and the next few verses show that it included Christian speculative theology in general, and drew conclusions with regard to Christian social and moral behaviour' (*op. cit.*, p. 189).

[29] Fee, *op. cit.*, p. 366.

[30] Fee says on 8:1–3, 'Christian behaviour is not predicated on the way of knowledge, which leads to pride and destroys others, but on the way of love, which is in fact the true way of knowledge. All of this will be spelled out in greater detail in vv. 7–13, and especially in chap.13' (*op. cit.*, pp. 368–69).

[31] *Ibid.*, p. 585–586. Hodge points out that elsewhere other gifts are mentioned which are not found here (*op. cit.*, p. 244); Guthrie surveys the other passages and says, 'From these evidences we may note that Paul never conceives of the Spirit as the giver of a certain number of circumscribed gifts' (*New Testament Theology*, p. 566).

[32] Fee says, 'Paul's concern at the outset is singular: To insist that "inspired utterance" in itself does not mark what is truly "spiritual", but the intelligible content of that utterance, content that is ultimately tested by the basic Christian confession of the lordship of Jesus Christ' (*op. cit.*, p. 575).

[33] Commentators discuss the great difficulty of imagining

circumstances under which someone in a Christian meeting could say, 'Jesus is accursed'. Perhaps Grosheide's comment is the most helpful, *'Jesus is anathema* is simply a brief statement, summarizing everything that could be said against Jesus' (*op. cit.*, p. 281).

[34] Grosheide thinks that this confession must be thought of as taking place by means of *glossolalia* (*op. cit.*, p. 280), but Fee indicates that in the circumstances of the early churches this was a real test: 'The use of "Lord" in such a context meant absolute allegiance to Jesus as one's deity and set believers apart from both Jews, for whom such a confession was blasphemy, and pagans, especially those in the cults, whose deities were called "lords" ' (*op. cit.*, pp. 581–82).

[35] Calvin says, 'I take knowledge to mean an understanding of holy things; but wisdom a thorough-going grasp of them' (*op. cit.*, p.262). But others suggest otherwise and Fee is almost certainly right when he says, 'The probability that both σοφία and γνῶσις were Corinthian terms taken over by Paul only increases our difficulty in determining the specific nature of these two gifts in Paul's own thinking' (*op. cit.*, p. 591, fn. 45).

[36] *Ibid.*, p. 592.

[37] Fee makes the link but appears to be saying that 'spirits' refers to the spirits of the prophets themselves, rather than evil spirits (*ibid.*, p. 597).

[38] Orr and Walther say, 'Apparently prophecy in these early churches functioned in a role filled now mainly by preaching. (But there seemed to be a greater sense of immediate Spirit direction as the sequel will show)' (*op. cit.*, p. 306). On the other hand Calvin says, 'I take the term *prophecy* to mean that unique and outstanding gift of revealing what is the secret will of God, so that the prophet is, so to speak, God's messenger to men' (*op. cit.*, p. 263). However, when he comes to verse 28 he says, 'I am certain, in my own mind, that he means by prophets ... those who were blessed with the unique gift of dealing with Scripture, not only by interpreting it, but also by the wisdom they showed in making it meet the needs of the hour' (*op. cit.*, p. 271). Wayne Grudem has argued very strongly that what we have here is 'a secondary type of prophecy with diminished authority' (hence the need for checking, 14:29) (*The Gift of Prophecy in 1 Corinthians* [Washington: University Press of America, 1982], p. 262). The quotation comes from his conclusion. Fee describes prophecy in this way: 'spontaneous, Spirit-inspired, intelligible

messages, orally delivered in the gathered assembly, intended for the edification or encouragement of the people' (*op. cit.*, p. 595).

[39] 'Prophecy addresses the human understanding and provides a *message* that *builds up a church*' (Orr and Walther, *op. cit.,* p. 306).

[40] Compare the section on Acts.

[41] Dunn says, 'First, they [early Christian prophets] helped to interpret the prophecies of the OT and the sayings of Jesus in the light of what had happened (death and resurrection of Jesus, and the outpouring of the Spirit), and in relation to their own (changing) situations' (*Jesus and the Spirit* [London: SCM], p. 172).

[42] See the section on Revelation and, in particular, the quotation in fn. 11.

[43] It is however implied; Fee comments, 'Thus, one of the sure signs of the presence of God in the believing community is this deep plowing work of the Spirit, whereby through prophetic revelations the secrets of the heart are laid bare.' He adds, 'No wonder the Corinthians preferred tongues; it not only gave them a sense of being more truly "spiritual" but it was safer!' (*op. cit.*, p. 687).

Chapter 6: 2 Corinthians

[1] Barrett says, 'There is a play on words in the Greek (Χριστὸς ... χρίσας) which the English only clumsily represents' (*A Commentary on the Second Epistle to the Corinthians* [London: A. & C. Black, 1973], p. 79).

[2] For example Stephen Smalley says, 'There are thus good grounds for understanding χρῖσμα in this verse, within a Jewish-Christian setting, as a reference to the gift of the Spirit, which is "the characteristic endowment" of believers (Westcott, 73).' He adds, 'Paul seems also to be (independently) indebted to this kind of interpretation when he speaks of God in Christ "anointing" the believer, and putting his Spirit in our hearts "as a deposit, guaranteeing what is to come" (2 Cor. 1:21–22)' (*1, 2, 3 John*, wbc [Dallas: Word Books, 1991], p. 106). The study by Gary Burge on the Holy Spirit in the Johannine Tradition also agrees that the χρῖσμα in 1 John 2:20, 27 refers to the Spirit (*The Anointed Community* [Grand Rapids: Eerdmans, 1987] pp. 174–75).

[3] 'In the thought of the New Testament, then, the Christian experiences of anointing, sealing, and receiving the earnest are all

associated with the operation of the Holy Spirit' (P. E. Hughes, *The Second Epistle to the Corinthians*, NICNT [Grand Rapids: Eerdmans, 1962], p. 42–43). The question of whether these are all to be related to baptism is considered by a number of writers. David Lull, who considers several similar passages, concludes, 'This means that 2 Cor. 1:21–22 presupposes proclamation, not baptism, as the setting in which the Spirit was initially received by his converts' (*The Spirit in Galatia* [Society of Biblical Literature, 1980; distributed by Scholars Press, California], pp. 63–64).

[4] 5:5 also refers to the Spirit as a guarantee. Here the context is of the hope Christians have after death. It may be that the reference to the Spirit as a guarantee accounts for the confidence expressed in the next verse and verse 8 (though the 'therefore' could apply to the whole of verses 1–5), and also for the confident words at the beginning of the chapter, 'For we *know* ...'

[5] Barrett says, 'Christians, being in Christ (that Paul here writes "into Christ", εἰς Χριστὸν, not "in Christ", ἐν Χριστῷ, may be due to the commercial metaphor; we are, as it were, 'entered to Christ's account'), share his vocation and mission and as themselves anointed are assured of this not by the steadfastness of their own faith, or by the warmth of its emotional accompaniments, but by God himself' *(op. cit.*, p. 79).

[6] Calvin says, 'For when God pours out upon us the heavenly gift of His Spirit, this is His way of sealing the certainty of His Word on our hearts.' And again, 'we should note that, since this degree of certainty is beyond the capacity of the human mind, it is the office of the Holy Spirit to confirm within us what God promises in His Word' (*The Second Epistle of Paul the Apostle to the Corinthians and the Epistles to Timothy, Titus and Philemon*, trans. T. A. Smail [Oliver and Boyd, 1964], p. 23).

[7] Writing on verse 17 Hughes says, 'Although, however, there is in our judgment no *direct* reference to the Holy Spirit here, yet there can be no doubt that the operation of the Holy Spirit is implicit in Paul's argument, especially in view of his plain teaching elsewhere that it is the Holy Spirit's office to apply the work of Christ to the believing heart. The distinction between "spirit" and "Spirit" accordingly becomes a fine one and explains the division of the commentators over this point' (*op. cit.*, p. 116). 'The Spirit of the living God' (v. 3), seems an unmistakeable reference to the Holy

Spirit and suggests that 'Spirit' should be understood similarly throughout the passage. 'The Spirit gives life' (v. 6) and 'the Spirit of the Lord' (v. 17) also both appear to be clear references to the Holy Spirit.

[8] I give evidence for this in my article, 'Lifting the Veil (2 Corinthians 3:13–18)'; (*Foundations,* Autumn 1993, No. 31), p. 10.

[9] Hughes, *op. cit.,* p. 97.

[10] 'Great authority has been given to a comment of Origen's to the effect that by the letter we should understand the grammatical and natural sense of Scripture, which he calls the literal sense, and by the Spirit the allegorical sense, which is commonly held to be spiritual. Thus for several centuries it was commonly said and accepted that here Paul is giving us a key for expounding the Scriptures allegorically, whereas in fact nothing could be further from his mind' (Calvin, *op. cit.,* pp. 41, 42).

[11] Calvin inclines to this view (p. 42). So does Nigel Watson (*The Second Epistle to the Corinthians* [London: Epworth Press, 1993]) when he writes: 'on the one hand, a way of knowing God's will as *letter*, as external code, as "something coldly strange to the depths of the heart", to use Allo's phrase; and on the other, a way of knowing God's will as *spirit*, that is, as power, in other words, a knowledge which is also an empowering to live by what one knows, a knowledge which carries the personality of the knower along with it' (p. 29).

[12] Perhaps the contrast is a little more subtle than that. Barrett says, '*Letter* thus points to the way in which (in Paul's view) many of his Jewish contemporaries understood the law on which their religion was based, and through this to man-made religion in general, whether legalistic or antinomian and mystical ... *Spirit* points to the new action of God in Christ, where man by faith leaves God to act creatively, no longer expecting to fend for himself' (*op. cit.,* p. 113).

Scott Hafemann expresses the point slightly differently: 'The "letter" (gramma) of 2 Corinthians 3:6 is therefore the Law apart from the power of the Spirit, which by itself can only declare God's will and pronounce judgment for not doing it, but cannot empower one to keep it. Only God's Spirit, which is now being poured out in the new covenant as a result of the work of Christ, can "make one alive" (2 Cor. 3:6) and bring about this righteousness (2 Cor. 3:8–9)' 'Letters to the Corinthians' in G.F. Hawthorne, R.P. Martin and D.G.Reid (eds.), *Dictionary of Paul and his Letters* [Leicester: IVP, 1993], p. 169).

[13] Many writers take the view that it was the glory that was fading. Scott Hafemann, however, says, 'Moses had to veil himself, therefore, not because the glory was fading, but so that the effects of God's glory against a stiff-necked people might be brought to an end ... This would make it possible for God's presence to continue in Israel's midst in spite of Israel's hardened nature. The veil of Moses thus becomes a metonymy for the hardness of Israel's heart under the old covenant (2 Cor. 3:14, 15)' (*ibid.*, p. 169).

[14] Taking 'the Lord' in verse 17 to refer back to 'the Lord' in verse 16; i.e. to 'the Lord' in Exodus 34.

[15] The verb κατοπτρίζειν could be translated either as 'beholding' or 'reflecting'. However as Martin says, 'The translation "we reflect" removes the contrast of the Christians with the Jews, who because of their veil cannot see; so the rendering "we behold" is to be preferred' (R. P. Martin, *2 Corinthians*, wbc [Dallas: Word Books, 1991], p.71).

[16] The last phrase presents another notorious crux of interpretation. Possibly 'the Lord who is the Spirit', following 17a, is the best rendering.

[17] So Hughes says: 'through the operation of the Holy Spirit who enables the believer constantly to behold the glory of the Lord.... In origin, process and consummation this whole work of redemption is "of the Lord the Spirit" ' (*op. cit.*, p. 120).

[18] 'The force of the phrase is concessive: "Even if, as I grant, my gospel is veiled in the case of some" ' (*ibid.*, p. 125, fn. 28).

[19] 'The dreadful consequence, then, of unbelief, of bowing down to "the god of this age" instead of to the only true God, is that the mind is blinded. The effect is attributed to Satan as the initiator of sin and therefore of its consequences; but it should not be overlooked that, despite the satanic revolt, God is still sovereign and that this blindness resulting from sin also has the nature of a judgment upon the wilful and persistent rebelliousness of the human heart. This, in turn, is attended by the inability to perceive and rejoice in the surpassing splendour of the gospel, and that means perdition. The tempter, in fact, sets in motion a kind of chain reaction: sin leads to blindness, and blindness leads to destruction. Impelled by hatred of the gospel, he has been a liar (= a blinder of men's minds) and a murderer (= a destroyer of men's souls) from the beginning (John 8:44f.) (*ibid.*, p. 129).

[20] 'It was on the road to Damascus that the light first shone into his heart. That outward light was a symbol of the glory of Christ

streaming into his heart' (Ernest Best, *Second Corinthians*, Interpretation [Louisville: John Knox Press, 1987], p. 39).

[21] REB.

[22] 'Unbelievers are helplessly blinded by the god of this age so that they cannot see the glory of the gospel (v. 4); spiritual sight and enlightenment can come, if they are to come at all, only through the intervening grace of Almighty God, for, left to himself, the sinner can only stumble in darkness' (Hughes, *op. cit.,* pp. 132–133).

[23] 'The shining, moreover, *is in the heart*, that is, in its scriptural significance, the centre of man's whole being, moral, intellectual, and spiritual' (*ibid.*, p. 134).

[24] 'The ἡμεῖς cannot mean Paul (and the other apostles) in particular, but embraces all believers who seize the possibility of verse 14. The term corresponds to the τις of verse 17' (R. Bultmann, *The Second Letter to the Corinthians*, trans. Roy A. Harrisville [Minneapolis: Augsburg Publishing House, 1985], pp. 153–154).

[25] 'Here "to know" is equivalent to "to judge", as if he had said, "We do not judge according to outward appearance so as to think that the man who seems to be most outstanding really is" ' (Calvin, *op. cit.*, p. 74).

[26] So, for example, Best: 'Since Paul's conversion and in the light of his conviction that Christ died for him, he thinks in a different kind of way, once "according to the flesh" but now "according to the Spirit". His judgments are now controlled by God's Spirit' (*op. cit.*, p. 53).

[27] 'It is noteworthy that Paul does not speak of "knowing Christ after the Spirit", though the contrast would seem to suggest it. Probably, as J. Louis Martyn has argued, he has avoided such an expression because it was the sort of thing that his opponents, with their claims to have arrived, would have said only too readily' (Watson, *op. cit.*, p. 61). So also Victor Paul Furnish, *II Corinthians,* AB (New York: Doubleday and Co. Inc., 1984), p. 331.

[28] J. Louis Martyn, '*Epistemology at the turn of the Ages: 2 Corinthians 5:16*', pp. 269–287 in W. R. Farmer, C. F. D. Moule and R. R. Niebuhr (eds.), *Christian History and Interpretation* (Cambridge: CUP, 1967), p. 280.

[29] Watson, *op. cit.*, and Furnish, *op. cit.*

[30] Hughes, *op. cit.*, p. 350.

[31] The dative τῷ θεῷ is explained in different ways. Hughes says, 'We prefer, however, to regard it as a semitism, or at any rate as

reflecting the influence of the LXX, and to translate δυνατά τῷ θεῷ as "divinely powerful" (Beza, Moffatt)' (*ibid.*, p. 351, fn. 6). C. F. D. Moule also takes it as a semitism, *An Idiom Book of New Testament Greek* (Cambridge: CUP, 1975), p. 184.

[32] Paul has used ὅπλα earlier in 6:7 and also in Romans 13:2, 'the armour of light', cf. also Romans 6:13a. Ephesians 6:10ff. does not seem to be an adequate parallel as Paul is thinking there primarily of a spiritual battle which is not with 'flesh and blood'. Here his battle, if not exactly with flesh and blood, is certainly with the ideas and teachings of human proponents.

[33] 'According to II Cor. 3:14, the veil which still exists over the heart (cf. 3:15) also exists "upon the reading of the old covenant". Thus, the work of the Spirit also carries a corresponding hermeneutical implication based on the important OT unity between the moral and the theoretical/practical spheres of life, epitomized in the maxim that "the fear of the Lord is the beginning of wisdom" (cf. Prov. 1:7; 9:10; 15:33; Job 28:28; Ps. 111:10). This means, in turn, that the barrier to a proper understanding of the law removed "in Christ" is not intellectual, but moral. The importance of this point for Paul's immediate argument is found in the fact that, according to 3:7–11, a proper understanding of the glory inherent in the law is an essential prerequisite for an understanding of the exceedingly glorious nature of the gospel ... But given both that the barrier to be removed is a moral one and the example of Paul's own reading of the OT in II Cor. 3:7–18 itself, the distinctively Christian OT hermeneutic cannot be said to consist in a new esoteric way of reading the OT, much less in a set of predetermined exegetical presuppositions which are only available to those already within the new covenant relationship to God' (J. Scott Hafemann, *Suffering and Ministry in the Spirit* [Grand Rapids: Eerdmans, 1990], pp. 231–32).

Chapter 7: Galatians

[1] D. Lull, *The Spirit in Galatia* (Society of Biblical Literature, 1980; distributed by the Scholars Press, California), p. 25.

[2] Ibid., p. 199.

[3] Richard Longenecker (*Galatians*, wbc [Dallas: Word Books, 1990], p. 23, 24) takes it to be 'from Jesus Christ' but he acknowledges that most commentators 'understand Jesus Christ as the content of the revelation mainly because of v. 16a'.

[4] H. Ridderbos, *The Epistle of Paul to the Churches of Galatia*, NICNT (Grand Rapids: Eerdmans, 1953), p. 63.

[5] Lull says, 'Thus, despite the different historical situations in Paul's churches, in 1 Thess.1:4–6, 1 Cor. 2:4–5 and Gal. 3:1–5, πνευμα [pneuma] is an empirical datum of Paul's converts' experience, which has its *Sitz im Leben* in missionary preaching' (*op. cit.*, p. 59).

[6] Paul switches from 'you' to 'our' and back again in order to stress that this is the experience of all Christians. There is some textual uncertainty but this probably arises from a scribal tendency towards consistency.

[7] So Betz, '["hope"] is the eschatalogical nature of the gift of salvation. It is not visible and obtainable now, but because of the gift of the Spirit which the Galatians have experienced, and the "arguments" which the readers have read in chapters 3–4, this hope could and should be a matter of certainty even in this life' (Hans Dieter Betz, *Galatians*, Hermeneia [Philadelphia: Fortress Press, 1979], p. 262).

Chapter 8: Ephesians

[1] J. Armitage Robinson defines the two words in this way: 'Wisdom is the knowledge which sees into the heart of things, which knows them as they really are. Prudence is the understanding which leads to right action' (*St Paul's Epistle to the Ephesians* [London: Macmillan and Co., 1903] p. 30).

[2] 'The New Testament writers find the word [i.e. μυστήριον] in ordinary use in this colourless sense ["secret"], and they start it upon a new career by appropriating it to the great truths of the Christian religion, which could not have been known to men except by Divine disclosure or revelation. A mystery in this sense is not a thing which *must* be kept secret. On the contrary it is a secret which God wills to make known and has charged His Apostles to declare to those who have ears to hear it' (Robinson, 'Excursus on μυστηριον', in *ibid.*, p.240.) Francis Foulkes says: 'the word does bear the significance of truth not previously known but now revealed (Rom. xvi.25), and the even more important fact that understanding depends on God's will to reveal, and on man's desire to receive insight that must be God-given' (*The Epistle of Paul to the Ephesians*, TNTC [London: Tyndale Press, 1963], p. 51).

[3] Arthur G. Patzia says, 'Most commentators suggest that the idea of guarantee (ἀρραβών) came into the Greek world from the

Phoenicians, who, in matters of trade, often would make a deposit or an instalment as earnest money with the balance to be paid in full at some later date.... But "the deal" included a sense of "quality" as well, for the person receiving the down payment looked forward to receiving full payment with goods of the same quality (Mitton, pp. 62–63). In the Christian life, the Holy Spirit is a pledge that God will complete his promise to deliver *our inheritance*.... One's present life *in* the Spirit is a foretaste of one's future life *with* the Spirit. Beyond *guaranteeing* one's *inheritance*, the Holy Spirit assures believers of *the redemption of those who are God's possession'* (*Ephesians, Colossians, Philemon*, NIBC [Peabody: Hendrickson, 1990], p. 160).

⁴ Compare Foulkes: 'The *experience* [my italics, and below] of the Holy Spirit in his life is the final proof to him, and indeed a demonstration to others, of the genuineness of what he has believed, and provides the inward assurance that he belongs to God as a son' (*op. cit.*, p. 56). 'The Christian's *experience* of the Spirit now is a foretaste and pledge of what will be his when he fully possesses his God-given inheritance' (p. 57).

⁵ 'ἐπιγνώσις has always a moral value and is used in the NT exclusively in reference to facts of the religious order and specially in reference to the knowledge which we are enabled to gain of God and of His purpose for man's salvation. It is peculiar to the epistle' (B. F. Westcott, *The Epistle to the Ephesians* [London: Macmillan & Co., 1906], p. 23).

⁶ This is assuming the perfect passive participle is to be given its usual value; so Patzia: 'The tense of the verb here prohibits taking "enlightened" in a progressive sense – that is, as becoming more and more enlightened' (*op. cit.*, p. 165–66). On the other hand Robert Bratcher and Eugene Nida say, 'The perfect passive participle "having been illumined" with which verse 18 begins in Greek, is syntactically related to the main verb "gave" (verse 17) and modifies it; strictly it should refer to an action previous to the action of the main verb, but here it seems to function as a circumstantial clause, showing the way in which the disclosure, the revelation of God's will, takes place; or else (as participles are often used in biblical Greek) it serves as an imperative: "the eyes of your heart be opened"; so TEV *I ask that ...* (Compare NEB and others "I pray that ...")' (*A Translators Handbook on Paul's Letter to the Ephesians* [London/New York/

Stuttgart: United Bible Societies, 1982], p. 32).

[7] 'Such a recognition, knowledge and becoming cognisant is only possible for people who have been enlightened by the divine Spirit which enables them to see with the eyes of the heart' (Rudolf Schnackenburg, *Ephesians,* trans. Helen Heron [Edinburgh: T. & T. Clark, 1991], p. 74).

[8] 'The people of the region had an extraordinary fear of the hostile spiritual "powers" .... This fear was not immediately allayed, however, when people became Christians. Demonstrating his sincere pastoral concern, Paul addressed their fear of this realm. More than any other Pauline letter, Ephesians stresses the hostile role of the principalities and powers ... against the church [C. E. Arnold, *Ephesians: Power and Magic,* SNTSMS 63; Cambridge: University Press, 1989]. In contrast to the power of the hostile supernatural realm, Paul emphasizes the superiority of the power of God and the supremacy of Christ (Eph. 1:19–23; 4:8–10)' (C. E. Arnold, 'Letter to the Ephesians' in G. F Hawthorne, R. P. Martin and D. G. Reid (eds.), *Dictionary of Paul and His Letters* [Downers Grove/Leicester: IVP, 1993], p. 247).

[9] 'the factors which favour an emphasis here on the divine Spirit as giver are weightier. They include the explicit mention of the divine Spirit in connection with revelation in 3:5 (cf. also 1 Cor. 2:6–16), the apparent dependence on Col. 1:9 where "spiritual" refers to the Spirit, and the close verbal parallel to Rom. 8:15 where πνευμα υἱοθεσίας, "Spirit of adoption", is to be taken as a reference to God's Spirit. So this is a petition for the Spirit himself to be at work, giving insights into and unveiling aspects of the purpose of God in Christ, an activity which could take place privately, to individuals, or in corporate assembly gathered for worship' (Andrew T. Lincoln, *Ephesians,* WBC [Dallas: Word Books, 1990], p. 57.

[10] Robinson says, 'But a distinction may often be rightly drawn in the New Testament between the usage of the word [πνεῦμα] with the definite article and its usage without it. With the article, very generally, the word indicates the personal Holy Spirit; while without it some special manifestation or bestowal of the Holy Spirit is signified' (*op. cit.,* p. 39).

[11] Schnackenburg, 'Hence we are not concerned here with the Spirit of prophecy with special "revelations" (cf. 1 Cor. 14:6, 26, 30), or a charismatic talent (cf. 1 Cor. 1:5, 7) but with a spiritual experience possible for all believers.... From this experience of salvation which is

bestowed on all believers through the Spirit we must distinguish that special revelation granted to Paul of the "holy apostles and prophets in the Spirit" (Eph. 3:3, 5)' *op. cit.*, p. 74. Patzia (and others) links 'enlightenment' with baptism; but Schnackenburg says, 'We may suspect it [i.e. the prayer] comes out of a liturgical tradition, but do not have to (as Schlier) think it refers to baptism' (*ibid*). Commenting on the word 'revelation' John Owen says: 'But there is an *internal subjective revelation*, whereby no *new things* are revealed unto our minds, or are not outwardly revealed *anew*, but our minds are enabled to discern the things that are revealed already' (*The Causes, Ways, and Means of Understanding the Mind of God as revealed in his Word*, in *Works of John Owen*, Vol. 4 [Edinburgh: reprinted Banner of Truth Trust, 1967], p. 134).

[12] Mitton says, 'As the light of day enables our physical eyes to see things hidden by the darkness, so the light which shines from Christ enables us to grasp the truth in what earlier seemed puzzling and obscure' (C. L. Mitton, *Ephesians*, NCB [Oliphants, 1976], p.61).

[13] John Owen, whose whole treatise (already referred to) is about spiritual illumination, finishes his remarks on these verses in this way: 'I have insisted the longer upon this testimony, because the whole of what we assert in general, in the nature, causes, and effects of it, is fully declared therein. And this was the way whereby they of old came to understand divine revelations, or the mind of God as revealed in the Scripture' (*op. cit.*, pp. 141–142).

[14] Westcott says, 'νεκρὸς describes generally the complete absence of the characteristic power of that to which it is referred.... Men are dead in respect to that which is the true characteristic of men when they are without that power through which they grow to the divine likeness for which men were made' (*op. cit.*, p. 29). Foulkes comments, 'Man's sinful condition is lifeless and motionless as far as any Godward activity is concerned' (*op. cit.*, p. 69). Hendriksen says of man, 'He lacks the ability to bestir himself so as to give heed to that which God demands of him (Ezek. 37; John 3:3, 5). Only when God turns him is he able to turn from his wicked way (Jer. 31:18, 19)' (William Hendriksen, *Ephesians*, NTC [Grand Rapids: Baker Book House, 1967], p. 112).

[15] The precise nuance of σάρξ depends on usage and context. BAGD says 'In Paul's thoughts especially the *flesh* is the willing instrument of sin, and is subject to sin to such a degree that wherever

flesh is, all forms of sin are likewise present and no good thing can live in the *sarx*. The second usage of the word seems to be more restricted because it is distinguished from "mind".'

[16] The Greek here is διανοιῶν ('thoughts'). Patzia says, '*Thoughts* includes one's intellectual and reasoning ability (cf. Col. 1:21)' (*op. cit.*, p. 178). 'The last word, a plural of a word more commonly used in the singular (διάνοια) meaning a "thought" or "purpose" or "intelligence", signifies clearly that the effects of man's evil and selfishness are not limited to the emotions but embrace his intellect and reasoning processes as well (Col. 1:21)' (Foulkes, *op. cit.*, p. 70).

[17] Foulkes says here, 'The personal Spirit of God is obviously intended' (*op. cit.*, p. 85). Robinson links *Spirit* with *body* in verse 16 saying, 'This phrase is the counterpart of the phrase "in one body" of v. 16. "In one body" we both were reconciled to God; "in one Spirit" we both have our access to the Father' (*op. cit.*, p. 66). He identifies 'body' with the 'Body of Christ' and says, 'the Body of Christ has a Spirit that dwells in it' (*ibid*). This seems doubtful; it seems more likely that 'body' refers to Christ's actual body (cf. vv. 13–14). However, Robinson is doubtless right to link the two phrases together.

[18] See 1 Corinthians 2:10, 'God has revealed them to us through his Spirit' (NKJV); and the discussion of this passage earlier.

[19] Robinson says, 'Here, as in some other places, the Apostle's language is so vague that we cannot tell with entire certainty whether he refers directly to the personal Divine Spirit, or rather desires to suggest that the reception of the revelation is a spiritual process' (*op. cit.*, p. 78). Westcott inclines to the former view, though he adds that when a person holds fellowship with God 'he is himself in the Holy Spirit and the Holy Spirit is in him' (*op. cit.*, p. 46). Comparison with 2:18, 22 suggest that 'Spirit' is intended. Schnackenburg takes the word to refer to the Spirit but, because of the position of αὐτοῦ after apostles, suggests that it only refers to the prophets, 'both groups are recipients of revelation, the prophets, however, in a different manner, as "in the Spirit" may signify' (*op. cit.*, p. 133–134).

[20] '"The saints" here is not a restricted group within the church, but, as regularly, the whole people of God' (N. T. Wright, *Colossians and Philemon*, TNTC [Leicester: Inter-Varsity Press, 1986], p. 91).

[21] BAGD, which gives Acts 4:13; 10:34 as the two other places in the

NT where καταλαμβάνω is used in this way. Its use in John 1:5 has already been discussed.

[22] Westcott says, 'Such knowledge is not an individual privilege but a common endowment. The co-operation of all is required for the attainment of the full conception.' He also adds on the word 'saints'; 'Sainthood – consecration – is the condition of spiritual knowledge' (*op. cit.,* p. 52). Robinson takes the thought a little further when he comments, 'The measures of the divine purpose are indeed beyond the comprehension of any individual intelligence: but in union "with all the saints" we may be able to comprehend them. Each saint may grasp some portion: the whole of the saints – when "we all come to the perfect man" – may know, as a whole, what must for ever transcend the knowledge of the isolated individual' (*op. cit.,* p. 86).

[23] *Ibid.,* p. 86.

[24] 'Christians experience Christ's inexhaustible and never fully comprehensible love "with all the saints" in the Church, but constantly have need of strengthening by the Holy Spirit in order to have an ever-increasing share in the riches of God's grace. In this way they are led more and more to God the Father in Christ through the Holy Spirit' (Schnackenburg, *op. cit.,* p. 152).

[25] 'There [Rom. 1] it is thrice said that "God gave them up": here it is said that, "having become reckless, they gave themselves up." The emphasis which in either case St Paul lays on want of knowledge corresponds with the stress which, as we have already seen, he lays upon true wisdom' (Robinson, *op. cit.,* p. 106). Lincoln notes, 'this ignorance does not provide an excuse for the broken relationship with God' (*op. cit.,* p. 278); and Markus Barth explains that in this way: 'ignorance is frequently a stance of the total man that includes his emotion, will, and action. Not to know the Lord is as much as to ignore him.... There is no cause to put the blame upon external, circumstantial reasons for what has its origin and seat in man himself' (*Ephesians,* AB [New York: Doubleday & Co.], 1974, p. 501).

[26] Martin refers to, '... "insensibility" which can refer to a spiritual condition that borders on indifference and leads to a way of life where all distinctions between good and bad, wholesome and destructive, are lost in a willful disregard of moral values' (Ralph P. Martin, *Ephesians, Colossians and Philemon,* Interpretation [Louisville: John Knox Press, 1992], p. 60).

[27] Foulkes says, 'Rather the original in this last clause is "in him"

repeating thus the key phrase of the Epistle. Christ was not only the subject, but "the sphere of the instruction" (Robinson)' (Foulkes, *op. cit.,* p. 129). So also Hendriksen, 'The addressed, then, had heard of Christ and had been taught not only *about* but "*in*" him; that is, the entire atmosphere had been Christian. Christ, speaking through his ambassadors, was the teacher. He was also the theme' (*op. cit.*, p. 212).

[28] Speaking for those who see a reference here to the Holy Spirit, Schnackenburg says, 'The double expression "spirit of your minds" could pleonastically mean the human spirit according to the style of Eph.; but since *pneuma* is nowhere else in Eph. used this way, what must be meant is the Christian mind guided by the divine Spirit (cf. 3:16; 4:3; 5:18; 6:18)' (*op. cit.*, p. 200). However, Lincoln's assessment seems definitive, 'The majority of recent commentators [he mentions Schlier, Gnilka, Houlden, Halter, Ernst, Schnackenburg and Mussner] opt for a reference to the divine Spirit on the grounds that nowhere else in Ephesians does πνεῦμα refer to the human spirit and elsewhere in the letter it is the Spirit who controls believers (cf. 1:17; 3:16; 4:3; 5:18; 6:18). Also in Titus 3:5 the Holy Spirit is the explicit agent of renewal. Houlden (319) even translates the verse "Be renewed by the Spirit in your mind." But this is not what the Greek text says. It speaks about the spirit *of* your mind. Since this is so, we must agree that "it is improbable that God's Spirit would be described as 'of your mind'" (Mitton, 165) ... In Ephesians' characteristic style of pleonastic accumulation of synonyms, both spirit and mind are employed to designate a person's innermost being (*cf.* also Meyer, 249; Abbott, 137; J. A. Robinson, 191; Westcott, 68; Barth, 508; Mitton, 165; Bratcher and Nida, *Handbook*, 114–115; RSV, NEB)', Lincoln, *op. cit.*, pp. 286-87.

[29] So, for example, Foulkes: 'Such a renewal in the mind (Rom. 12:2) or in *the spirit of* the *mind*, is possible by the indwelling of the Spirit of God' (*op. cit.*, p. 131); and Hendriksen: 'This renewal is basically an act of God's Spirit powerfully influencing man's *spirit*, here, as also in 1 Cor. 4:21; Gal. 6:1; and 1 Peter 3:4, *mental attitude, state of mind, disposition*, with respect to God and spiritual realities' (*op. cit.*, p. 215).

[30] Hendriksen says, 'We may call this a highly anthropomorphic expression, and so it is, both here and in Isa. 63:10 from which it is borrowed' (*op. cit.*, p. 222).

[31] 'So had the night of spiritual ignorance and sin penetrated them that they were, as it were, night itself, night embodied' (C. F. D. Moule, *Ephesians* [Cambridge: CUP, 1953], quoted in Patzia, *op. cit.*, p. 131).

[32] ἐν κυρίῳ, taking up again the idea of Christians being 'in Christ'. 'It is only "in the Lord", that is, in vital connection with him, that they are now light' (Hendriksen, *op. cit.*, p. 231). 'He says in effect, "If you are in the Lord, you are in the light, and the light is in you"' (Foulkes, *op. cit.*, p. 145).

[33] Martin especially, 'Yet another title is "children of light" (vv. 8–14). This title is interesting not only for its association with the community of the Dead Sea scrolls who also used this description to set off their group from the surrounding "children of darkness" but for the example in verse 14 of a baptismal reminder. At the commencement of their new life as believers these men and women had been brought into the full light of Christ. We may overhear the very terms of their initiation in a three-line baptismal chant contained in verse 14:

> Awake, o sleeper,
> And get up from the dead;
> And Christ's light will shine upon you!

'The life situation of this snatch of early hymnody is evidently baptism, which was frequently known in the church as a person's "enlightenment" and depicted as the rising of the new convert from the death of sin into union with the living Lord (Heb. 6:4; Rom. 6:4–12)' (*op. cit.*, p. 63).

[34] *The Greek New Testament* (United Bible Societies, 3rd edn.).

[35] Foulkes notes that 'there is a certain strangeness about the construction in the Greek here' (πληροῦσθε ἐν πνεύματι), but he adds, 'It is as if the two thoughts of being filled with the Spirit, and living a life "in the Spirit" (see on 2:18), are being expressed at the same time; and this may be assisted by the fact that the little preposition *en* in the New Testament can often have a meaning equivalent to "with".... To take the expression as meaning merely to be filled in spirit would be to deprive it of the force of meaning that it clearly has in the context' (*op. cit.*, p. 152).

[36] ' "With your hearts" does not mean that their mouths should

remain silent.... It means rather that the Spirit with his power should take hold of the "inner person" (*cf.* 3:16ff) and the outward song should be produced by the inner dynamic' (Schnackenburg, *op. cit.*, p. 238).

[37] Wright notes that 'the word of Christ' in Colossians 3:16 might refer 'just possibly, to the word which Christ speaks in the present by his Spirit' (*op. cit.*, p. 144).

[38] Westcott: 'The sword which the Spirit provides and through which it acts' (*op. cit.*, p. 97).

[39] See fn. 8 above.

[40] Hendriksen says, 'Through it [i.e. the sword of the Spirit] doubts are dispelled, fears are driven away, assurance of salvation given, and Satan put to flight' (*op. cit.*, p. 280).

Chapter 9: Philippians to 2 Timothy

[1] 'But the Philippians who were in Christ were to make such choices of what was vital... on the basis of an ever-increasing love – a love that penetrated more deeply into the knowledge of God and the treasures of Christ, and imparted to the Christian a keener and more delicate moral sense for specific situations' (P. T. O'Brien, *The Epistle to the Philippians*, NIGTC [Grand Rapids: Eerdmans, 1991], p. 78).

[2] However, it is interesting to note the comment of Collange, 'Hence agape is an object of prayer (*proseuchomai*), the Spirit is the source of it (Rom. 5:5; Gal. 5:22) supplying the eschatological bounty (*puissere*; Rom. 5:13; 1 Cor. 14:12; 2 Cor. 3:9 etc.) which is typical of the ultimate acts of God' (Jean-Francois Collange, *The Epistle of Saint Paul to the Philippians,* trans. A.W. Heathcote [London: Epworth Press, 1979], p. 49).

[3] Martin says, 'Almost certainly we should interpret the word for "spirit" to refer to the Holy Spirit and not the human spirit' (Ralph P. Martin, *Philippians*, NCBC [Grand Rapids: Eerdmans, 1976], p. 86). So also Meyer, 'This is to be explained of the Holy Spirit' (*Critical and Exegetical Handbook to the Epistles to the Philippians and Colossians* [Edinburgh: T. & T. Clark, 1875], p. 70).

[4] So Martin, Meyer and O'Brien, who say, 'The arguments in favour of ... "participation in the Spirit", are in our view the most weighty, even if final certainty as to the precise meaning is not attainable' (O'Brien, *op. cit.*, p. 174).

[5] So M. Silva, 'the fellowship produced by the Spirit' (Moises

The Holy Spirit and The Bible

Silva, *Philippians*, WEC [Chicago: Moody Press, 1988], p. 99); 'a fellowship the Holy Spirit provides', R. Melick Jr., *Philippians, Colossians, Philemon*, NAC, 32 (Nashville: Boardman Press, 1991), p. 93. Hendriksen says, 'This genitive transcends both objective and subjective; one might call it adjectival' and thus tries to combine both meanings (*Philippians*, NTC [London: The Banner of Truth Trust, reprinted 1973], p. 98).

[6] ' "Participation in the Spirit" should sound the death knell to all factiousness and party spirit, for it is by this "one Spirit" that they were all baptized into one body (1 Cor. 12:13)' (O'Brien, *op. cit.*, p. 174).

[7] O'Brien notes that nothing is said about the manner in which God will reveal this, but emphasizes that it is a 'divine disclosure' (*op. cit.*, p. 439–440). Both Hendriksen and Meyer refer to the Spirit as the agent in this; Meyer says, 'The ἀποκαλύψει, which is to be taken as purely future, is conceived by Paul as taking place through the Holy Spirit (see Eph. 1:17; Col. 1:10)' (*op. cit.*, p. 176).

[8] Among those who see some reference or allusion to the Spirit are Martin (NCBC [Grand Rapids: Eerdmans, 1982], p. 103); Bruce (E. K. Simpson and F. F. Bruce, *Commentary on the Epistles to the Ephesians and the Colossians*, NLCNT [London: Marshall, Morgan & Scott, 1957], p. 185); Patzia (*Ephesians, Colossians, Philemon*, NIBC [Peabody: Hendriksen, 1990], pp. 21–22); Meyer (*op. cit.*, p. 263). Those who retain 'spiritual' include Wright (*Colossians and Philemon*, TNTC [Leicester: Inter-Varsity Press, 1986], p. 58), Melick (*op. cit.*, p. 202), and C. F. D. Moule (*The Epistles of Paul the Apostle to the Colossians and to Philemon*, CGTC [Cambridge: CUP, 1957], p. 53). Radford makes the best case for a direct reference to the Holy Spirit: 'we may recognize in the word spiritual in the preceding clause a reference to the Holy Spirit, and see a trinitarian sequence – the will of the Father, the guidance of the Spirit, the example of the Son. "The Spirit of the Lord" in Isaiah 11:2 is described as "the spirit of wisdom and understanding"; and the two Greek words in the LXX there are the sophia and synesis of the present passage' (Lewis B. Radford, *The Epistle to the Colossians and the Epistle to Philemon*, WC, [London: Methuen & Co., 1931], p. 158–59).

[9] There is considerable debate about the exact nature of the 'Colossian heresy'. O'Brien says, 'The teaching was set forth as "philosophy" (Col. 2:8), based on "tradition" (*paradosis* denotes its

antiquity, dignity and revelational character), which was supposed to impart true knowledge (Col. 2:18, 23). Paul seems to be quoting catchwords of the opponents in his attack on their teaching' ('Colossians' in *Dictionary of Paul and his Letters,* eds. G.F. Hawthorne, R.P. Martin, and D.G. Reid, Leicester, IVP, 1993, p. 148).

[10] Melick says of διανοίᾳ, 'Here it is a dative of reference so that the text is "with reference to the mind, by their evil works".' He continues, 'Paul characterized the mind (disposition) as evil, and the evidence he used was their evil works. The cause of their sinfulness was not their evil deeds: their evil deeds came from their sinfulness' (*op. cit.,* p. 230).

[11] Moule has an appendix entitled *A Note on the Knowledge of God* in which he says, 'the Christian γνῶσις was not the knowledge merely of certain propositions about the nature of God ... it was a relationship with a personal God who had revealed himself in Jesus Christ. Just as in the O.T. "to know God" meant far more than to know about God – it meant obedience and a response of the will ... so, still more, Christian γνῶσις meant a response of the whole person – will as well as mind – to God as revealed in the supreme historical event, the ministry, death and resurrection of Jesus' (*op. cit.,* p. 163).

[12] This translation is supported by Wright, *op. cit.* p. 95, Hendriksen, *Colossians and Philemon,* NTC (Baker, 1964), Melick and Moule; but it is rejected by Meyer, who maintains the phrase must mean 'of the God of Christ, i.e. to whom Christ belongs in a special way, as to His Father, Sender, Head, etc' (*op. cit.,* p.342).

[13] There are two more references (other than 1:8, 9) to πνεῦμα: 2:5 and 3:16. It may be that in Colosse a reference to πνεῦμα might be misunderstood.

[14] Wright says, 'In other words, while the process of knitting together the church into a united body clearly includes the growth of love, it also includes the growth, on the part of the whole community, of that proper understanding of the gospel which leads to the rich blessings of a settled conviction and assurance. Living in a loving and forgiving community will assist growth in understanding, and vice versa, as truth is confirmed in practice and practice enables truth to be seen in action and so to be fully grasped (*cf.* 1:9–11)' (*op. cit.,* pp. 94–95).

[15] Lunemann says, 'By δύναμις is not to be understood miracles by which the power of the preached gospel was attested ... for if so, the plural would have been necessary' (Gottlieb Lunemann, *Critical*

and Exegetical Handbook to the Epistles of St Paul to the Thessalonians, ET P. J. Gloag [Edinburgh: T. & T. Clark, 1880], p. 27). On the other hand Charles Wanamaker (*The Epistles to the Thessalonians*, NIGTC [Grand Rapids/Exeter: Eerdmans/Paternoster, 1990]) thinks there is a probable reference to miracles. Nygren says, 'The gospel is not the presentation of an idea, but the operation of a power. When the gospel is preached ... the power of God is at work for the salvation of men' (*op. cit.*, p. 67, quoted in Leon Morris *The Epistles of Paul to the Thessalonians*, TNTC [London: Tyndale Press, 1956], p. 37).

[16] 'Paul probably still has the preachers in mind, their conviction about the gospel being a factor in the Thessalonians' response. But it is possible (as Bruce and others) to take the word as applying to the hearers and to the Spirit's role in convincing them of the truth of what they heard and, beyond that perhaps, in giving them a general confidence in God' (David J. Williams, *1 and 2 Thessalonians*, NIBC [Peabody: Hendrikson, 1992], p. 30). William Hendriksen also mentions both aspects but considers that Paul primarily has in mind the 'full assurance of the missionaries as they spoke the word' (*I and II Thessalonians*, NTC [Grand Rapids: Baker, 1955], p. 51).

[17] Williams says, 'the present tense of the verb *energeo*, "to be at work", implies that the work is still in process' (*op. cit.*, p. 45). Morris says, 'Armitage Robinson, in a valuable note on *energein* and its cognates in his commentary on Ephesians (pp. 241-247), argues that it should be understood as passive, i.e. "is made operative", his point being that, while another writer might well have used the active, Paul prefers the passive which implies that God is the One who works. Whether we accept Robinson's linguistics or not, this is certainly the thought of Paul, for God is the effective power and the word his instrument' (*op. cit.*, p. 55).

[18] 'Paul does not specify here how the gospel is effective, but undoubtedly the Thessalonians would have understood it in terms of the way in which they experienced the work of the Spirit (*cf.* 1:5-6), both at the time of their conversion and later in the life of their community (*cf.* 5:19f.)' (Wanamaker, *op. cit.*, p. 112).

[19] Lunemann comments on this, 'But the verbal idea is not ... to be weakened into the idea of the divine permission, but must be taken in its proper sense. For according to the Pauline view it is a holy ordinance of God that the wicked by their wickedness should lose themselves

always the more in wickedness, and thus sin is punished by sin. But what is an ordinance of God is also accomplished by God Himself' (*op. cit.*, pp. 221–222).

[20] Williams calls this, 'a most unusual expression; there is nothing like it elsewhere in the Greek Bible' (*op. cit.*, p. 130).

[21] Plummer translates 'are already on the road to perdition' and adds, 'the present participle (τοῖς ἀπολλυμένοις) implies that perishing has already begun, not that perdition has already taken place' (Alfred Plummer, *A Commentary on St Paul's Second Epistle to the Thessalonians* [London, Robert Scott: 1918], p. 67).

[22] 'these verses offer an explanation for why people outside the community of faith are perishing: they have chosen to reject the truth of the gospel when it was presented to them, taking pleasure in wickedness instead. For this reason God has made certain that their own decision against the truth will result in their condemnation in the judgment, thereby sealing their destruction' (Wanamaker, *op. cit.*, p. 263).

[23] Wanamaker points out, 'The two phrases ... are governed by the preposition ἐν ("in") and describe the means by which salvation comes about' (*ibid.*, p. 266).

[24] There is fairly widespread agreement that 'Spirit' here refers to the Holy Spirit; so Plummer, *ad loc.*, Lunemann, Wanamaker, Morris, Hendriksen. Williams says, 'Some exegetes see in this a reference to the human spirit – "through the sanctification of the whole person, body and spirit". It is far more likely, however, that Paul is speaking of the work of God's Spirit' (*op. cit.*, p. 134).

[25] So Fee, 'For Paul, the "mystery" of the faith was not something "secret" but rather a truth once hidden (in God) and now revealed by the Spirit, hence revealed truth' (Gordon D. Fee, *1 & 2 Timothy & Titus* [San Francisco: Harper and Row, 1984], p. 49. Also Calvin in *Commentaries on the Epistles to Timothy, Titus and Philemon,* trans. William Pringle [Edinburgh: CTS, 1856], p. 86).

[26] George W. Knight III says, 'Rom. 1:4 serves as the best commentary on this compact statement'. He goes on to say, 'The next use of πνεῦμα in the PE (4:1, without qualification, as here) refers to the Holy Spirit (see also Tit. 3:5; 2 Tim. 1:14; probably 1:7) and not the human spirit (as indicated by ὑμῶν in 2 Tim. 4:22), and there is no indication of shift in meaning, which favours that same identification here. If this understanding is correct, then ἐν is used

with the meaning "by", indicating means, in contrast to the preceding line where it is used with the meaning "in", indicating place' (*The Pastoral Epistles*, NIGTC [Grand Rapids: Eerdmans/Carlisle: Paternoster, 1992], pp. 184–85). However because of the parallelism with 'flesh' in the previous line a number of commentators come down on 'spirit'; so J. N. D. Kelly (*A Commentary on the Pastoral Epistles*, BNTC [London: A. & C. Black, 1963]; Fee (*op. cit.*,), and D. Guthrie (*The Pastoral Epistles*, TNTC [London: Tyndale Press, 1957]).

[27] 'The Spirit attested his Sonship. The same Spirit present at Jesus' baptism, who empowered his ministry, finally vindicated him by raising him from the dead (*cf.* 1 Peter 3:18)' (Thomas C. Oden, *First and Second Timothy and Titus*, Interpretation [Louisville: John Knox Press, 1989], pp. 44–45).

[28] Fee says, 'But whether this refers to the prophetic Spirit's having spoken in the church (as Barrett) or to the Spirit speaking to Paul as he writes (or earlier, as in Acts 20) cannot be known' (*op. cit.*, p. 60).

[29] Scott says, 'Intimations of the Spirit were often given in riddles, but this one had been made in clear, unmistakeable terms. The allusion may be to some well-known oracle which was current in the Church. Christian prophets, under the influence of the Spirit, were continually making forecasts of future events, and an important announcement of this kind would be preserved and circulated' (E. F. Scott, *The Pastoral Epistles*, MNTC [London: Hodder and Stoughton, 1947], p. 44).

[30] Knight thinks that Paul 'most likely' has the words of Jesus himself in mind. He writes, 'The numerous occurrences of τὸ πνεῦμα λεγει in Revelation (2:7, 11, 17, 25; 3:6, 13, 22) demonstrate that this phrase can be used to refer to the revelation given by Jesus Christ (*cf.* Rev. 1:1–3, 9–20, especially vv. 1, 19, 20). Such usage brings to mind the warning of Jesus concerning apostasy in Mt. 24:10, 11 and Mk. 13:22. The warning of Jesus is conceptually the closest to this clause in that both speak of "falling away" (1 Tim. 4:1 with ἀφίστημι, Mt. 24:10 with σκανδαλίζω; these words can be used interchangeably as in Lk. 8:13 [ἀφίστημι] pr. Mt. 13:21; Mk. 4:17 [σκανδαλίζω])' (*op. cit.*, p. 188). He adds, 'That he [i.e. Paul] writes τὸ πνεῦμα λεγει emphasizes the ongoing and present significance of this warning, which has been reiterated by the Spirit through him and others (*cf. e.g.*, Acts 20:28–31; 2 Tim. 3:1ff.; 4:3, 4)' *ibid*.

[31] Kelly says, 'Paul mentions both these functions together in Rom. 12:7, implying that their exercise called for a special charisma, or

endowment, of the Spirit' (*op. cit.*, p. 105).

[32] Kelly says: 'In Paul's letters ... charisma, or "gift", denotes a special endowment of the Spirit enabling the recipient to carry out some function in the community' (*op. cit.*, p. 106). So also Scott, though he adds: 'The word seems here to be applied to an office, conferred by the Spirit, inasmuch as those appointed to it were designated by inspired prophets' (*op. cit.*, p. 53). There is general agreement linking χάρισμα with some sort of gift of the Spirit.

[33] Scott says: 'The reference cannot be to baptism, for the "gift", as the sequel shows, is the specific one of leadership in the Church, and this was conferred by ordination' (*op. cit.*, p. 91). Most writers refer to ordination. Oden remarks: 'The spiritual gifts that enable ministry are related to, but distinguishable from, those gifts given and received in repentance and baptism' (*op. cit.*, p. 31). However it is difficult to think of 'power, love and self-discipline' as being gifts that can be distinguished from those given at the time of conversion.

[34] Knight comments on the use of πνεῦμα in verse 7 as follows: 'But since the statement here begins with the negative, the generic lower-case "spirit" is probably the best decision after all, as long as one recognizes that the positive affirmation beginning with ἀλλὰ does, indeed, refer to the Spirit of God.' He continues, 'If this understanding is correct, then ἡμῖν, "us", refers to Christians in general (as in v. 9) rather than just to Paul and Timothy as those who have received a special χάρισμα (so *e.g.*, Lock and Parry), and aorist ἔδωκεν refers to the past action of God at the beginning of every Christian's life in giving his "Spirit" (*cf.* 1 Cor. 12:13; Rom. 8:9, 11, 14–16)' (*op. cit.*, p.371).

[35] 'spirit of: the expression goes back to Isaiah 11:2; while none of the words of the passage appears here, "strength" there matches power.... In view of both the Isaiah background ("the Spirit of the Lord") and the writer's use of *pneuma* (e.g. 1 Tim. 3:16; 4:1; Tit. 3:5), it is likely that the meaning of spirit is more concrete than appears at first glance: God's spirit issuing in the qualities mentioned, which are the specific content of the gift in v. 6' (J. L. Houlden, *The Pastoral Epistles*, TPI NTC [London/Philadelphia: SCM/Trinity Press International, 1989], p. 110). Scott says that 'the idea of a spiritual gift here blends with that of the Spirit itself' (*op. cit.*, p. 91); and Calvin says, 'The word Spirit is here taken for the gifts which proceed from him, agreeably to the figure called Metonymy' (*op. cit.*, p. 192, fn. from *French Sermons*).

[36] Fee says, 'Sophronismos is a cognate, and here probably a synonym, for the "sound-mindedness" of Titus 2:2, 5, and so forth. In all likelihood Paul intended to call for a "wise head" in the face of the deceptive and unhealthy teaching of the errorists' (op. cit., p. 177).

[37] 'Since what has been entrusted is described as good, it almost certainly refers to the "sound teaching of the gospel" ' (ibid., pp. 182–83).

[38] 'It was his view, of course (cf. 1 Cor. 12:4ff.), that every ministerial function in the community had its appropriate endowment of the Spirit, and it was natural that, as the need for preventing heretics from tampering with the gospel became more pressing and obvious, he should extend this to the special responsibilities of men like Timothy and himself in this regard' (Kelly, op. cit., p. 167).

[39] Calvin says: 'to this mortal contagion Paul elegantly compares false doctrines; for if you once give entrance to them, they spread till they have completed the destruction of the church' (op. cit., p. 224). So also Kelly: 'It is not just the dangers of false teaching to its adherents that worry Paul, but its insidious tendency to spread and infect other people, just as gangrene spreads to and eats up the neighbouring tissues' (op. cit., p. 184).

[40] 'In effect it is equivalent to being drunk and besotted, for the verb (Gk. ananephein) literally means "return to sobriety" ' (Kelly, op. cit., p. 191).

[41] It is probable that verse 7 refers to the women spoken about in the previous verse, while in verse 8 Paul turns again to the false teachers themselves; so Knight (op. cit., p. 434).

Chapter 10: General Epistles

[1] These are 2:4; 3:7; 6:4; 9:8, 14; 10:15, 29. There is some doubt whether 9:14 refers to the Holy Spirit, but the verse is widely understood in this way. Note, for example, the change from NEB 'a spiritual and eternal sacrifice' to REB 'through the eternal Spirit'.

[2] As F. F. Bruce points out, 'the Epistle to the Hebrews is not an epistle or letter in the strict sense of the term.' He quotes from Zuntz (The Text of the Epistles, p. 286), 'It is a midrash in rhetorical Greek prose – it is a homily' (F. F. Bruce, The Epistle to the Hebrews, NICNT [Grand Rapids: Eerdmans, reprinted 1985], pp. xlvii–xlviii).

[3] For example λέγει is used at 1:6, 7; 3:7; 5:6; 8:8; 10:5. Guthrie says [on 1:6], 'The formula he says (legei), which introduces the

quotation, is a familiar one in this epistle. The subject is omitted, but God is clearly meant. The scriptural quotations are not simply formal Old Testament statements, but God himself speaking personally out of the text' (Donald Guthrie, *Hebrews*, TNTC [Leicester/Grand Rapids: IVP/Eerdmans, reprinted 1986], p. 74).

[4] In several references the verb is in the passive, *e.g.* 3:15; 4:7; 7:8, 17, and the implication here is that God is the speaker; there is no reference to Scripture speaking in the letter.

[5] 'From our author's point of view the identity of the human writer of an OT passage is a matter of minor importance; this appears, *e.g.*, from the introduction of a quotation from Ps. 8:4–6 in Heb. 2:6 with the words "someone has testified somewhere". (*Cf.* also the treatment of the narrative statement of Gen. 2:2 as a divine utterance in Heb. 4:4)' (Bruce, *op. cit.*, p. l, fn. 117).

[6] 2:12, 13; 10:5–7. Simon Kistemaker, *Hebrews* (Welwyn: Evangelical Press, 1984), p. 90, esp. fn. 8.

[7] 'And repeatedly, when quoting the Old Testament Scriptures, the writer uses this formula: God, Jesus, or the Holy Spirit says ... The Word is not a written document of past centuries. It is alive and current; it is powerful and effective; and it is undivided and unchanged' (*Ibid*. p. 118).

[8] 'As the word of the living God it cannot fail itself to be living' (P. E. Hughes, *A Commentary on the Epistle to the Hebrews* [Grand Rapids: Eerdmans, 1977], p. 164).

[9] Westcott says: 'The language is not directly applicable to the Personal Word Himself, He cannot properly be likened to a sword' (B. F. Westcott, *The Epistle to the Hebrews* [London and New York: Macmillan & Co., 1889], p. 101). Moffatt points out: 'Here the writer personifies the revelation of God for a moment' (J. Moffatt, *Epistle to the Hebrews*, ICC [Edinburgh: T. & T. Clark, 1924], p. 55).

[10] Δηλόω is used in 12:27 [the text says 12:17, but presumably 12:27 is intended] of what is implicitly shown by an OT text, and which the author's interpretation makes explicit. The meaning is similar here' (Paul Ellingworth, *The Epistle to the Hebrews*, NICGT [Grand Rapids/Carlisle: Eerdmans/Paternoster, 1993], p. 451). Westcott points out, 'The Spirit which inspired the teaching and fixed the ritual Himself discloses it, and this he does continuously (δηλοῦντος not δηλωσάντος) as long as the veil rests over any part of the record' (*op. cit.*, p.251).

[11] 'The Spirit speaks and interprets the Word of God. He discloses the meaning of the Word (John 14:26; 15:26) and guides the believer in the truth' (Kistemaker on 9:8; *op. cit.,* p. 243). So also Guthrie; '... his [the writer's] doctrine of the Spirit in relation to Scripture reaches to the significance of the imagery used, as 9:8 shows.' And on 9:8 itself; 'This statement shows something of the writer's approach to inspiration, for the Spirit is continually demonstrating (present tense) how the cultus may now be *applied*. This explanatory ministry of the Spirit is in harmony with the promise of Jesus in John's Gospel (*cf.* Jn. 16:12ff.)' (Guthrie, *op. cit.,* p. 103, 183, my italics).

[12] 'In this case it seems that the special function of the Holy Spirit is to draw attention to the combining of the idea of an inner law and the complete putting away of sin' (*ibid.,* p. 209).

[13] REB.

[14] ἐν ἁγιασμῷ πνεύματος εἰς ὑπακοήν...

[15] 'the ending -μος of the noun ἁγιασμός (sanctification) expresses progressive activity' (Simon J. Kistemaker, *Peter and Jude,* NTC [Welwyn: Evangelical Press, 1987], p. 38).

[16] 'The end in view is obedience' (Alan M. Stibbs, *The First Epistle General of Peter,* TNTC [London: Tyndale Press,1959], p. 72. So also Kistemaker (*op. cit.,* p. 37).

[17] Wayne Grudem, *1 Peter,* TNTC [Leicester/Grand Rapids; Inter-Varsity Press/Eerdmans, 1988).

[18] The link with 'chosen' tends to make it appear that sanctification refers to an act in the past, whereas Grudem's view does much more justice to the idea of a progressive work of the Spirit.

[19] Grudem, *op. cit.,* pp. 51–52.

[20] Bo Reicke says, 'By "living hope" is meant a hope by which one may live' (*The Epistles of James, Peter and Jude,* AB [New York: Doubleday, 1964]; p .79). This does not seem to be nearly a dynamic enough concept.

[21] 'This hope is the eager, confident expectation of the life to come' (Grudem, *op. cit.,* p. 55).

[22] Moffatt says: 'your heart, if not your eyes, can possess him, Peter claims.... Out of sight, but not out of reach: such is Peter's description of Christ. It is one of the most inward and moving sentences in the epistle' (*The General Epistles,* MNTC [London: Hodder & Stoughton, 1928], p. 98).

[23] Stibbs says: 'There is a contrast here between the sight of Jesus,

possibly both at his first and at his second advents, and the knowledge of Him by faith, which is the present experience of His people' (*op. cit.*, p. 79).

[24] 'It is thus the joy that results from being in the presence of God himself, and joy that even now partakes of the character of heaven. It is the joy of heaven before heaven, experienced now in fellowship with the unseen Christ' (Grudem; *op. cit.*, p. 66).

[25] REB has 'spirit', but it is difficult to think of a NT writer not associating 'spirit' in a context like this with the Holy Spirit. Peter probably calls the Spirit the Spirit of Christ because the prophets are speaking of the Christ.

[26] Bigg says, 'Here the Holy Ghost who was "sent from heaven" on the day of Pentecost and inspired the preachers of the gospel, is introduced as a guarantee that the gospel cannot contradict the message of the prophets who were inspired by the Πνεῦμα Χριστοῦ' (Rev. Charles Bigg, *Epistles of St Peter and St Jude*, ICC [Edinburgh: T. & T. Clark, 1901], p. 109).

[27] There has been considerable debate about the precise meaning of εἰς τίνα ἢ ποῖον καιρὸν. Walter Kaiser applies them only to time, 'I strongly affirm that the prophets claimed ignorance only on the matter of *time*.' Scholars who translate differently 'err badly' (Walter C. Kaiser, 'Legitimate Hermeneutics,' in Donald McKim (ed.), *A Guide to Contemporary Hermeneutics* [Grand Rapids: Eerdmans, 1986], p. 118, 119). Perhaps a majority of scholars and translations have 'the time and circumstances' (see *e.g.* NIV, REB). Kistemaker and Selwyn support this understanding (E. G. Selwyn, *The First Epistle of Peter* [London: MacMillan & Co. Ltd., 1946]). Kelly speaks of 'only a blurred vision of its details and timing' (J. N. D. Kelly, *The Epistles of Peter and Jude*, BNTC [London: A. & C. Black, 1969], p. 60). Thirdly, Grudem in an additional note argues persuasively for the RSV's 'what person or time' (*op. cit.*, pp. 74, 75). Of these alternatives the first appears to be the least likely.

[28] Stibbs notes, 'We do well, therefore, not to let the so-called scientific and critical approach rob us of the distinctive and divinely-intended Christian use of the Old Testament' (*op. cit.*, p. 82).

[29] Kelly prefers the translation 'the Lord Christ', saying, 'since the author is adapting the LXX "sanctify the Lord [i.e. Jahweh] himself", it seems more natural to construe Christ (τὸν Χριστὸν) as appositional, intended to clarify the reference of the Lord' (*op. cit.*, p. 142).

[30] 'The whole passage recalls Lk.12:1–12 (*cf.* Lk. 21:14, 15), with its teaching as to what to fear in persecution and what not to fear, and its promise of the Holy Spirit's guidance when confronted with the question πῶς ἢ τίς ἀπολογήσησθε' (Selwyn, *op. cit.*, p. 193).

[31] Bauckham draws attention to Peter's use of ἐπιγνώσις and γνῶσιν: 'It seems clear that 2 Peter's use of ἐπιγνώσις (a favourite term: 1:2, 3, 8; 2:20) conforms to this usage: it is the "decisive knowledge of God which is implied in conversion to the Christian religion" (Bultmann in TDNT 1,707). In contrast to γνῶσις, which is used in 2 Peter for knowledge which can be acquired and developed in the course of the Christian life (1:5, 6; 3:18), ἐπιγνώσις always refers to the fundamental saving knowledge on which the whole of Christian life is based. Similarly ἐπιγινώσκειν (2:21 *bis*) refers to the conversion experience of coming to knowledge (whereas γινώσκειν has an ordinary sense in 1:20; 3:3)' (R. Bauckham, *Jude, 2 Peter*, WBC [Waco: Word Books, 1983], p. 170).

[32] There is considerable textual variation in the last phrase but this does not affect the general sense of the verse.

[33] Moffat, *op cit.*, p. 189.

[34] Bo Reicke, *op. cit.*, p. 159. Kelly, calling this understanding of the verses, 'much the most natural meaning, and the one which suits the context best as well as agreeing with the lexical evidence for ἐπίλυσις' goes on to say: 'But if one's own interpretation is excluded what is the approved alternative? The next verse makes this clear: it is the interpretation intended by the Holy Spirit, whose inspiration lies behind prophecy. In view of his attitude and date there can be no doubt that he is not thinking of the Spirit-endowed individual or prophet in the community, but rather of apostolic authority as embodied in the recognized ministers and charismatic teachers of the local churches who, as he understands it, bear the Spirit's commission. The notion of the official Church as the appointed custodian of scripture is evidently taking shape' (*op. cit.*, p. 324).

[35] Bauckham, *op. cit.*, p. 233.

Chapter 11: The Letters of John

[1] There is some debate about whether 'word' means message or the personal 'Word' at this point. Smalley says, 'However, these two interpretations of λόγος need not be opposed to each other; and possibly there is an intentional ambivalence at this point. For the life-

giving word of the gospel is essentially a proclamation about Jesus who is the living Word of God. "Jesus gave the word and embodied it." (Houlden, 52)' (*1, 2, 3 John*, WBC, 51 [Dallas: Word Incorporated; UK edition 1991], p. 6).

[2] 'He [i.e. John] is not, like St. Luke, a sedulous investigator and recorder of the facts as certified by the most trustworthy witnesses; but he is himself such a witness' (Robert Law, *The Tests of Life* [reprint of 3rd ed; Grand Rapids: Baker Book House, 1979], p. 109).

[3] Stott comments, 'It is not the person who claims to be a Christian and to know God who is presumptuous, but he whose claim is contradicted by his conduct. He is a *liar* (4)' (J. R. W. Stott, *Epistles of John*, TNTC [London: Tyndale Press, 1966], p. 90).

[4] It is possible to take 'love of God' in three different ways. Smalley says, 'all three senses may belong to the phrase.... In obedient Christian behaviour is manifested a love for God which responds to God's (kind of) love (*cf.* 4:19). At the same time the similar expressions at 2:15 and 5:3, using ἀγάπη (love) with a genitive, suggest that the predominant, but not the exclusive, meaning here is man's love for God.' He adds, 'True love for God is expressed in moral rectitude: if we love God at all, we shall *want* to obey him' (*op. cit.*, p. 49). Calvin says, 'How then is it possible for you to know God and yet be touched by no feeling? Nor indeed does it proceed only from God's nature that, if we know him, we immediately love Him. For the same Spirit who enlightens our minds also inspires our hearts with an affection corresponding to our knowledge. And the knowledge of God causes us to fear and love Him' (*The Gospel according to St John 11–21 and The First Epistle of John* [Edinburgh: The Saint Andrew Press, 1972], p. 245).

[5] Stott says, 'But their knowledge of Him ripens with the years. The little children know Him as *the Father*; the fathers have come to know him as *him that is from the beginning*' (*op. cit.*, p. 97).

[6] Although writers refer to the Holy Spirit there is considerable debate about whether in fact the anointing actually refers to the Word of God. Several combine the two ideas, e.g. Marshall, 'we should probably take the step of combining the two interpretations of our passage. The anointing is the Word taught to converts before their baptism and apprehended by them through the work of the Spirit in their hearts'. He quotes de la Potterie, 'The anointing is indeed *God's word*, not as it is preached externally in the community, but as it is

received by faith into men's hearts and remains active, *thanks to the work* of the *Spirit*' (I. H. Marshall, *The Epistles of John*, NICNT [Grand Rapids: Eerdmans, 1978], p. 155). However Burge says, 'One of the chief arguments against the interpretation that sees this anointing as only the word of God or the orthodox *kerygma* is that this anointing dwells within the believer (τὸ χρῖσμα μένει ἐν ὑμῖν, 2:27). Therefore the anointing stands apart from the word as independent but finds its primary function in confirming the word and applying it in the present schism' (*op. cit.*, p. 175). This seems a more satisfactory way of understanding χρῖσμα.

⁷ Houlden explains the use of χρῖσμα in this way: 'The crucial point of faith is to hold that Jesus is the anointed one (= Messiah = *Christos*); the opponents are in effect opponents of Jesus, and so *antichristoi*. The faithful supporters of Jesus have (like him – in his baptism?) received an anointing (*chrisma*) from God' (J. L. Houlden, *A Commentary on the Johannine Epistles*, BNTC [London: A. & C. Black, 1976], p. 79). Thompson says, 'Despite the denials of Brown (1982:341), it is likely that the secessionists would have claimed an *anointing* as well' (Marianne Meye Thompson, *1–3 John*, IVP NTCS [Leicester/Downers Grove: IVP, 1992], p. 76).

⁸ 'the use of the word without explanation assumes that it was familiar to both writers and readers as denoting the abiding gift of the Holy Ghost' (Law, *op. cit.*, p. 112).

⁹ 'Some manuscripts read "you know all things" (οἴδατε πάντα) while others read "you all know" (πάντες οἴδατε), leaving the object to be supplied (NIV, the truth, from v. 21). Πάντες has better textual support. The stress falls on what all, not a few, know' (Thompson, *op. cit.*, p. 77).

¹⁰ Westcott comments, 'The object of the Apostle in writing was not to communicate fresh knowledge, but to bring into active and decisive use the knowledge which his readers already possessed' (B. F. Westcott, *The Epistles of St John: the Greek text with notes and essays* [London: Macmillan & Co., 1902], p. 74).

¹¹ Marshall says, 'In the present case, two points may clarify what he means. On the one hand, Schnackenburg stresses that the instruction given by church teachers must be accompanied by inner teaching by the Spirit which enables the hearers to sift out and accept what is true. On the other hand, Bruce comments that the Spirit's instruction comes through teachers who themselves possess the

anointing; Christians possessed by the Spirit give one another mutual instruction, without which no single individual can appreciate the whole of God's truth (Eph. 3:18)' (*op. cit.*, p. 163).

[12] 'The Word is an objective safeguard, while the anointing of the Spirit is a subjective experience; but both the apostolic teaching and the heavenly Teacher are necessary for continuance in the truth. And both are to be personally and inwardly grasped' (Stott, *op. cit.*, p. 115). 'The Spirit is not a source of independent revelation, but makes the Revelation of Christ effectual' (Law, *op. cit.*, p. 115).

[13] 'A case in which εἰδέναι can scarcely be differentiated from γινώσκειν. It probably expresses a stronger feeling of the certainty of the thing known; *cf.* 5:19' (Law, *op. cit.*, p. 390).

[14] 'But as love is the special fruit of the Spirit, it is also a sure symbol of regeneration. For, since none sincerely loves his brethren unless he is born again by God's Spirit, he rightly concludes that this same Spirit of God, who is life, dwells in all who love the brethren' (Calvin, *op. cit.*, p. 275).

[15] Houlden: 'The chapter finishes with the introduction of a quite new idea – that of the Spirit. We know that God dwells in us, not now because we keep his commands or because we love the brothers (3:14), as we might expect, but because of the Spirit he has given to us' (*op. cit.*, p. 104).

[16] Marshall comments, 'John does not explain how this assurance manifests itself. Is he thinking of the way in which the believer realizes that he can confidently address God as Abba, Father? Or is it some inner consciousness of being loved by God? Or is it some "charismatic" experience of the power of the Spirit? John has not told us, and in this there may be an element of divine wisdom' (*op. cit.*, pp. 202–203).

[17] 'A transition from the previous section (3:10–24) to this verse is provided by the reference to "spirit(s)" in 3:24b and 4:1. John may either have developed his teaching in 4:1–6 from the allusion to the Spirit of God at 3:24b (so Dodd, 94), or included the linking phrase about the Spirit in that verse in order to anticipate the present section (so Marshall, 203; following Schnackenburg, 208)' (Smalley, *op. cit.*, p. 217).

[18] Marshall says, 'The word "spirit" here must mean either "utterance inspired by a spirit" or "person inspired by a spirit". In the latter case the thought is perhaps of the individual spirit of a prophet, which might be inspired by God or Satan' (*op. cit.*, p. 204).

[19] 'But the very office of the Divine Spirit, the promised Paraclete, is to testify to Jesus as the Christ come in the flesh' (Law, *op. cit.*, p. 267).

[20] 'Listening means far more than simply giving them a hearing; it implies agreement with what is heard' (Thompson, *op. cit.*, p. 117).

[21] Stott emphasizes apostolic authority at this point, 'The fact is that he is not speaking in his own name, nor even in the name of the Church, but as one of the apostles, who were conscious of the special authority bestowed upon them by Jesus Christ' (*op. cit.*, p. 158).

[22] Stott links this with the words of Jesus in John's Gospel, 'There is a certain affinity between God's Word and God's people. Jesus had taught that His sheep hear His voice (Jn. x. 4, 5, 8, 16, 26, 27), that everyone who is of the truth listens to His witness to the truth (Jn. xviii. 37), and that "he who is of God hears the words of God" (Jn. viii. 47, RSV). In the same way John asserts that since *we are of God* (6) and *ye are of God* (4), you listen to us. There is a correspondence between message and hearers. The Spirit who is in you (4) enables you to discern His own voice speaking through us (2)' (*op. cit.*, p. 158).

[23] '(Here, *the Spirit is truth*, that is, it belongs to the sphere of truth and what it inspires is genuine and trustworthy)' (Houlden, *op. cit.*, p. 127).

[24] 'The majority of commentators rightly see that the chief reference of the "water and blood" in v. 6 is neither to the sacraments of baptism and the eucharist nor to the blood and water which flowed from the side of Jesus according to John 19:34. Rather, John is speaking here of the terminal points in the earthly ministry of Jesus: his baptism at the beginning, and his crucifixion at the end.... Historically Jesus "came" into his power and authority by the "water" of his baptism, at which point he was declared to be God's Son (Mark 1:11; John 1:34); and he "came" into his power and authority in an even more ultimate sense by the "blood" of his cross, a moment which the fourth evangelist describes as the "glorification" of Christ (John 17:1). Cf. 4:2' (Smalley, *op. cit.*, p. 278).

[25] Marshall (*op. cit.*, p. 235), who quotes Dodd, 'In history, the descent of the Spirit was evidence of the Messiahship of Jesus. In the present experience of the Church, the activity of the Spirit is evidence of His power to baptize with the Spirit, and therefore of His divine Sonship.'

[26] Calvin says, 'He adds a third witness, the Holy Spirit, who in fact holds the first place, for otherwise the water and the blood would have flowed in vain. He it is who seals in our hearts the testimony of the water and the blood. He it is who by His power makes the fruit of Christ's death come to us, who makes the blood shed for our redemption penetrate our souls' (*op. cit.*, p. 304).

[27] 'Absolute self-surrender to the Son of God brings to the believer a direct consciousness of His Divine Nature and work' (Westcott, p.186).

[28] 'That which for others is external is for the believer experimental. The witness of Spirit and water and blood becomes an inner conviction of life and cleansing and redemption' (*ibid.*).

[29] 'behind the "divine testimony" of "the Spirit and the water and the blood" (v. 8) lies the sovereign being of God himself. God's own authority, that is to say, has been stamped on the truth of the Christian gospel (Williams, 55)' (Smalley, *op. cit.*, p. 283).

[30] There is a variant reading here: 'the true God' (*cf.* REB), but this does not alter the sense. Stott says, 'God is here described not as "true", *alethes*, but as "real" (NEB), *alethinos*' (*op. cit.*, p. 194).

[31] 'Bultmann, 89, argues that the gift of insight mentioned here corresponds to the "anointing" (χρῖσμα) which the believer receives as a means of true knowledge' (Smalley, *op. cit.,* p. 306).

Chapter 12: Revelation of John
[1] R. J. Bauckham, *The Climax of Prophecy* (Edinburgh: T. & T. Clark, 1993); Chapter 5 'The Role of the Spirit', p. 150.

[2] Bauckham, *op. cit.,* p. 162.

[3] *Ibid.*, p. 150.

[4] *Ibid.*, p. 158.

[5] 'There is no reason to doubt that he was in the Spirit throughout the time that he was the recipient of the revelations recorded in this book; but here it is being in the Spirit, perhaps to an intensified degree and for an immediate purpose, that enables him to respond to the invitation, "Come up hither", and to describe what he saw and heard after passing through "the door opened to heaven" ' (P. E. Hughes, *The Book of Revelation* [Leicester/Grand Rapids: Inter-Varsity Press/ Eerdmans, 1990], p. 72).

[6] *Ibid.*, p. 158.

[7] *Ibid.*, p. 160.

[8] *Ibid.*, p. 168. But others understand the word to mean 'allegorically'. So Hughes, *op. cit.*, p. 127 and G. E. Ladd, *A Commentary on the Revelation of John* (Grand Rapids: Eerdmans, 1978), p. 157.

[9] Bauckham, *op. cit.*, p. 169.

[10] *Ibid.*, p.172–173.

[11] *Ibid.*, p.xi.

Conclusion

[1] The emphasis here is on the words 'grasp and appreciate'. Paul assumes that everyone knows of the existence and specific characteristics of God, but this knowledge is suppressed (Rom. 1:18–21).

[2] 'Obviously readers cannot distance themselves absolutely from their own baggage. But even if distanciation is never perfect, it can be remarkably effective. Such readers not only try to understand the social setting, meaning of words, cultural context, emotional overtones and symbolic associations of the text to be studied, but self-consciously distance themselves, as far as that is possible, from the automatic assumptions brought to bear by uncritical reading' (D. A. Carson, *The Gagging of God* [Leicester: Apollos, 1996], p. 120).

[3] Thomas F. Torrance, *The Hermeneutics of John Calvin* (Scottish Academic Press, 1988), p. 65.

[4] 'Instead of going round and round an endless hermeneutical circle, one can as it were "spiral in" on the truth, as one asks better questions of a text, and hears more accurate answers' (Carson, *op. cit.,* p. 121).

[5] Torrance, *op. cit.,* p. 61.

[6] 2 Timothy 3:16; 2 Peter 1:21.

[7] This is an essential part of the thesis of Stephen Prickett in *Words and The Word*: 'This book begins from the suspicion that the current problems of biblical hermeneutics are unlikely to be solved without some historical understanding of how the present situation arose, and that its roots cannot be understood simply in terms of development of theology or of literary theory considered as separate disciplines in isolation, but that they must be approached through their interaction and subsequent separation in the late eighteenth and early nineteenth centuries' (Stephen Prickett, *Words and The Word* [Cambridge: Cambridge University Press, 1986], p. 2).

[8] The word 'church' is used here for convenience, as the word most usually used. It raises questions about what constitutes the church and what its limits are. Moreover it would be more true to the New Testament to use the plural 'churches', which might also be more suitable to the contemporary situation.

[9] This raises what Robert Morgan and John Barton call 'the central problem of biblical interpretation in the West today: the tension between uses of the Bible as Scripture in religious contexts and the frequently non-religious aims of modern biblical scholarship' (*Biblical Interpretation* [Oxford: Oxford University Press, 1989], p. 271). There is no way to avoid this tension and it seems perfectly proper for the church to adopt an 'advocacy stance' in its use of the Bible.

[10] It is interesting and important to note that Augustine made *love* one of the keys to interpret the Scripture, 'What Augustine always stressed was that the entire canonical text should produce love for God and for neighbour in the lives of those in the church' (David S. Dockery, *Biblical Interpretation Then and Now* [Grand Rapids: Baker Book House, 1992], p. 146).

[11] Owen, pp. 122,124.

[12] *Ibid.*, p. 229.

[13] *Ibid.*, p. 226.

[14] For example, it may be doubted whether the precise shape of the Colossian heresy, if it was one heresy, will ever be discovered, or that we will know that it has, if it has! It may also be doubted whether that will in any way affect the continuing use and usefulness of the letter to the Colossians.

[15] Romans 15:4; 1 Corinthians 10:11; 2 Timothy 3:15–17; 1 Peter 1:11,12; 2 Peter 1:19.

[16] 2 Timothy 3:16, 17.

[17] For example Eliot says,

What we call the beginning is often the end
And to make an end is to make a beginning.
The end is where we start from. And every phrase
And sentence that is right (where every word is at home,
Taking its place to support the others, ...)
Every phrase and every sentence is an end and a beginning,
Every poem an epitaph.
(Four Quartets; Little Gidding, V, lines 214 –225).

[18] See, for example, Grant R. Osborne, *The Hermeneutical Spiral* (Downers Grove: InterVarsity Press, 1991). The phrase appears to have been first used by Roger Lundin, 'It might be more accurate to describe Gadamer's phenomenological study of understanding as a hermeneutical spiral rather than a hermeneutical circle' (Roger Lundin, Anthony Thiselton and Clarence Walhout, *The Responsibility of Hermeneutics* [Grand Rapids: Eerdmans, 1986], p. 25).

[19] 'If the mistaken interpretation tends to build up love, which is the end of the commandment, the interpreter goes astray in much the same way as a man who, by mistake, quits the high road, but yet reaches, through the fields, the same place to which the road leads' (Augustine, *On Christian Doctrine, I.* 36–41; quoted in Dockery, *op. cit.,* p. 144).

[20] *Ibid.*

[21] *Ibid.,* p. 170.

[22] *Ibid.,* p. 181.

Subject Index

Persons Index

Scripture Index

Christian Focus Publications
publishes books for all ages

Our mission statement -

STAYING FAITHFUL
In dependence upon God we seek to help make his infallible word, the Bible, relevant. Our aim is to ensure that the Lord Jesus Christ is presented as the only hope to obtain forgiveness of sin, live a useful life and look forward to heaven with him.

REACHING OUT
Christ's last command requires us to reach out to our world with his gospel. We seek to help fulfill that by publishing books that point people towards Jesus and help them to develop a Christ-like maturity. We aim to equip all levels of readers for life, work ministry and mission.

Books in our adult range are published in three imprints.

Christian Focus contains popular works including biographies, commentaries, basic doctrine, and Christian living. Our children's books are also published in this imprint.

Mentor focuses on books written at a level suitable for Bible College and seminary students, pastors, and other serious readers; the imprint includes commentaries, doctrinal studies, examination of current issues, and church history.

Christian Heritage contains classic writings from the past.

For a free catalogue of all our titles, please write to:

Christian Focus Publications, Ltd
Geanies House, Fearn,
Ross-shire, IV20 1TW, Scotland, United Kingdom

info@christianfocus.com